MISSIONARY COMPANION

Published by Covenant Communications, Inc.
American Fork, Utah

Printed in China
First Printing: March 2012

24 23 22 21 20 19 18 17 16 12 11 10 9 8 7 6 5 4 3

ISBN 978-1-60861-445-5

Easy Reference Guide for
Missionaries and Teachers

Richard J. Allen

Covenant Communications, Inc.

TABLE OF CONTENTS

INTRODUCTION The purpose for this compact handbook is to help students of the gospel—missionaries, families, teachers—have rapid and convenient access to the actual wording of important scriptural passages and groups of passages relating to the key themes of the gospel of Jesus Christ. The word of God—given unto His children by His own voice, by the voice of holy angels, or through His chosen prophets (see D&C 136:37)—is compelling evidence of His unbounded love and mercy. His word honors and fulfills the covenant promises leading to eternal joy and exaltation. As Alma confirms, the word of God, when planted in faithful hearts and yearning minds, unfolds as a living entity, destined to become "a tree springing up unto everlasting life" (Alma 32:41). In this way, the scriptures provide a continual flow of light to illuminate the pathway that leads to Christ. By following the word of God, we can come unto Christ and partake of the blessings of the gospel and prepare ourselves and our families for eternal life and exaltation. Then, by lifting the ensign of the restored gospel and sharing saving truths with others—using "boldness, but not overbearance" and being "filled with love" (Alma 38:12)—we can bring magnificent blessings into the lives of the honest at heart.

A word about the method used in preparing these materials: From the outset, the selected scriptures didn't come from any list. For each one of the topics, I started from scratch—reading and pondering all of the scriptures containing the key word (or related variant) in question—ranging from a modest count to many hundreds or more, depending on the topic—plus numerous other passages of relevance that do not contain the key word but convey a similar meaning and help with the understanding of the principles involved. This modus operandi had three advantages: first, it helped to unfold a more panoramic perspective of the wealth of wisdom pertaining to each of the topics; secondly, it enabled the selection of those passages with the greatest universal essence and import (i.e., the key scriptures featured after the introductory essay for each topic in the book); and thirdly—equally important—it allowed the discovery of patterns and interrelationships within the flow of scriptures so that stimulating questions and revealing answers could be formulated. I have characterized this methodology as Gospel Analytics™—an approach recommended to any reader with the aspiration to "feast upon the words of Christ" (2 Nephi 32:3) in a prayerful, meditative, and all-embracing way, thus experiencing the joy that comes from the guidance of the Spirit (see D&C 50:14).

Though it was not possible to include all of my findings, the harvest of this system of learning and pondering is the present guidebook, designed for the purpose of empowering missionaries or any student of the gospel to penetrate quickly and with ease the grand and all-encompassing forest of available scriptural wisdom to find the very trees, the very branches, and the very fruit needed to provide light and truth for a given situation. It is my sincere hope that the *Missionary Companion* will be just that—a companion and friend along the pathway of gospel service to help open vistas of understanding, answer vital questions, magnify callings, and help the missionary prepare the hearts and minds of the honest at heart to learn the truth and come into the fold of the Savior.

My sincere gratitude is extended to Covenant Communications for the honor granted me to prepare the *Missionary Companion* and to their editors and designers for the patient and skillful service provided in completing the project. I also express warm thanks to my dear wife, Carol Lynn, for her support and encouragement. It is a joy and privilege to make the Missionary Companion available to you, the readers. Your response and observations concerning this volume are always welcome.

A footnote in conclusion: After the heading for each of the topics in the book a number in brackets is given, indicating the number of occurrences of the topic's key word or phrase (or a variant thereof) contained in the sacred canon of scripture—Old Testament, New Testament, Book of Mormon, Doctrine and Covenants, and Pearl of Great Price. If the topic's specific key word or phrase does not occur in the scriptures, then a zero is placed in the bracket. Each topic starts with an introductory paragraph that defines and illustrates its importance to the gospel. This is followed by a number of key scriptures where the topic or a variant is found. For many of the topics, a guiding Q&A segment is also provided as a means of generating further discussion and pondering. The scriptural materials included have also been supplemented in a number of cases with relevant quotations from modern-day prophets, plus other supportive materials of interest. Where applicable, cross references to the monumental missionary manual *Preach My Gospel* have also been added.

Richard J. Allen

ABRAHAMIC COVENANT [0]. The covenant established between the Lord and Abraham extends forward the blessings and obligations associated with the priesthood of God and the gospel of salvation and exaltation. The Saints of this last dispensation are servants of the Most High, commissioned under the Abrahamic covenant to bring the blessings of the gospel to the entire world. According to this divine covenant, Israel was (and is) assured a homeland upon the earth and an inheritance in the mansions of heaven, a bounteous earthly progeny and (in keeping with the new and everlasting covenant of marriage) eternal increase in the hereafter, and the blessings of the fulness of gospel truth in the temporal sphere, as well as salvation and exaltation in the hereafter for the faithful and obedient. By divine decree, the obligation under this magnificent covenant was (and is) that the chosen people (see 1 Peter 2:9) are to convey priesthood blessings to the entire world and spread the gospel of saving ordinances to the receptive children of God in all lands. All those who receive the gospel of Jesus Christ through faith, repentance, baptism, and the gift of the Holy Ghost are counted as the seed of Abraham. Those not of direct Israelite heritage are welcomed into the fold by adoption (see Matthew 3:9; JST Matthew 3:36; Luke 3:8; JST Luke 3:5–7; Romans 8:15; Galatians 4:5–7; Ephesians 1:5).

D&C 110:12. "After this, Elias appeared, and committed the dispensation of the gospel of Abraham, saying that in us and our seed all generations after us should be blessed." (This event took place on April 3, 1836, in the Kirtland Temple, along with the appearance there of Jesus Christ, Moses, and Elijah, bringing blessings, keys, and powers to Joseph Smith and Oliver Cowdery as part of the Restoration.)

Abraham 2:8–11. "My name is Jehovah, and I know the end from the beginning; therefore my hand shall be over thee. And I will make of thee a great nation, and I will bless thee above measure, and make thy name great among all nations, and thou shalt be a blessing unto thy seed after thee, that in their hands they shall bear this ministry and Priesthood unto all nations; And I will bless them through thy name; for as many as receive this Gospel shall be called after thy name, and shall be accounted thy seed, and shall rise up and bless thee, as their father; And I will bless them that bless thee, and curse them that curse thee; and in thee (that is, in thy Priesthood) and in thy seed (that is, thy Priesthood), for I give unto thee a promise that this right shall continue in thee, and in thy seed after thee (that is to say, the literal seed, or the seed of the body) shall all the families of the earth be blessed, even with the blessings of the Gospel, which are the blessings of salvation, even of life eternal." (See also Genesis 17:6–7; 22:15–18; D&C 84:34.)

ACCOUNTABILITY [160]. The gift of moral agency requires that we all be accountable for our desires, thoughts, deeds, and actions. There are consequences (blessings or punishments) that follow our choices in the context of knowing right from wrong and acting on that knowledge.

Alma 12:14. "For our words will condemn us, yea, all our works will condemn us; we shall not be found spotless; and our thoughts will also condemn us; and in this awful state we shall not dare to look up to our God."

Alma 41:3–4. "And it is requisite with the justice of God that men should be judged according to their works; and if their works were good in this life, and the desires of their hearts were good, that they should also, at the last day, be restored unto that which is good. And if their works are evil they shall be restored unto them for evil."

D&C 72:3. "For it is required of the Lord, at the hand of every steward, to render an account of his stewardship, both in time and in eternity."

D&C 101:78. "That every man may act in doctrine and principle pertaining to futurity, according to the moral agency which I have given unto him, that every man may be accountable for his own sins in the day of judgment." (There will one day be a time of ultimate reckoning for each of us concerning our performance in this mortal life.)

D&C 137:10. "And I also beheld that all children who die before they arrive at the years of accountability are saved in the celestial kingdom of heaven." (The grace and mercy of the Lord cover all who are not capable of judging right from wrong; see also D&C 18:42; 20:71; Moroni 8:19.)

Second Article of Faith. "We believe that men will be punished for their own sins, and not for Adam's transgression."

Words of the Prophets | **Joseph F. Smith on accountability.** "If there is one principle of the gospel of Jesus Christ that goes directly to the very foundation of justice and righteousness, it is that great and glorious and God-like principle that every man will have to render an account for that which he does, and every man will be rewarded for his works, whether they be good or evil." —Joseph F. Smith, *Gospel Doctrine: Selections from the Sermons and Writings of Joseph F. Smith*, compiled by John A. Widtsoe (Salt Lake City: Deseret Book, 1939), 69.

ADVERSITY [13]. Adversity is a reality of life. Without adversity, we could not understand or appreciate joy in contrast to sorrow, righteousness in contrast to wickedness. Often, the problem is not so much the situation itself but rather our attitude toward the situation and the events and relationships around us. How we view the situation is the key to dealing with adversity. Perceiving things from a higher perspective invariably leads to greater understanding and frequently to the discovery of effective solutions.

2 Nephi 2:11. "For it must needs be, that there is an opposition in all things. If not so, my first-born in the wilderness, righteousness could not be brought to pass, neither wickedness, neither holiness nor misery, neither good nor bad. Wherefore, all things must needs be a compound in one; wherefore, if it should be one body it must needs remain as dead, having no life neither death, nor corruption nor incorruption, happiness nor misery, neither sense nor insensibility." (See also 2 Nephi 2:12, 15.)

D&C 24:8. "Be patient in afflictions, for thou shalt have many; but endure them, for, lo, I am with thee, even unto the end of thy days."

D&C 98:3. "Therefore, he giveth this promise unto you, with an immutable covenant that they [your prayers] shall be fulfilled; and all things wherewith you have been afflicted shall work together for your good, and to my name's glory, saith the Lord."

D&C 122:7. "And if thou shouldst be cast into the pit, or into the hands of murderers, and the sentence of death passed upon thee; if thou be cast into the deep; if the billowing surge conspire against thee; if fierce winds become thine enemy; if the heavens gather blackness, and all the elements combine to hedge up the way; and above all, if the very jaws of hell shall gape open the mouth wide after thee, know thou, my son, that all these things shall give thee experience, and shall be for thy good." (The Lord is comforting Joseph Smith during his incarceration in Liberty Jail; see also Alma 7:11–12.)

D&C 136:31. "My people must be tried in all things, that they may be prepared to receive the glory that I have for them, even the glory of Zion; and he that will not bear chastisement is not worthy of my kingdom." (See also Proverbs 3:5–6; Mosiah 3:19).

WORDS OF THE PROPHETS | **Ezra Taft Benson on adversity.** "Our great purpose in life is to overcome adversity and worldly consideration as we strive for things of the Spirit." —Ezra Taft Benson, *The Teachings of Ezra Taft Benson* (Salt Lake City: Bookcraft, 1988), 450.

AGENCY [28]. From the beginning, Heavenly Father decreed that His children would be blessed with the gift of agency—the right to choose for themselves what course of action to take. Only by learning to use agency, congruent with eternal principles of righteousness, would we become like our Maker. Agency is a gift from God. It is necessary for our growth. Our choices and decisions determine our blessings or the consequences of our actions. Agency can operate because there is (1) opposition in all things, (2) knowledge of good and evil, (3) laws and commandments given by God, and (4) the freedom to choose. This moral agency connotes responsibility and accountability in regard to our choices.

Joshua 24:15. "Choose you this day whom ye will serve . . . but as for me and my house, we will serve the Lord." (See also Alma 30:8; Moses 6:33.)

2 Nephi 2:15–16. "And to bring about his eternal purposes in the end of man, after he had created our first parents, and the beasts of the field and the fowls of the air, and in fine, all things which are created, it must needs be that there was an opposition; even the forbidden fruit in opposition to the tree of life; the one being sweet and the other bitter. Wherefore, the Lord God gave unto man that he should act for himself. Wherefore, man could not act for himself save it should be that he was enticed by the one or the other."

2 Nephi 2:27. "Wherefore, men are free according to the flesh; and all things are given them which are expedient unto man. And they are free to choose liberty and eternal life, through the great Mediator of all men, or to choose captivity and death, according to the captivity and power of the devil; for he seeketh that all men might be miserable like unto himself."

D&C 58:27–28. "Verily I say, men should be anxiously engaged in a good cause, and do many things of their own free will, and bring to pass much righteousness; For the power is in them, wherein they are agents unto themselves. And inasmuch as men do good they shall in nowise lose their reward."

D&C 93:30–31. "All truth is independent in that sphere in which God has placed it, to act for itself, as all intelligence also; otherwise there is no existence. Behold, here is the agency of man."

D&C 101:78. "That every man may act in doctrine and principle pertaining to futurity, according to the moral agency which I have given unto him, that every man may be accountable for his own sins in the day of judgment."

Moses 4:3. "Wherefore, because that Satan rebelled against me, and sought to destroy the agency of man, which I, the Lord God, had given him, and also, that I should give unto him mine own power; by the power of mine Only Begotten, I caused that he should be cast down."

Words of the Prophets | Lorenzo Snow on agency. "There is the principle of God in every individual. It is designed that man should act as God, and not be constrained and controlled in everything, but have an independency, an agency and the power to spread abroad and act according to the principle of godliness that is in him, act according to the power and intelligence and enlightenment of God, that he possesses, and not that he should be watched continually, and be controlled, and act as a slave in these matters."
—Lorenzo Snow, *Journal of Discourses*, 20:367.

ANGELS [543]. Angels, meaning "messengers," are ministering servants of the Lord. From the time of Adam onward, angels have been called to participate in making the gospel message available to mankind (Moses 5:58–59). The message of the Lord at the Second Coming will remind the world that He has continually reached out with saving truth through multiple channels of communication, including the stewardship of angels (D&C 43:25; see also D&C 84:42; 136:37). The holy scriptures contain a rich treasure of information about angels—what Paul referred to as "ministering spirits, sent forth to minister for them who shall be heirs of salvation" (Hebrews 1:14).

Matthew 16:27. "For the Son of man shall come in the glory of his Father with his angels; and then he shall reward every man according to his works."

Luke 15:10. "Likewise, I say unto you, there is joy in the presence of the angels of God over one sinner that repenteth."

1 Corinthians 13:1. "Though I speak with the tongues of men and of angels, and have not charity, I am become as sounding brass, or a tinkling cymbal."

1 Timothy 3:16. "And without controversy great is the mystery of godliness: God was manifest in the flesh, justified in the Spirit, seen of angels, preached unto the Gentiles, believed on in the world, received up into glory."

Hebrews 2:7, 9. "Thou madest him a little lower than the angels; thou crownedst him with glory and honour, and didst set him over the works of thy hands. . . . But we see Jesus, who was made a little lower than the angels for the suffering of death, crowned with glory and honour; that he by the grace of God should taste death for every man." (See also Hebrews 2:16.)

D&C 129:1–3. "There are two kinds of beings in heaven, namely: Angels, who are resurrected personages, having bodies of flesh and bones—For instance, Jesus said: Handle me and see, for a spirit hath not flesh and bones, as ye see me have. Secondly: the spirits of just men made perfect, they who are not resurrected, but inherit the same glory."

D&C 130:5–7. "There are no angels who minister to this earth but those who do belong or have belonged to it. The angels do not reside on a planet like this earth; But they reside in the presence of God, on a globe like a sea of glass and fire, where all things for their glory are manifest, past, present, and future, and are continually before the Lord."

ADDITIONAL INFORMATION—**Description of an angel**. After the angel Moroni appeared to the young Joseph Smith on September 21, 1823, Joseph gave this account: "He had on a loose robe of most exquisite whiteness. It was a whiteness beyond anything earthly I had ever seen; nor do I believe that any earthly thing could be made to appear so exceedingly white and brilliant. His hands were naked, and his arms also, a little above the wrist; so, also, were his feet naked, as were his legs, a little above the ankles. His head and neck were also bare. I could discover that he had no other clothing on but this robe, as it was open, so that I could see into his bosom. Not only was his robe exceedingly white, but his whole person was glorious beyond description, and his countenance truly like lightning." —Joseph Smith, JS—H 1:32–33.

Note: Not all angels are heavenly in character. The Savior spoke of the devil and his angels (see Matthew 25:41). Paul warned that Satan can appear as "an angel of light" (2 Corinthians 11:14; see also Alma 30:53). Peter also spoke of the angels cast "down to hell" (2 Peter 2:4; see also Jude 1:6).

APOSTASY [4]. The word *apostasy* derives from the Greek roots *apo* (away from) and *sta* (to stand)—hence implying standing away from something; in this case, it means "to be separated from a set of principles or values," thus abandoning one's beliefs or standing far away from the truth. Apostasy and restoration are key interdependent themes in the historical unfolding of the gospel plan through the dispensations of time. It is the widespread falling away from covenant principles (such as occurred among the Saints following the earthly mission of the Savior and His apostolic leaders) that necessitates a restoration of divine truth to mankind through divine intervention. Where there has been an apostasy—or a falling away—there is a vacuum that can be redressed only through a restoration, or a coming back once again into a closeness with the Lord and His gospel. Such a restoration, on a grand scale, was launched through the First Vision proffered to the boy Joseph Smith in the spring of 1820. That magnificent event inaugurated a series of significant happenings that resulted in the reestablishment of the kingdom of God upon the earth once again as an enduring blessing to God's children:"unto the bringing of them out of darkness unto light—yea, out of hidden darkness and out of captivity unto freedom" (2 Nephi 3:5). The radiant miracle of the Restoration in our time is best perceived and understood against the blackness of the Apostasy.

Amos 8:11–12. "Behold, the days come, saith the Lord God, that I will send a famine in the land, not a famine of bread, nor a thirst for water, but of hearing the words of the Lord: And they shall wander from sea to sea, and from the north even to the east, they shall run to and fro to seek the word of the Lord, and shall not find it."

Matthew 7:15–17. "Beware of false prophets, which come to you in sheep's clothing, but inwardly they are ravening wolves. Ye shall know them by their fruits. Do men gather grapes of thorns, or figs of thistles? Even so every good tree bringeth forth good fruit; but a corrupt tree bringeth forth evil fruit." (See also 3 Nephi 14:15–17.)

Matthew 24:9–13, 23–24. "Then shall they deliver you up to be afflicted, and shall kill you: and ye shall be hated of all nations for my name's sake. And then shall many be offended, and shall betray one another, and shall hate one another. And many false prophets shall rise, and shall deceive many. And because iniquity shall abound, the love of many shall wax cold. But he that shall endure unto the end, the same shall be saved. . . . Then if any man shall say unto you, Lo, here is Christ, or there; believe it not. For there shall arise false Christs, and false prophets, and shall shew great signs and wonders; insomuch that, if it were possible, they shall deceive the very elect."

John 16:1–4. "These things have I spoken unto you, that ye should not be offended. They shall put you out of the synagogues: yea, the time cometh, that whosoever killeth you will think that he doeth God service. And these things will they do unto you, because they have not known the Father, nor me. But these things have I told you, that when the time shall come, ye may remember that I told you of them. And these things I said not unto you at the beginning, because I was with you."

Acts 20:28–30. "Take heed therefore unto yourselves, and to all the flock, over the which the Holy Ghost hath made you overseers, to feed the church of God, which he hath purchased with his own blood. For I [Paul] know this, that after my departing shall grievous wolves enter in among you, not sparing the flock. Also of your own selves shall men arise, speaking perverse things, to draw away disciples after them."

2 Thessalonians 2:2–3. "Be not soon shaken in mind, or be troubled, neither by spirit, nor by word, nor by letter as from us, as that the day of Christ is at hand. Let no man deceive you by any means: for that day shall not come, except there come a falling away first, and that man of sin be revealed, the son of perdition." Note the JST version of verse 9 in this passage: *"Yea, the Lord, even Jesus,* whose coming is *not until* after *there cometh a falling away, by* the working of Satan with all power, and signs and lying wonders." (Added words shown in italics.)

2 Nephi 26:20–21. "And the Gentiles are lifted up in the pride of their eyes, and have stumbled, because of the greatness of their stumbling block, that they have built up many churches; nevertheless, they put down the power and miracles of God, and preach up unto themselves their own wisdom and their own learning, that they may get gain and grind upon the face of the poor. And there are many churches built up which cause envyings, and strifes, and malice."

Examples of apostasy underway (then and now).

Matthew 15:8–9. "This people draweth nigh unto me with their mouth, and honoureth me with their lips; but their heart is far from me. But in vain they do worship me, teaching for doctrines the commandments of men." (See also Mark 7:7; Isaiah 29:13)

John 12:40. "He hath blinded their eyes, and hardened their heart; that they should not see with their eyes, nor understand with their heart, and be converted, and I should heal them." (See also Isaiah 53:1.)

Galatians 1:6–7. "I marvel that ye are so soon removed from him that called you into the grace of Christ unto another gospel: Which is not another; but there be some that trouble you, and would pervert the gospel of Christ." (See also Romans 10:2–3; 1 Corinthians 1:11–13; Galatians 2:4; Titus 1:9–10; Jude 1:4.)

1 John 2:18–19. "Little children, it is the last time: and as ye have heard that antichrist shall come, even now are there many antichrists; whereby we know that it is the last time.

They went out from us, but they were not of us; for if they had been of us, they would no doubt have continued with us." (See also Titus 1:16; 2 Corinthians 11:13.)

Mormon 1:13–14. "But wickedness did prevail upon the face of the whole land, insomuch that the Lord did take away his beloved disciples, and the work of miracles and of healing did cease because of the iniquity of the people. And there were no gifts from the Lord, and the Holy Ghost did not come upon any, because of their wickedness and unbelief."

D&C 84:49–50. "And the whole world lieth in sin, and groaneth under darkness and under the bondage of sin. And by this you may know they are under the bondage of sin, because they come not unto me." (See also D&C 33:4; 38:11.)

D&C 86:3–4. "And after they [the apostles] have fallen asleep the great persecutor of the church . . . even Satan, sitteth to reign. . . . But behold, in the last days, even now while the Lord is beginning to bring forth the word, and the blade is springing up and is yet tender—"

D&C 123:12. "For there are many yet on the earth among all sects, parties, and denominations, who are blinded by the subtle craftiness of men, whereby they lie in wait to deceive, and who are only kept from the truth because they know not where to find it—"

Revelation, chapters 2–3. At the conclusion of the apostolic administration, only seven churches (congregations of Saints) remained, with dire apostate trends and tendencies manifest among them.

D&C 38:39. "And if ye seek the riches which it is the will of the Father to give unto you, ye shall be the richest of all people, for ye shall have the riches of eternity; and it must needs be that the riches of the earth are mine to give; but beware of pride, lest ye become as the Nephites of old." (See also Daniel 2:44.)

WORDS OF THE PROPHETS | Joseph Smith on the Lord's instructions concerning apostate Christianity. "It no sooner appeared than I found myself delivered from the enemy which held me bound. When the light rested upon me I saw two Personages, whose brightness and glory defy all description, standing above me in the air. One of them spake unto me, calling me by name and said, pointing to the other—*This is My Beloved Son. Hear Him!* My object in going to inquire of the Lord was to know which of all the sects was right, that I might know which to join. No sooner, therefore, did I get possession of myself, so as to be able to speak, than I asked the Personages who stood above me in the light, which of all the sects was right (for at this time it had never entered into my heart that all were wrong)—and which I should join. I was answered that I must join none of them, for they were all wrong." —JS—H 1:17–19.

ADDITIONAL INFORMATION—**How is the Savior the source of light to dispel the night of the Apostasy?** John 3:19–20—"And this is the condemnation, that light is come into the world, and men loved darkness rather than light, because their deeds were evil. For every one that doeth evil hateth the light, neither cometh to the light, lest his deeds should be reproved."

The scriptures are replete with references to the Savior as being the source of light and life: "Behold, I am Jesus Christ, the Son of God. I am the life and the light of the world" (D&C 11:28). "I am the light and the life of the world. I am Alpha and Omega, the beginning and the end" (3 Nephi 9:18; see also 3 Nephi 11:11; 15:9; Ether 4:12; D&C 12:9; 45:7; John 9:5; 12:46). "And that which doth not edify is not of God, and is darkness. That which is of God is light; and he that receiveth light, and continueth in God, receiveth more light; and that light groweth brighter and brighter until the perfect day" (D&C 50:23–24). Our charge is to stay close to the Savior, to be part of His plan of life and perfection—the plan of salvation.

Cross reference to "Apostasy": see Preach My Gospel, *35–36.*

APOSTLES [143]. The word *apostle* derives from the Greek word *apostolos*, meaning "messenger," or "one who has been sent." The first reference to Apostles occurs relative to the calling of the twelve disciples by Jesus Christ (Matthew 10:1–4; also Luke 6:13–16; 9:1–2; Mark 3:14; 6:7). Apostles are called to be special witnesses of Jesus Christ to the world and are leaders at the head of Christ's Church.

Matthew 28:19–20. "Go ye therefore, and teach all nations, baptizing them in the name of the Father, and of the Son, and of the Holy Ghost: Teaching them to observe all things whatsoever I have commanded you: and, lo, I am with you alway, even unto the end of the world. Amen." (See also Mark 16:14–16.)

John 15:14–17. "Ye are my friends, if ye do whatsoever I command you. Henceforth I call you not servants; for the servant knoweth not what his lord doeth: but I have called you friends; for all things that I have heard of my Father I have made known unto you. Ye have not chosen me, but I have chosen you, and ordained you, that ye should go and bring forth fruit, and that your fruit should remain: that whatsoever ye shall ask of the Father in my name, he may give it you. These things I command you, that ye love one another."

Acts 1:21–22. "Wherefore of these men which have companied with us all the time that the Lord Jesus went in and out among us, Beginning from the baptism of John, unto that same day that he was taken up from us, must one be ordained to be a witness with us of his resurrection." (See also Acts 4:33.)

D&C 107:23. "The twelve traveling councilors are called to be the Twelve Apostles, or special witnesses of the name of Christ in all the world—thus differing from other officers in the church in the duties of their calling." (See also D&C 107:30.)

D&C 107:33, 35. "The Twelve are a Traveling Presiding High Council, to officiate in the name of the Lord, under the direction of the Presidency of the Church, agreeable to the institution of heaven; to build up the church, and regulate all the affairs of the same in all nations, first unto the Gentiles and secondly unto the Jews. . . . The Twelve being sent out, holding the keys, to open the door by the proclamation of the gospel of Jesus Christ, and first unto the Gentiles and then unto the Jews."

ADDITIONAL INFORMATION—**The original Twelve.**

1. Simon (Peter)
2. Andrew (brother of Peter)
3. James (son of Zebedee; the Lord called him and his brother John "Boanerges" or "sons of thunder," as in Mark 3:17)

4. John (brother of James)
5. Philip
6. Bartholomew (generally identified as Nathanael—see John 1:45–49; 21:2)
7. Thomas
8. Matthew (the publican, also called Levi as in Mark 2:14 and Luke 5:27–29)
9. James (son of Alphaeus)
10. Lebbaeus (with surname Thaddaeus, probably the same as Judas in Luke 6:16)
11. Simon the Canaanite (probably more accurately translated as Cananaean, i.e., one with an attachment to certain political leanings in favor of an independent Israel in the days of Roman imperial sovereignty)
12. Judas Iscariot

The original Twelve of the Restoration

1. Thomas B. Marsh (fell away but returned)
2. David W. Patten (faithful and martyred)
3. Brigham Young (always faithful)
4. Heber C. Kimball (always faithful)
5. Orson Hyde (fell away but returned)
6. William E. McLellin (fell away and became hostile)
7. Parley P. Pratt (faithful and penitent)
8. Luke S. Johnson (fell away but returned)
9. William Smith (fell away and never returned)
10. Orson Pratt (fell away but returned)
11. John F. Boynton (fell away and never returned)
12. Lyman E. Johnson (fell away and never returned)

ATONEMENT [128]. The Atonement is central to all aspects of the gospel. It is the empowering crux of the plan of salvation and the pillar of God's design for "the immortality and eternal life of man" (Moses 1:39). Because the Son accommodated Himself fully to the will of the Father (Moses 4:2), the Atonement, in all of its glory, unfolded as a magnificent gift to mankind, empowering the resurrection for everyone and giving the opportunity for the faithful and obedient to gain access once again to the presence of God. When we diligently apply the principles of the Atonement to our lives through the covenant process—through faith, repentance, baptism, receiving the gift of the Holy Ghost, and enduring to the end—we become liberated from the fallen state we are in through the "merits, and mercy, and grace of the Holy Messiah" (2 Nephi 2:8). We become free through Christ by obedience.

John 3:16–17. "For God so loved the world, that he gave his only begotten Son, that whosoever believeth in him should not perish, but have everlasting life. For God sent not his Son into the world to condemn the world; but that the world through him might be saved."

Romans 6:23. "For the wages of sin is death; but the gift of God is eternal life through Jesus Christ our Lord."

1 Corinthians 15:19–22. "If in this life only we have hope in Christ, we are of all men most miserable. But now is Christ risen from the dead, and become the firstfruits of them that slept. For since by man came death, by man came also the resurrection of the dead. For as in Adam all die, even so in Christ shall all be made alive."

Hebrews 5:9. "And being made perfect, he became the author of eternal salvation unto all them that obey him."

2 Nephi 25:23. "For we labor diligently to write, to persuade our children, and also our brethren, to believe in Christ, and to be reconciled to God; for we know that it is by grace that we are saved, after all we can do." (See also Ephesians 2:8–10; James 2:17.)

Alma 7:11–12. "And he shall go forth, suffering pains and afflictions and temptations of every kind; and this that the word might be fulfilled which saith he will take upon him the pains and the sicknesses of his people. And he will take upon him death, that he may loose the bands of death which bind his people; and he will take upon him their infirmities, that his bowels may be filled with mercy, according to the flesh, that he may know according to the flesh how to succor his people according to their infirmities." (Note: The suffering of our Savior through the Atonement makes possible the Lord's understanding of our needs. He will succor us. He will help us in our trials, tribulations, and all our infirmities. We can come to realize, as did father Lehi, that "I am encircled about eternally in the arms of his love"—2 Nephi 1:15.)

Alma 34:9–10. "For it is expedient that an atonement should be made; for according to the great plan of the Eternal God there must be an atonement made, or else all mankind must unavoidably perish; yea, all are hardened; yea, all are fallen and are lost, and must perish except it be through the atonement which it is expedient should be made. For it is expedient that there should be a great and last sacrifice; yea, not a sacrifice of man, neither of beast, neither of any manner of fowl; for it shall not be a human sacrifice; but it must be an infinite and eternal sacrifice."

Alma 34:15–16. "And thus he shall bring salvation to all those who shall believe on his name; this being the intent of this last sacrifice, to bring about the bowels of mercy, which overpowereth justice, and bringeth about means unto men that they may have faith unto repentance. And thus mercy can satisfy the demands of justice, and encircles them in the arms of safety, while he that exercises no faith unto repentance is exposed to the whole law of the demands of justice; therefore only unto him that has faith unto repentance is brought about the great and eternal plan of redemption."

3 Nephi 27:13–16. "Behold I have given unto you my gospel, and this is the gospel which I have given unto you—that I came into the world to do the will of my Father, because my Father sent me. And my Father sent me that I might be lifted up upon the cross; and after that I had been lifted up upon the cross, that I might draw all men unto me, that as I have been lifted up by men even so should men be lifted up by the Father, to stand before me, to be judged of their works, whether they be good or whether they be evil—And for this cause have I been lifted up; therefore, according to the power of the Father I will draw all men unto me, that they may be judged according to their works. And it shall come to pass, that whoso repenteth and is baptized in my name shall be filled; and if he endureth to the end, behold, him will I hold guiltless before my Father at that day when I shall stand to judge the world." (See also John 12:32—"And I, if I be lifted up from the earth, will draw all men unto me.")

3 Nephi 27:20. "Now this is the commandment: Repent, all ye ends of the earth, and come unto me and be baptized in my name, that ye may be sanctified by the reception of the Holy Ghost, that ye may stand spotless before me at the last day. Verily, verily, I say unto you, this is my gospel; and ye know the things that ye must do in my church; for the works which ye have seen me do that shall ye also do; for that which ye have seen me do even that shall ye do."

D&C 19:15–19. "Therefore I command you to repent—repent, lest I smite you by the rod of my mouth, and by my wrath, and by my anger, and your sufferings be sore—how sore you know not, how exquisite you know not, yea, how hard to bear you know not. For behold, I, God, have suffered these things for all, that they might not suffer if they would repent; But if they would not repent they must suffer even as I; Which suffering caused myself, even God, the greatest of all, to tremble because of pain, and to bleed at every pore, and to suffer both body and spirit—and would that I might not drink the bitter cup, and shrink—Nevertheless, glory be to the Father, and I partook and finished my preparations unto the children of men." (See also Luke 22:44.)

D&C 76:40–43. "And this is the gospel, the glad tidings, which the voice out of the heavens bore record unto us—That he came into the world, even Jesus, to be crucified for the world, and to bear the sins of the world, and to sanctify the world, and to cleanse it from all unrighteousness; That through him all might be saved whom the Father had put into his power and made by him; Who glorifies the Father, and saves all the works of his hands, except those sons of perdition who deny the Son after the Father has revealed him."

D&C 88:14–17. "Now, verily I say unto you, that through the redemption which is made for you is brought to pass the resurrection from the dead. And the spirit and the body are the soul of man. And the resurrection from the dead is the redemption of the soul. And the redemption of the soul is through him that quickeneth all things, in whose bosom it is decreed that the poor and the meek of the earth shall inherit it."

Moses 6:59–60. "That by reason of transgression cometh the fall, which fall bringeth death, and inasmuch as ye were born into the world by water, and blood, and the spirit, which I have made, and so became of dust a living soul, even so ye must be born again into the kingdom of heaven, of water, and of the Spirit, and be cleansed by blood, even the blood of mine Only Begotten; that ye might be sanctified from all sin, and enjoy the words of eternal life in this world, and eternal life in the world to come, even immortal glory; For by the water ye keep the commandment; by the Spirit ye are justified, and by the blood ye are sanctified."

Third Article of Faith. "We believe that through the Atonement of Christ, all mankind may be saved, by obedience to the laws and ordinances of the Gospel."

Words of the Prophets | Joseph Smith on the Atonement. "How indescribably glorious are these things to mankind! Of a truth they may be considered tidings of great joy to all people; and tidings, too, that ought to fill the earth and cheer the hearts of every one when sounded in his ears." —Joseph Smith, *HC* 2:5–6.

John Taylor on man becoming gods through the Atonement. "It is for the exaltation of man to this state of superior intelligence and Godhead that the *mediation* and *atonement* of Jesus Christ is instituted" —John Taylor, Mediation and Atonement (Salt Lake City: Deseret Book, 1892), 140.

Joseph F. Smith on repentance through the Atonement. "By the atonement of Jesus Christ, the sins of the repentant shall be washed away, though they be crimson they shall be made white as wool." —Joseph F. Smith, *CR*, October, 1899, 41.

ADDITIONAL INFORMATION—**What was the greatest moment in the history of mankind?** The Atonement is three-fold: Christ's suffering in Gethsemane for our trials and sins, His death on the cross, and His Resurrection to bring new life. The suffering of the Savior on the cross at Golgotha was unspeakable and intense; and yet, it was during His travail in the Garden of Gethsemane that the transcendent triumph of redemption leading to eternal life was ultimately attained, followed by the sequential triumph over death on the cross brought about through the resurrection, as He later confirmed: "Nevertheless, glory be to the Father, and I partook and finished my preparations unto the children of men" (D&C 19:19).

That moment in the Garden of Gethsemane was at the center of the flow of all history, both human and divine. This was a moment in time unlike any other. It was a moment of both infinite agony and redeeming charity, both sorrow "unto death" (Matthew 26:38) and atonement unto life, both suffering unspeakable and triumph immeasurable—the ultimate result of eternal design and heavenly will. What did this moment mean to humankind? Just this: it meant the victory over the Fall; the hope of liberty over the reality of everlasting spiritual imprisonment; the possibility of eternal joy in the presence of God over the horror of a never-ending separation from one's heavenly roots. This was the moment when faith for all God's children was raised to a higher power—"this being the intent of this last sacrifice, to bring about the bowels of mercy, which overpowereth justice, and bringeth about means unto men that they may have faith unto repentance" (Alma 34:15). This moment in time, coupled with Christ's victory over life and death, was motivated by love and empowered by grace to accomplish the inexorable will of God unto the saving of all mankind.

Cross reference to "Atonement": see Preach My Gospel, *31–34, 48, 51–52, 58, 60–61.*

BAPTISM [85]. Baptism is the universal covenant ordinance that opens the gateway to salvation for all those with a broken heart and contrite spirit, those who desire to take upon themselves the name of Jesus Christ, enter His fold, and receive a remission of their sins through faith and repentance, with the baptism of fire (gift of the Holy Ghost) following. Baptism is only appropriate for those who are of the age of accountability, which the Lord, through revelation, has revealed to be eight years old. Baptism is emblematic of a rebirth—a coming forth from a state of sinfulness to a state of spiritual rejuvenation and purification through the blessings of the Atonement, much like rising from the grave to a new life through the resurrection. The word *baptism* derives from the Greek verb baptizein, meaning "to immerse or dip."

John 3:3–5. "Jesus answered and said unto him, Verily, verily, I say unto thee, Except a man be born again, he cannot see the kingdom of God. Nicodemus saith unto him, How can a man be born when he is old? can he enter the second time into his mother's womb, and be born? Jesus answered, Verily, verily, I say unto thee, Except a man be born of water and of the Spirit, he cannot enter into the kingdom of God."

2 Nephi 31:13. "Wherefore, my beloved brethren, I know that if ye shall follow the Son, with full purpose of heart, acting no hypocrisy and no deception before God, but with real intent, repenting of your sins, witnessing unto the Father that ye are willing to take upon you the name of Christ, by baptism—yea, by following your Lord and your Savior down into the water, according to his word, behold, then shall ye receive the Holy Ghost; yea, then cometh the baptism of fire and of the Holy Ghost; and then can ye speak with the tongue of angels, and shout praises unto the Holy One of Israel."

3 Nephi 11:37–39. "And again I say unto you, ye must repent, and become as a little child, and be baptized in my name, or ye can in nowise receive these things. And again I say unto you, ye must repent, and be baptized in my name, and become as a little child, or ye can in nowise inherit the kingdom of God. Verily, verily, I say unto you, that this is my doctrine, and whoso buildeth upon this buildeth upon my rock, and the gates of hell shall not prevail against them."

Moroni 6:1–4. "And now I speak concerning baptism. Behold, elders, priests, and teachers were baptized; and they were not baptized save they brought forth fruit meet that they were worthy of it. Neither did they receive any unto baptism save they came forth with a broken heart and a contrite spirit, and witnessed unto the church that they truly repented of all their sins. And none were received unto baptism save they took upon them the name of Christ, having a determination to serve him to the end. And after they had been received unto baptism, and were wrought upon and cleansed by the power of the Holy Ghost, they were numbered among the people of the church of Christ; and their names were taken, that they might be remembered and nourished by the good word of God, to keep them in the right way, to keep them continually watchful unto prayer, relying alone upon the merits of Christ, who was the author and the finisher of their faith."

D&C 33:11–13. "Yea, repent and be baptized, every one of you, for a remission of your sins; yea, be baptized even by water, and then cometh the baptism of fire and of the Holy Ghost. Behold, verily, verily, I say unto you, this is my gospel; and remember that they shall have faith in me or they can in nowise be saved; And upon this rock I will build my church; yea, upon this rock ye are built, and if ye continue, the gates of hell shall not prevail against you."

D&C 20:37. "And again, by way of commandment to the church concerning the manner of baptism—All those who humble themselves before God, and desire to be baptized, and come forth with broken hearts and contrite spirits, and witness before the church that they have truly repented of all their sins, and are willing to take upon them the name of Jesus Christ, having a determination to serve him to the end, and truly manifest by their works that they have received of the Spirit of Christ unto the remission of their sins, shall be received by baptism into his church."

Moses 6:58–60. "Therefore I give unto you [Adam] a commandment, to teach these things freely unto your children, saying: That by reason of transgression cometh the fall, which fall bringeth death, and inasmuch as ye were born into the world by water, and blood, and the spirit, which I have made, and so became of dust a living soul, even so ye must be born again into the kingdom of heaven, of water, and of the Spirit, and be cleansed by blood, even the blood of mine Only Begotten; that ye might be sanctified from all sin, and enjoy the words of eternal life in this world, and eternal life in the world to come, even immortal glory; For by the water ye keep the commandment; by the Spirit ye are justified, and by the blood ye are sanctified."

Fourth Article of Faith. "We believe that the first principles and ordinances of the Gospel are: first, Faith in the Lord Jesus Christ; second, Repentance; third, Baptism by immersion for the remission of sins; fourth, Laying on of hands for the gift of the Holy Ghost."

Cross reference to "Baptism": see Preach My Gospel, *63–65, 203–210.*

BAPTISM FOR THE DEAD [8]. The doctrine and practice of baptism for the dead is a glorious confirmation of the universal love, compassion, and grace of our Father in Heaven and His Son Jesus Christ. In the wake of the restoration of the keys and powers of vicarious temple work in our day, the Prophet Joseph Smith declared in an epistle dated September 6, 1842: "Let your hearts rejoice, and be exceedingly glad. Let the earth break forth into singing. Let the dead speak forth anthems of eternal praise to the King Immanuel, who hath ordained, before the world was, that which would enable us to redeem them out of their prison; for the prisoners shall go free. . . . And let the sun, moon, and the morning stars sing together, and let all the sons of God shout for joy! And let the eternal creations declare his name forever and ever! And again I say, how glorious is the voice we hear from heaven, proclaiming in our ears, glory, and salvation, and honor, and immortality, and eternal life; kingdoms, principalities, and powers!" (D&C 128:22–23). Elijah restored the binding and sealing powers for the ordinances of the priesthood, including temple ordinances, on April 3, 1836, in the Kirtland Temple (see D&C 110:13–16).

This "welding link . . . between the fathers and the children" (D&C 128:18), empowered through vicarious work for the dead, enables the living to serve in love on behalf of the salvation of their deceased family and friends as "saviours . . . on mount Zion" (Obadiah 1:21). Baptism in the flesh being a universal commandment (see John 3:3–5), the divine institution of vicarious work for the dead also allows the good news of salvation to be disseminated in the spirit world to give all of God's children a chance to accept the gospel message and then receive saving ordinances by proxy (1 Peter 4:6).

John 5:25–26. "Verily, verily, I say unto you, The hour is coming, and now is, when the dead shall hear the voice of the Son of God: and they that hear shall live. For as the Father hath life in himself; so hath he given to the Son to have life in himself."

1 Corinthians 15:29. "Else what shall they do which are baptized for the dead, if the dead rise not at all? why are they then baptized for the dead?"

1 Peter 3:18–21. "For Christ also hath once suffered for sins, the just for the unjust, that he might bring us to God, being put to death in the flesh, but quickened by the Spirit: By which also he went and preached unto the spirits in prison; Which sometime were disobedient, when once the longsuffering of God waited in the days of Noah, while the ark was a preparing, wherein few, that is, eight souls were saved by water. The like figure whereunto even baptism doth also now save us (not the putting away of the filth of the flesh, but the answer of a good conscience toward God,) by the resurrection of Jesus Christ."

D&C 124:28–31. "For there is not a place found on earth that he may come to and restore again that which was lost unto you, or which he hath taken away, even the fulness of the priesthood. For a baptismal font there is not upon the earth, that they, my saints, may be baptized for those who are dead—For this ordinance belongeth to my house, and cannot be acceptable to me, only in the days of your poverty, wherein ye are not able to build a house unto me. But I command you, all ye my saints, to build a house unto me; and I grant unto you a sufficient time to build a house unto me; and during this time your baptisms shall be acceptable unto me."

D&C 127:5–7. "And again, I give unto you a word in relation to the baptism for your dead. Verily, thus saith the Lord unto you concerning your dead: When any of you are baptized for your dead, let there be a recorder, and let him be eye-witness of your baptisms; let him hear with his ears, that he may testify of a truth, saith the Lord; That in all your recordings it may be recorded in heaven; whatsoever you bind on earth, may be bound in heaven; whatsoever you loose on earth, may be loosed in heaven."

D&C 128:12–13. "Herein is glory and honor, and immortality and eternal life—The ordinance of baptism by water, to be immersed therein in order to answer to the likeness of the dead, that one principle might accord with the other; to be immersed in the water and come forth out of the water is in the likeness of the resurrection of the dead in coming forth out of their graves; hence, this ordinance was instituted to form a relationship with the ordinance of baptism for the dead, being in likeness of the dead. Consequently, the baptismal font was instituted as a similitude of the grave, and was commanded to be in a place underneath where the living are wont to assemble, to show forth the living and the dead, and that all things may have their likeness, and that they may accord one with another—that which is earthly conforming to that which is heavenly, as Paul hath declared."

D&C 128:18. "For we without them [our kindred dead] cannot be made perfect; neither can they without us be made perfect. Neither can they nor we be made perfect without those who have died in the gospel also; for it is necessary in the ushering in of the dispensation of the fulness of times, which dispensation is now beginning to usher in, that a whole and complete and perfect union, and welding together of dispensations, and keys, and powers, and glories should take place, and be revealed from the days of Adam even to the present time. And not only this, but those things which never have been revealed from the foundation of the world, but have been kept hid from the wise and prudent, shall be revealed unto babes and sucklings in this, the dispensation of the fulness of times."

D&C 137:5–7. "I saw Father Adam and Abraham; and my father and my mother; my brother Alvin, that has long since slept; And marveled how it was that he had obtained an inheritance in that kingdom, seeing that he had departed this life before the Lord had set his hand to gather Israel the second time, and had not been baptized for the remission of sins. Thus came the voice of the Lord unto me, saying: All who have died without a knowledge of this gospel, who would have received it if they had been permitted to tarry, shall be heirs of the celestial kingdom of God."

D&C 138:32–34. "Thus was the gospel preached to those who had died in their sins, without a knowledge of the truth, or in transgression, having rejected the prophets. These were taught faith in God, repentance from sin, vicarious baptism for the remission of sins, the gift of the Holy Ghost by the laying on of hands, And all other principles of the gospel that were necessary for them to know in order to qualify themselves that they might be judged according to men in the flesh, but live according to God in the spirit."

BIBLE, WORD OF GOD AS FAR AS IT IS TRANSLATED CORRECTLY [Bible: 16]. In the words of Ezekiel, the Bible is the stick of Judah that is to be combined with the stick of Joseph (the Book of Mormon) in the latter days (Ezekiel 37:16–17). The Bible, with the thirty-nine books of the Old Testament and the twenty-seven books of the New Testament, is the record of God's covenant dealings with His people from the beginning of time through the mortal ministry of the Messiah and His servants.

The Prophet Joseph Smith, who translated the Book of Mormon from ancient plates through divine inspiration, characterized that book as "the most correct of any book on earth, and the keystone of our religion, and a man would get nearer to God by abiding by its precepts, than by any other book" (*HC* 4:461). Concerning the Bible, Joseph Smith spent much time from June 1830 to July 1833 examining the text and providing an inspired translation, or rewording, to render the account more accurate (see *HC* 1:98, 369). Unlike the Book of Mormon, given fresh from its prophetic source, the Bible consists of multiple documents that had passed through many hands over the generations, and by the time it was constituted as the amalgam volume passed down to us under the title *Bible* (meaning "book" from its Latin and Greek word origin), it had undergone various changes and revisions—some of them not always consonant with divine principles. Hence the need for modern revisions and adjustments brought about through inspired guidance from the Lord. Joseph Smith characterized the position of the Church concerning the word of God as follows: "We believe the Bible to be the word of God as far as it is translated correctly; we also believe the Book of Mormon to be the word of God" (Articles of Faith 1:8).

In vision, Nephi was shown the coming forth of the Bible in its purity (1 Nephi 13:24–25). Thereafter, Nephi was shown the subsequent adjustments and dilutions imposed upon the Bible at the hands of its purveyors and the losses of plain doctrine that caused the people of the Gentiles to stumble (1 Nephi 13:26, 28–29).

ADDITIONAL INFORMATION—**What are examples of the major adjustments and rewordings to the Bible completed by Joseph Smith?**

• Eight chapters of the Book of Moses in the Pearl of Great Price, including chapter 1, a major prefatory addition to the book of Genesis. This material makes clear that the gospel principles of faith, repentance, baptism, and the gift of the Holy Ghost were taught from the earliest days of mankind, beginning with Adam; by contrast, the words *baptism* and *Holy Ghost* do not even appear in the KJV of the Bible.

• Five chapters of the Book of Abraham in the Pearl of Great Price, including much insight into the premortal existence, the Creation, and the magnificent contours and breadth of the Abrahamic covenant.

• The JST restores to our understanding the covenant continuity of the priesthood throughout the dispensations of time and the interconnected ministries of the ancient prophets, including Enoch, Noah, and Abraham. Thus, for example, a fuller account of the ministry of Melchizedek given in the JST Genesis 14:25–40.

• Matthew 23:39 and Matthew 24, included in the Pearl of Great Price, giving insight into the events associated with the final chapter of the earth's history

• Multiple smaller corrections and additions included in the footnotes of the current LDS edition of the KJV of the Bible.

Are there factual errors or inconsistencies in the Bible? Yes, there are, since the accounts contained therein have come forth through various hands and at various times. An example, concerning the conversion of Saul (Paul): "And the men which journeyed with him stood speechless, hearing a voice, but seeing no man" (Acts 9:7); "And they that were with me saw indeed the light, and were afraid; but they heard not the voice of him that spake to me" (Acts 22:9). The JST renders the text as follows: "And they who were journeying with him saw indeed the light, and were afraid; but they heard not the voice of him who spake to him" (JST Acts 9:7).

Consider the death of Judas: "And he cast down the pieces of silver in the temple, and departed, and went and hanged himself" (Matthew 27:5); "Now this man purchased a field with the reward of iniquity; and falling headlong, he burst asunder in the midst, and all his bowels gushed out" (Acts 1:18). The JST renders the text as follows: "And he cast down the pieces of silver in the temple, and departed, and went and hanged himself on a tree. And straightway he fell down, and his bowels gushed out, and he died" (JST Matthew 27:6).

Clearly the inconsistencies illustrated above (and corrected by the JST) came about through errors of transmission in the handling of the text. Moroni, the last historian of the Book of Mormon text, gives good advice concerning such shortcomings: "Condemn me not because of mine imperfection, neither my father [Mormon], because of his imperfection, neither them who have written before him; but rather give thanks unto God that he hath made manifest unto you our imperfections, that ye may learn to be more wise than we have been" (Mormon 9:31).

Cross reference to "Bible": see Preach My Gospel, *106.*

BOOK OF MORMON [18]. The Book of Mormon is the word of God. It contains the fulness of the gospel of Jesus Christ and stands as another witness that Jesus is the Christ. Throughout the Book of Mormon, we are privileged to view panoramically the great blessings and tender mercies the Lord has shown to His children here upon the earth and especially on the American continent through His everlasting Atonement.

Isaiah 29:4, 11. "And thou shalt be brought down, and shalt speak out of the ground, and thy speech shall be low out of the dust, and thy voice shall be, as of one that hath a familiar spirit, out of the ground, and thy speech shall whisper out of the dust . . . And the vision of all is become unto you as the words of a book that is sealed, which men deliver to one that is learned, saying, Read this, I pray thee: and he saith, I cannot; for it is sealed." Note: Martin Harris delivered some characters and rendered passages from the Book of Mormon to Professor Charles Anthon, who confirmed the authenticity of the translation but declined to proceed when he learned that he could not see the original (which was sealed). This encounter with the learned man had been prophesied and was thus fulfilled.

Isaiah 29:14. "Therefore, behold, I will proceed to do a marvellous work among this people, even a marvellous work and a wonder: for the wisdom of their wise men shall perish, and the understanding of their prudent men shall be hid."

Ezekiel 37:16–19. "Moreover, thou son of man, take thee one stick, and write upon it, For Judah [the Bible], and for the children of Israel his companions: then take another stick, and write upon it, For Joseph [the Book of Mormon], the stick of Ephraim, and for all the house of Israel his companions: And join them one to another into one stick; and they shall become one in thine hand. And when the children of thy people shall speak unto thee, saying, Wilt thou not shew us what thou meanest by these? Say unto them, Thus saith the Lord God; Behold, I will take the stick of Joseph, which is in the hand of Ephraim, and the tribes of Israel his fellows, and will put them with him, even with the stick of Judah, and make them one stick, and they shall be one in mine hand." (See also 2 Nephi 3:12.)

John 10:16. "And other sheep I have, which are not of this fold: them also I must bring, and they shall hear my voice; and there shall be one fold, and one shepherd." (See also 2 Nephi 29:8; 3 Nephi 15:21; Revelation 14:6.)

2 Nephi 29:10–11. "Wherefore, because that ye have a Bible ye need not suppose that it contains all my words; neither need ye suppose that I have not caused more to be written. For I command all men, both in the east and in the west, and in the north, and in the south, and in the islands of the sea, that they shall write the words which I speak unto them; for out of the books which shall be written I will judge the world, every man according to their works, according to that which is written."

D&C 20:8–12. "And gave him [Joseph Smith] power from on high, by the means which were before prepared, to translate the Book of Mormon; Which contains a record of a fallen people, and the fulness of the gospel of Jesus Christ to the Gentiles and to the Jews also; Which was given by inspiration, and is confirmed to others by the ministering of angels, and is declared unto the world by them—Proving to the world that the holy scriptures are true, and that God does inspire men and call them to his holy work in this age and generation, as well as in generations of old; Thereby showing that he is the same God yesterday, today, and forever. Amen."

What are some of the priceless scriptural gems given to us through the Book of Mormon?

Depending on the Lord. 1 Nephi 3:7. "And it came to pass that I, Nephi, said unto my father: I will go and do the things which the Lord hath commanded, for I know that the Lord giveth no commandments unto the children of men, save he shall prepare a way for them that they may accomplish the thing which he commandeth them."

Power of the redemption. 2 Nephi 2:8. "Wherefore, how great the importance to make these things known unto the inhabitants of the earth, that they may know that there is no flesh that can dwell in the presence of God, save it be through the merits, and mercy, and grace of the Holy Messiah, who layeth down his life according to the flesh, and taketh it again by the power of the Spirit, that he may bring to pass the resurrection of the dead, being the first that should rise."

Agency. 2 Nephi 2:27. "Wherefore, men are free according to the flesh; and all things are given them which are expedient unto man. And they are free to choose liberty and eternal life, through the great Mediator of all men, or to choose captivity and death, according to the captivity and power of the devil; for he seeketh that all men might be miserable like unto himself."

Parental purpose. 2 Nephi 2:30. "I have spoken these few words unto you all, my sons, in the last days of my probation; and I have chosen the good part, according to the words of the prophet. And I have none other object save it be the everlasting welfare of your souls. Amen."

Means of salvation. 2 Nephi 25:23. "For we labor diligently to write, to persuade our children, and also our brethren, to believe in Christ, and to be reconciled to God; for we know that it is by grace that we are saved, after all we can do."

Key to service. Mosiah 2:17. "And behold, I tell you these things that ye may learn wisdom; that ye may learn that when ye are in the service of your fellow beings ye are only in the service of your God."

The only name to bring salvation. Mosiah 3:17. "And moreover, I say unto you, that there shall be no other name given nor any other way nor means whereby salvation can come unto the children of men, only in and through the name of Christ, the Lord Omnipotent."

Becoming a Saint through Christ. Mosiah 3:19. "For the natural man is an enemy to God, and has been from the fall of Adam, and will be, forever and ever, unless he yields to the enticings of the Holy Spirit, and putteth off the natural man and becometh a saint through the atonement of Christ the Lord, and becometh as a child, submissive, meek, humble, patient, full of love, willing to submit to all things which the Lord seeth fit to inflict upon him, even as a child doth submit to his father."

Covenant of baptism. Mosiah 18:8–10. "And it came to pass that he said unto them: Behold, here are the waters of Mormon (for thus were they called) and now, as ye are desirous to come into the fold of God, and to be called his people, and are willing to bear one another's burdens, that they may be light; Yea, and are willing to mourn with those that mourn; yea, and comfort those that stand in need of comfort, and to stand as witnesses of God at all times and in all things, and in all places that ye may be in, even until death, that ye may be redeemed of God, and be numbered with those of the first resurrection, that ye may have eternal life—Now I say unto you, if this be the desire of your hearts, what have you against being baptized in the name of the Lord, as a witness before him that ye have entered into a covenant with him, that ye will serve him and keep his commandments, that he may pour out his Spirit more abundantly upon you?"

The mighty change. Alma 5:14. "And now behold, I ask of you, my brethren of the church, have ye spiritually been born of God? Have ye received his image in your countenances? Have ye experienced this mighty change in your hearts?"

Purpose of life. Alma 12:24. "There was a space granted unto man in which he might repent; therefore this life became a probationary state; a time to prepare to meet God; a time to prepare for that endless state which has been spoken of by us, which is after the resurrection of the dead."

Essence of faith. Alma 32:21. "And now as I said concerning faith—faith is not to have a perfect knowledge of things; therefore if ye have faith ye hope for things which are not seen, which are true."

Atoning sacrifice. Alma 34:14–15. "And behold, this is the whole meaning of the law, every whit pointing to that great and last sacrifice; and that great and last sacrifice will be the Son of God, yea, infinite and eternal. And thus he shall bring salvation to all those who shall believe on his name; this being the intent of this last sacrifice, to bring about the bowels of mercy, which overpowereth justice, and bringeth about means unto men that they may have faith unto repentance."

Obedience. Alma 37:35. "O, remember, my son, and learn wisdom in thy youth; yea, learn in thy youth to keep the commandments of God."

Postmortal world. Alma 40:11–13. "Now, concerning the state of the soul between death and the resurrection—Behold, it has been made known unto me by an angel, that the spirits of all men, as soon as they are departed from this mortal body, yea, the spirits of all men, whether they be good or evil, are taken home to that God who gave them life. And then shall it come to pass, that the spirits of those who are righteous are received into a state of happiness, which is called paradise, a state of rest, a state of peace, where they shall rest from all their troubles and from all care, and sorrow. And then shall it come to pass, that the spirits of the wicked . . . shall be cast out into outer darkness."

Resurrection. Alma 40:23. "The soul shall be restored to the body, and the body to the soul; yea, and every limb and joint shall be restored to its body; yea, even a hair of the head shall not be lost; but all things shall be restored to their proper and perfect frame."

Avoiding sin. Alma 41:10. "Behold, I say unto you, wickedness never was happiness."

Counsel of the mothers. Alma 56:47. "Now they [the sons of Helaman] never had fought, yet they did not fear death; and they did think more upon the liberty of their fathers than they did upon their lives; yea, they had been taught by their mothers, that if they did not doubt, God would deliver them."

The testimony of the Father. 3 Nephi 11:7. "Behold my Beloved Son, in whom I am well pleased, in whom I have glorified my name—hear ye him."

The testimony of the Son. 3 Nephi 11:10–11. "Behold, I am Jesus Christ, whom the prophets testified shall come into the world. And behold, I am the light and the life of the world; and I have drunk out of that bitter cup which the Father hath given me, and have glorified the Father in taking upon me the sins of the world, in the which I have suffered the will of the Father in all things from the beginning."

The pattern for our lives. 3 Nephi 27:27. "Therefore, what manner of men ought ye to be? Verily I say unto you, even as I am."

Charity. Moroni 7:47. "But charity is the pure love of Christ, and it endureth forever; and whoso is found possessed of it at the last day, it shall be well with him."

Accountability. Moroni 8:10–12. "Behold I say unto you that this thing shall ye teach—repentance and baptism unto those who are accountable and capable of committing sin; yea, teach parents that they must repent and be baptized, and humble themselves as their little children, and they shall all be saved with their little children. And their little children need no repentance, neither baptism. . . . But little children are alive in Christ, even from the foundation of the world."

Personal revelation. Moroni 10:4–5. "And when ye shall receive these things, I would exhort you that ye would ask God, the Eternal Father, in the name of Christ, if these things are not true; and if ye shall ask with a sincere heart, with real intent, having faith in Christ, he will manifest the truth of it unto you, by the power of the Holy Ghost. And by the power of the Holy Ghost ye may know the truth of all things."

Words of the Prophets | Ezra Taft Benson on the Book of Mormon. "The honest seeker after truth can gain the testimony that Jesus is the Christ as he prayerfully ponders the inspired words of the Book of Mormon. Over one-half of all the verses in the Book of Mormon refer to our Lord. Some form of Christ's name is mentioned more frequently per verse in the Book of Mormon than even in the New Testament. He is given over one hundred different names in the Book of Mormon. Those names have a particular significance in describing His divine nature." Ezra Taft Benson, "Come Unto Christ," *Ensign*, November 1987, 83. "The Book of Mormon must be reenthroned in the minds and hearts of our people. We must honor it by reading it, by studying it, by taking its precepts into our lives and transforming them into lives required of the true followers of Christ." Ezra Taft Benson, "The Gift of Modern Revelation," *Ensign*, November 1986, 80. "I have a conviction: The more we teach and preach from the Book of Mormon, the more we shall please the Lord and the greater will be our power of speaking. By so doing, we shall greatly increase our converts, both within the Church and among those we proselyte. The Lord expects us to use this book, and we remain under His condemnation if we do not (see D&C 84:57)." Ezra Taft Benson, *The Teachings of Ezra Taft Benson* [Salt Lake City: Bookcraft, 1988], 58.
Cross reference to "Book of Mormon": see Preach My Gospel, *103–114.*

CHASTITY [7]. A key part of righteous living is chastity, the cultivation of a moral and virtuous character. The Lord will have a pure house and pure servants. Purity and cleanliness of mind and body are absolutely essential to qualify for the Spirit. Immorality in any form has a devastating effect upon the mind and spirit of individuals and families. Recognizing that we are the divine offspring of God should give us hope and help us to be clean and pure in order to enjoy the Spirit in our lives.

Isaiah 52:11. "Depart ye, depart ye, go ye out from thence, touch no unclean thing; go ye out of the midst of her; be ye clean, that bear the vessels of the Lord."

Matthew 5:8. "Blessed are the pure in heart: for they shall see God." (See also 3 Nephi 12:8.)

John 17:19. "And for their sakes I sanctify myself, that they also might be sanctified through the truth."

1 Corinthians 3:16–17. "Know ye not that ye are the temple of God, and that the Spirit of God dwelleth in you? If any man defile the temple of God, him shall God destroy; for the temple of God is holy, which temple ye are." (See also 1 Corinthians 6:19–20; 7.)

Thirteenth Article of Faith. "We believe in being honest, true, chaste, benevolent, virtuous, and in doing good to all men; indeed, we may say that we follow the admonition of Paul—We believe all things, we hope all things, we have endured many things, and hope to be able to endure all things. If there is anything virtuous, lovely, or of good report or praiseworthy, we seek after these things."

CHRISTIAN/CHRISTIANS [7]. Christians are devoted and sincere followers of Jesus Christ. The faithful members of The Church of Jesus Christ of Latter-day Saints—the restored Church of the Lord—are honored to be identified as Christians and strive with all their "heart, might, mind and strength" (D&C 4:2) to comply with the Lord's directives and covenants. The name of the Church to which they belong confirms the essential and fundamental Christian nature of their cause and belief.

Acts 11:25-26. "Then departed Barnabas to Tarsus, for to seek Saul: And when he had found him, he brought him unto Antioch. And it came to pass, that a whole year they assembled themselves with the church, and taught much people. And the disciples were called Christians first in Antioch."

Acts 26:28. "Then Agrippa said unto Paul, Almost thou persuadest me to be a Christian."

1 Peter 4:16. "Yet if any man suffer as a Christian, let him not be ashamed; but let him glorify God on this behalf."

Alma 46:13–16. "And he [Moroni] fastened on his head-plate, and his breastplate, and his shields, and girded on his armor about his loins; and he took the pole, which had on the end thereof his rent coat, (and he called it the title of liberty) and he bowed himself to the earth, and he prayed mightily unto his God for the blessings of liberty to rest upon his brethren, so long as there should a band of Christians remain to possess the land—For thus were all the true believers of Christ, who belonged to the church of God, called by those who did not belong to the church. And those who did belong to the church were faithful; yea, all those who were true believers in Christ took upon them, gladly, the name of Christ, or Christians as they were called, because of their belief in Christ who should come. And therefore, at this time, Moroni prayed that the cause of the Christians, and the freedom of the land might be favored."

Alma 48:10. "And thus he [Moroni] was preparing to support their liberty, their lands, their wives, and their children, and their peace, and that they might live unto the Lord their God, and that they might maintain that which was called by their enemies the cause of Christians."

How do the scriptures of the Restoration confirm that The Church of Jesus Christ of Latter-day Saints is Christian?

Subtitle of the Book of Mormon. "Another Testament of Jesus Christ." The Book of Mormon is thus a further scriptural witness of the divinity of Jesus Christ and His atoning sacrifice.

Preface to the Book of Mormon. "Which is to show unto the remnant of the House of Israel what great things the Lord hath done for their fathers; and that they may know the covenants of the Lord, that they are not cast off forever—And also to the convincing of the Jew and Gentile that JESUS is the CHRIST, the ETERNAL God, manifesting himself unto all nations."

Occurrence of the name of Jesus Christ in the scriptures. The name *Christ* appears 555 times in the Bible (New Testament) and 527 times in the scriptures of the Restoration: 384 times in the Book of Mormon, 128 times in the Doctrine and Covenants, and 15 times in the Pearl of Great Price. The name *Jesus Christ* appears 270 times in the Bible (New

Testament) and 175 times in scriptures of the Restoration: 82 times in the Book of Mormon, 85 times in the Doctrine and Covenants, and 8 times in the Pearl of Great Price. In addition, alternate names for Jesus Christ, such as Son of God, Lamb of God, Savior, and Redeemer, among others, are replete in LDS scriptures, which reflect the substance and essence of the gospel of Jesus Christ and His teachings. (See also the First Article of Faith.)

Name of the Church. 3 Nephi 27:7–8. "Therefore, whatsoever ye shall do, ye shall do it in my name; therefore ye shall call the church in my name; and ye shall call upon the Father in my name that he will bless the church for my sake. And how be it my church save it be called in my name?" (See also D&C 115:3–4; 127:12; 128:21; 136:2.)

Jesus Christ being the only name by which salvation can come. Acts 4:10–12. "Be it known unto you all, and to all the people of Israel, that by the name of Jesus Christ of Nazareth, whom ye crucified, whom God raised from the dead, even by him doth this man stand here before you whole. This is the stone which was set at nought of you builders, which is become the head of the corner. Neither is there salvation in any other: for there is none other name under heaven given among men, whereby we must be saved." (See also 2 Nephi 25:20; Mosiah 3: 1–8, 17; 4:6–8; 5:8–12, 15; Alma 11:40; D&C 18:2–5; 109:4; Moses 6:51–52.)

Book of Mormon—containing the "fulness of the gospel of Jesus Christ"—serves to confirm the truth of the Christian Bible. 1 Nephi 13:38–41. "And it came to pass that I beheld the remnant of the seed of my brethren, and also the book of the Lamb of God, which had proceeded forth from the mouth of the Jew, that it came forth from the Gentiles unto the remnant of the seed of my brethren. And after it had come forth unto them I beheld other books, which came forth by the power of the Lamb, from the Gentiles unto them, unto the convincing of the Gentiles and the remnant of the seed of my brethren, and also the Jews who were scattered upon all the face of the earth, that the records of the prophets and of the twelve apostles of the Lamb are true. And the angel spake unto me, saying: These last records, which thou hast seen among the Gentiles, shall establish the truth of the first, which are of the twelve apostles of the Lamb, and shall make known the plain and precious things which have been taken away from them; and shall make known to all kindreds, tongues, and people, that the Lamb of God is the Son of the Eternal Father, and the Savior of the world; and that all men must come unto him, or they cannot be saved." (See also 2 Nephi 3:11–12; D&C 20:6–12.)

Principle of continuing revelation is an inviolate part of the Church of Jesus Christ. Amos 3:7. "Surely the Lord God will do nothing, but he revealeth his secret unto his servants the prophets."(See also 2 Nephi 29:10–14.)

Restored Church is organized and empowered according to the pattern given by Jesus Christ in the primitive Church. Sixth Article of Faith. "We believe in the same organization that existed in the Primitive Church, namely, apostles, prophets, pastors, teachers, evangelists, and so forth." (See also Ephesians 4:1–3; Fifth Article of Faith.)

Confirmation of the Christian essence of the restored Church comes through the Holy Ghost. 1 Corinthians 12:3. "No man can say that Jesus is the Lord, but by the Holy Ghost." (See also Moroni 10:4–5.)

CHURCH, ANCIENT [Church: 840]. Through the dispensations of time, the Lord has ordained and arranged for a divine organization to govern the unfolding of His kingdom as a means to bless and sanctify His people. The structure and organization of the Church, with its various offices and circles of leadership, did not evolve by chance but was a prepared gift from heaven to optimize the process of making saving truths and ordinances available to the sons and daughters of God in their quest to return home once again. The celestial kingdom itself is organized on principles of glory and eternal light; thus, the earthly kingdom is a type and likeness of what awaits the faithful in the coming world (D&C 105:5). During the meridian of time, the Lord organized His Church and kingdom according to specific principles and stewardships. In the space of only three years, the Savior put in place a dynamic, empowered, and orderly institution that bore the signature of divine perfection. It was complex yet unified, domestic in its outreach yet authorized directly by Deity, designed for the everyday yet governed by keys extending to eternity.

Matthew 5:16. "Let your light so shine before men, that they may see your good works, and glorify your Father which is in heaven." (See also 3 Nephi 12:16.)

JST Matthew 6:38. "Wherefore, seek not the things of this world but seek ye first to build up the kingdom of God, and to establish his righteousness, and all these things shall be added unto you."

Matthew 13:31–32. "Another parable put he forth unto them, saying, The kingdom of heaven is like to a grain of mustard seed, which a man took, and sowed in his field: Which indeed is the least of all seeds: but when it is grown, it is the greatest among herbs, and becometh a tree, so that the birds of the air come and lodge in the branches thereof."

Matthew 16:17–19. "And Jesus answered and said unto him, Blessed art thou, Simon Bar-jona: for flesh and blood hath not revealed it unto thee, but my Father which is in heaven. And I say also unto thee, That thou art Peter, and upon this rock [i.e., the rock of Jesus Christ as the divine empowerment of the principle of revelation] I will build my church; and the gates of hell shall not prevail against it. And I will give unto thee the keys of the kingdom of heaven: and whatsoever thou shalt bind on earth shall be bound in heaven: and whatsoever thou shalt loose on earth shall be loosed in heaven."

Matthew 17:1–3. "And after six days Jesus taketh Peter, James, and John his brother, and bringeth them up into an high mountain apart, And was transfigured before them: and his face did shine as the sun, and his raiment was white as the light. And, behold, there appeared unto them Moses and Elias talking with him."

Matthew 28:18–20. "And Jesus came and spake unto them, saying, All power is given unto me in heaven and in earth. Go ye therefore, and teach all nations, baptizing them in the name of the Father, and of the Son, and of the Holy Ghost: Teaching them to observe all things whatsoever I have commanded you: and, lo, I am with you alway, even unto the end of the world. Amen."

Mark 3:14. "And he ordained twelve, that they should be with him, and that he might send them forth to preach."

Luke 9:1–2. "Then he called his twelve disciples together, and gave them power and authority over all devils, and to cure diseases. And he sent them to preach the kingdom of God, and to heal the sick."

Luke 10:1–3. "After these things the Lord appointed other seventy also, and sent them two and two before his face into every city and place, whither he himself would come. Therefore said he unto them, The harvest truly is great, but the labourers are few: pray ye therefore the Lord of the harvest, that he would send forth labourers into his harvest. Go your ways: behold, I send you forth as lambs among wolves."

John 15:16. "Ye have not chosen me, but I have chosen you, and ordained you, that ye should go and bring forth fruit, and that your fruit should remain: that whatsoever ye shall ask of the Father in my name, he may give it you."

Words of the Prophets | **Harold B. Lee on the ancient Church.** "The Master's church was an orderly, organized body 'built upon the foundation of the apostles and prophets, Jesus Christ himself being the chief corner stone' (Ephesians 2:20). This organization with teachers, helps, and a complete government (see 1 Corinthians 12:28) was 'for the perfecting of the Saints, for the work of the ministry, for the edifying of the body of Christ' (Ephesians 4:12). The officers in the true church had to have divine authority from authorized ordinances and not just 'assumed' authority. The Lord told His apostles: 'Ye have not chosen me, but I have chosen you, and ordained you, that ye should go and bring forth fruit. . . .' (John 15:16) and to the chiefest of the apostles He gave the 'keys' of the kingdom of God, or in other words, the keys of authority to the Church of Jesus Christ, that whatsoever would be bound in earth should be bound in heaven." —Harold B. Lee, *Stand Ye in Holy Places* (Salt Lake City: Deseret Book, 1974), 315.

CHURCH, RESTORED IN THE FULNESS OF TIMES [Church: 840]. On April 6, 1830, an event of singular importance in the history of the world took place in a humble cabin in the small town of Fayette, New York (see D&C 20:1). On that occasion the Lord's Church was formally organized in this dispensation as a divine blessing for all who would come with broken hearts and contrite spirits and covenant to be His children by taking upon them His name and serving Him forever in righteousness. The Church is indeed the organized and authorized structure through which the Saints are to be perfected, the gospel preached unto all the world, and salvation administered and secured for all the hosts of creation—both living and dead—who become heirs of immortality and eternal life.

D&C 1:30. "And also those to whom these commandments were given, might have power to lay the foundation of this church, and to bring it forth out of obscurity and out of darkness, the only true and living church upon the face of the whole earth, with which I, the Lord, am well pleased, speaking unto the church collectively and not individually—" (See also D&C 109:73.)

D&C 1:38. "What I the Lord have spoken, I have spoken, and I excuse not myself; and though the heavens and the earth pass away, my word shall not pass away, but shall all be fulfilled, whether by mine own voice or by the voice of my servants, it is the same."

D&C 5:14. "And to none else [beyond the Three Witnesses of the plates translated by Joseph Smith: Oliver Cowdery, David Whitmer, and Martin Harris] will I grant this power, to receive this same testimony among this generation, in this the beginning of the rising up and the coming forth of my church out of the wilderness—clear as the moon, and fair as the sun, and terrible as an army with banners."

D&C 13:1. "Upon you my fellow servants, in the name of Messiah I [John the Baptist] confer the Priesthood of Aaron, which holds the keys of the ministering of angels, and of the gospel of repentance, and of baptism by immersion for the remission of sins; and this shall never be taken again from the earth, until the sons of Levi do offer again an offering unto the Lord in righteousness."

D&C 20:1. "The rise of the Church of Christ in these last days, being one thousand eight hundred and thirty years since the coming of our Lord and Savior Jesus Christ in the flesh, it being regularly organized and established agreeable to the laws of our country, by the will and commandments of God, in the fourth month, and on the sixth day of the month which is called April." (See also D&C 21:3.)

D&C 20:8–11. "And gave him [Joseph Smith] power from on high, by the means which were before prepared, to translate the Book of Mormon; Which contains a record of a fallen people, and the fulness of the gospel of Jesus Christ to the Gentiles and to the Jews also; Which was given by inspiration, and is confirmed to others by the ministering of angels, and is declared unto the world by them—Proving to the world that the holy scriptures are true, and that God does inspire men and call them to his holy work in this age and generation, as well as in generations of old."

D&C 21:4–6. "Wherefore, meaning the church, thou shalt give heed unto all his words and commandments which he shall give unto you as he receiveth them, walking in all holiness before me; For his word ye shall receive, as if from mine own mouth, in all patience and faith. For by doing these things the gates of hell shall not prevail against you; yea, and the Lord God will disperse the powers of darkness from before you, and cause the heavens to shake for your good, and his name's glory."

D&C 27:12–13. "And also with Peter, and James, and John, whom I have sent unto you, by whom I have ordained you and confirmed you to be apostles, and especial witnesses of my name, and bear the keys of your ministry and of the same things which I revealed unto them; Unto whom I have committed the keys of my kingdom, and a dispensation of the gospel for the last times; and for the fulness of times, in the which I will gather together in one all things, both which are in heaven, and which are on earth."

D&C 65:2. "The keys of the kingdom of God are committed unto man on the earth, and from thence shall the gospel roll forth unto the ends of the earth, as the stone which is cut out of the mountain without hands shall roll forth, until it has filled the whole earth."

D&C 101:22–23. "Behold, it is my will, that all they who call on my name, and worship me according to mine everlasting gospel, should gather together, and stand in holy places; And prepare for the revelation which is to come, when the veil of the covering of my temple, in my tabernacle, which hideth the earth, shall be taken off, and all flesh shall see me together." (See also D&C 124:36; 127; 128; 132.)

D&C 110:16. "Therefore, the keys of this dispensation are committed into your hands; and by this ye may know that the great and dreadful day of the Lord is near, even at the doors."

D&C 115:4. "For thus shall my church be called in the last days, even The Church of Jesus Christ of Latter-day Saints."

Sixth Article of Faith. "We believe in the same organization that existed in the Primitive Church, namely, apostles, prophets, pastors, teachers, evangelists, and so forth."

What passages of scripture prefigured the coming Restoration of the Church and the gospel?

Isaiah 11:12. "And he shall set up an ensign for the nations, and shall assemble the outcasts of Israel, and gather together the dispersed of Judah from the four corners of the earth." (See also 2 Nephi 21:12.)

Isaiah 29:13–14. "Wherefore the Lord said, Forasmuch as this people draw near me with their mouth, and with their lips do honour me, but have removed their heart far from me, and their fear toward me is taught by the precept of men: Therefore, behold, I will proceed to do a marvelous work among this people, even a marvellous work and a wonder." (See also D&C 4:1–2.)

Jeremiah 31:31–33. "Behold, the days come, saith the Lord, that I will make a new covenant with the house of Israel, and with the house of Judah: Not according to the covenant that I made with their fathers in the day that I took them by the hand to bring them out of the land of Egypt; which my covenant they brake, although I was an husband unto them, saith the Lord: But this shall be the covenant that I will make with the house of Israel; After those days, saith the Lord, I will put my law in their inward parts, and write it in their hearts; and will be their God, and they shall be my people."

Daniel 2:34–35, 44–45. "Thou sawest till that a stone was cut out without hands. . . and the stone . . . became a great mountain, and filled the whole earth. . . . And in the days of these kings shall the God of heaven set up a kingdom, which shall never be destroyed . . . and it shall stand for ever. Forasmuch as thou sawest that the stone was cut out of the mountain without hands . . . and the dream is certain, and the interpretation thereof sure." (See also D&C 65:2.)

Acts 3:19–21. "Repent ye therefore, and be converted, that your sins may be blotted out, when the times of refreshing shall come from the presence of the Lord; And he shall send Jesus Christ, which before was preached unto you: Whom the heaven must receive until the times of restitution of all things, which God hath spoken by the mouth of all his holy prophets since the world began."

Ephesians 1:10. "That in the dispensation of the fulness of times he might gather together in one all things in Christ, both which are in heaven, and which are on earth; even in him."

James 1:5–7. "If any of you lack wisdom, let him ask of God, that giveth to all men liberally, and upbraideth not; and it shall be given him. But let him ask in faith, nothing wavering. For he that wavereth is like a wave of the sea driven with the wind and tossed. For let not that man think that he shall receive any thing of the Lord."

Revelation 14:6–7. "And I saw another angel fly in the midst of heaven, having the everlasting gospel to preach unto them that dwell on the earth, and to every nation, and kindred, and tongue, and people, Saying with a loud voice, Fear God, and give glory to him; for the hour of his judgment is come: and worship him that made heaven, and earth, and the sea, and the fountains of waters."

Words of the Prophets | Joseph F. Smith on the organization of the Church. "The house of God is a house of order, and not a house of confusion; and it could not be thus, if there were not those who had authority to preside, to direct, to counsel, to lead in the affairs of the Church. . . . Take away the organization of the Church, and its power would cease. Every part of its organization is necessary, and essential to its perfect existence. Disregard, ignore, or omit any part and you start imperfection in the Church." —Joseph F. Smith, *CR,* April 1915, 5.

COMMANDMENTS [867]. Heavenly Father, through His Beloved Son, Jesus Christ, has given us the laws and commandments essential for gaining eternal life. Obedience to these commandments will ensure our happiness here and in the hereafter. The commandments have been established according to divine design, and when we honor and keep them by enduring steadfastly and obediently to the end, blessings of everlasting joy await us. When we truly love God, we will keep His commandments faithfully.

Exodus 20:3. "Thou shalt have no other gods before me."

Deuteronomy 6:17. "Ye shall diligently keep the commandments of the Lord your God, and his testimonies, and his statutes, which he hath commanded thee."

Ecclesiastes 12:13. "Let us hear the conclusion of the whole matter: Fear God, and keep his commandments: for this is the whole duty of man."

Matthew 22:36–40. "Master, which is the great commandment in the law? Jesus said unto him, Thou shalt love the Lord thy God with all thy heart, and with all thy soul, and with all thy mind. This is the first and great commandment. And the second is like unto it, Thou shalt love thy neighbour as thyself. On these two commandments hang all the law and the prophets." (See also D&C 59:5–6.)

John 13:34–35. "A new commandment I give unto you, That ye love one another; as I have loved you, that ye also love one another. By this shall all men know that ye are my disciples, if ye have love one to another."

John 14:15. "If ye love me, keep my commandments."

Mosiah 2:41. "And moreover, I would desire that ye should consider on the blessed and happy state of those that keep the commandments of God. For behold, they are blessed in all things, both temporal and spiritual; and if they hold out faithful to the end they are received into heaven, that thereby they may dwell with God in a state of never-ending happiness. O remember, remember that these things are true; for the Lord God hath spoken it."

D&C 20:77. "O God, the Eternal Father, we ask thee in the name of thy Son, Jesus Christ, to bless and sanctify this bread to the souls of all those who partake of it, that they may eat in remembrance of the body of thy Son, and witness unto thee, O God, the Eternal Father, that they are willing to take upon them the name of thy Son, and always remember him and keep his commandments which he has given them; that they may always have his Spirit to be with them. Amen."

D&C 29:35. "Behold, I gave unto him that he should be an agent unto himself; and I gave unto him commandment, but no temporal commandment gave I unto him, for my commandments are spiritual; they are not natural nor temporal, neither carnal nor sensual."

D&C 84:44. "For you shall live by every word that proceedeth forth from the mouth of God."

D&C 93:1. "Verily, thus saith the Lord: It shall come to pass that every soul who forsaketh his sins and cometh unto me, and calleth on my name, and obeyeth my voice, and keepeth my commandments, shall see my face and know that I am."

Abraham 3:24–25. "And there stood one among them that was like unto God, and he said unto those who were with him: We will go down, for there is space there, and we will take of these materials, and we will make an earth whereon these may dwell; And we will prove them herewith, to see if they will do all things whatsoever the Lord their God shall command them."

Words of the Prophets | Ezra Taft Benson on the meaning of "after all we can do." "Yes, it is 'by grace that we are saved, after all we can do' (2 Nephi 25:23). What is meant by 'after all we can do'? 'After all we can do' includes extending our best effort. 'After all we can do' includes living His commandments. 'After all we can do' includes loving our fellowmen and praying for those who regard us as their adversary. 'After all we can do' means clothing the naked, feeding the hungry, visiting the sick and giving 'succor [to] those [who] stand in need of [our] succor' (Mosiah 4:16—remembering that what we do unto one of the least of God's children, we do unto Him (see Matthew 25:34–40; D&C 42:38). 'After all we can do' means leading chaste, clean, pure lives, being scrupulously honest in all our dealings and treating others the way we would want to be treated." —Ezra Taft Benson, *The Teachings of Ezra Taft Benson* (Salt Lake City: Bookcraft, 1988), 354.

Cross reference to "Commandments": see Preach My Gospel*, 71–81.*

CONSCIENCE [44]. Conscience is the light of Christ, a voice from within, that moral sense that helps us determine right from wrong and then helps us try to do that which is morally right. We all have that voice within. When we listen intently to the voice of our conscience and follow its guidance, we are led into pathways that bring us closer to our Father in Heaven and His Beloved Son.

1 Peter 3:15–16. "But sanctify the Lord God in your hearts: and be ready always to give an answer to every man that asketh you a reason of the hope that is in you with meekness and fear: Having a good conscience; that, whereas they speak evil of you, as of evildoers, they may be ashamed that falsely accuse your good conversation in Christ."

Alma 42:17–18. "Now, how could a man repent except he should sin? How could he sin if there was no law? How could there be a law save there was a punishment? Now, there was a punishment affixed, and a just law given, which brought remorse of conscience unto man."

Moroni 7:15–19. "For behold, my brethren, it is given unto you to judge, that ye may know good from evil; and the way to judge is as plain, that ye may know with a perfect knowledge, as the daylight is from the dark night. For behold, the Spirit of Christ is given to every man, that he may know good from evil; wherefore, I show unto you the way to judge; for every thing which inviteth to do good, and to persuade to believe in Christ, is sent forth by the power and gift of Christ; wherefore ye may know with a perfect knowledge it is of God. But whatsoever thing persuadeth men to do evil, and believe not in Christ, and deny him, and serve not God, then ye may know with a perfect knowledge it is of the devil; for after this manner doth the devil work, for he persuadeth no man to do good, no, not one; neither do his angels; neither do they who subject themselves unto him. And now, my brethren, seeing that ye know the light by which ye may judge, which light is the light of Christ, see that ye do not judge wrongfully; for with that same judgment which ye judge ye shall also be judged. Wherefore, I beseech of you, brethren, that ye should search diligently in the light of Christ that ye may know good from evil; and if ye will lay hold upon every good thing, and condemn it not, ye certainly will be a child of Christ."

D&C 84:45–47. "For the word of the Lord is truth, and whatsoever is truth is light, and whatsoever is light is Spirit, even the Spirit of Jesus Christ. And the Spirit giveth light to every man that cometh into the world; and the Spirit enlighteneth every man through the world, that hearkeneth to the voice of the Spirit. And every one that hearkeneth to the voice of the Spirit cometh unto God, even the Father."

Words of the Prophets | Spencer W. Kimball on conscience. "How wonderful that God should endow us with this sensitive yet strong guide we call a conscience! Someone has aptly remarked that 'conscience is a celestial spark which God has put into every man for the purpose of saving his soul' . . . To be sorry is an approach, to abandon the act of error is a beginning, but until one's conscience has been sufficiently stirred to cause him to move in the matter, so long as there are excuses and rationalizations, one has hardly begun his approach to forgiveness." —Spencer W. Kimball, *The Miracle of Forgiveness*, (Salt Lake City: Bookcraft, 1969), 152.

CONSECRATION [98]. The Lord has asked His righteous sons and daughters to consecrate their lives for the building up of the kingdom of God. When we consecrate our lives, we dedicate and set apart our time, talents, and material goods for the cause of Zion. Consecration is uniquely related to the depth of our conversion to our Savior Jesus Christ. Through consecration, we truly sacrifice all things for the Lord. We begin the process by purifying our own lives, thus becoming better able to assist our brothers and sisters as they seek to enjoy the blessings of eternal life. Part of this law, as we now live it, requires us to provide for our own family and be an instrument in the Lord's hands to assist all those with whom we associate. We also consecrate one tenth of our income annually for the Church (see D&C 119:4) and pay a generous fast offering (see Isaiah 58:6–7). Consecration is an attitude of magnanimity and charity, as well as an observable act of goodness.

Matthew 6:33. "But seek ye first the kingdom of God, and his righteousness; and all these things shall be added unto you." (See also JST Matthew 6:38.)

Matthew 25:40. "And the King shall answer and say unto them, Verily I say unto you, Inasmuch as ye have done it unto one of the least of these my brethren, ye have done it unto me."

2 Nephi 10:19. "Wherefore, I will consecrate this land unto thy seed, and them who shall be numbered among thy seed, forever, for the land of their inheritance; for it is a choice land, saith God unto me, above all other lands, wherefore I will have all men that dwell thereon that they shall worship me, saith God."

2 Nephi 32:9. "But behold, I say unto you that ye must pray always, and not faint; that ye must not perform any thing unto the Lord save in the first place ye shall pray unto the Father in the name of Christ, that he will consecrate thy performance unto thee, that thy performance may be for the welfare of thy soul."

2 Nephi 33:4. "And I know that the Lord God will consecrate my prayers for the gain of my people. And the words which I have written in weakness will be made strong unto them; for it persuadeth them to do good; it maketh known unto them of their fathers; and it speaketh of Jesus, and persuadeth them to believe in him, and to endure to the end, which is life eternal."

Mosiah 4:21. "And now, if God, who has created you, on whom you are dependent for your lives and for all that ye have and are, doth grant unto you whatsoever ye ask that is right, in faith, believing that ye shall receive, O then, how ye ought to impart of the substance that ye have one to another."

Mosiah 18:27–29. "And again Alma commanded that the people of the church should impart of their substance, every one according to that which he had; if he have more abundantly he should impart more abundantly; and of him that had but little, but little should be required; and to him that had not should be given. And thus they should impart of their substance of their own free will and good desires towards God, and to those priests that stood in need, yea, and to every needy, naked soul. And this he said unto them, having been commanded of God; and they did walk uprightly before God, imparting to one another both temporally and spiritually according to their needs and their wants."

Mosiah 23:17. "And it came to pass that none received authority to preach or to teach except it were by him from God. Therefore he [Alma] consecrated all their priests and all their teachers; and none were consecrated except they were just men."

3 Nephi 9:20. "And ye shall offer for a sacrifice unto me a broken heart and a contrite spirit. And whoso cometh unto me with a broken heart and a contrite spirit, him will I baptize with fire and with the Holy Ghost, even as the Lamanites, because of their faith in me at the time of their conversion, were baptized with fire and with the Holy Ghost, and they knew it not."

D&C 42:31. "And inasmuch as ye impart of your substance unto the poor, ye will do it unto me."

D&C 88:119. "Organize yourselves; prepare every needful thing; and establish a house, even a house of prayer, a house of fasting, a house of faith, a house of learning, a house of glory, a house of order, a house of God."

D&C 97:8. "Verily I say unto you, all among them who know their hearts are honest, and are broken, and their spirits contrite, and are willing to observe their covenants by sacrifice—yea, every sacrifice which I, the Lord, shall command—they are accepted of me."

D&C 105:5. "And Zion cannot be built up unless it is by the principles of the law of the celestial kingdom; otherwise I cannot receive her unto myself."

Words of the Prophets | Ezra Taft Benson on consecration. "We covenant to live the law of consecration. This law is that we consecrate our time, talents, strength, property, and money for the upbuilding of the kingdom of God on this earth and the establishment of Zion. Until one abides by the laws of obedience, sacrifice, the gospel, and chastity, he cannot abide the law of consecration, which is the law pertaining to the celestial kingdom." —Ezra Taft Benson, *The Teachings of Ezra Taft Benson* (Salt Lake City: Bookcraft, 1988), 121–123. "The law of consecration is a law for an inheritance in the celestial kingdom. God, the Eternal Father, his Son Jesus Christ, and all holy beings abide by this law. It is an eternal law. It is a revelation by God to his Church in this dispensation. Though not in full operation today, it will be mandatory for all Saints to live the law in its fulness to receive celestial inheritance." —Ezra Taft Benson, "A Vision and a Hope for the Youth of Zion," in *1977 Devotional Speeches of the Year* (Provo, Utah: BYU, 1978), April 12, 1977, 75.

CONVERSION [63]. Conversion is the process of being born again—the spiritual transformation through which our sins are forgiven and we embark on the pathway of perfection with the promise that if we endure to the end in obedience to the commandments, we will inherit eternal life. To be born again of God implies a sanctifying process by which the old, or natural, man or woman is supplanted by the new spiritual man or woman who enjoys the companionship of the Holy Ghost and hence is no longer disposed to commit sin. In this manner, through compliance with the principles and ordinances of the gospel, we become spiritually begotten sons and daughters of God. The process of perfection is a divine gift of heaven (Moroni 10:32–33).

Matthew 18:1–4. "At the same time came the disciples unto Jesus, saying, Who is the greatest in the kingdom of heaven? And Jesus called a little child unto him, and set him in the midst of them, And said, Verily I say unto you, Except ye be converted, and become as little children, ye shall not enter into the kingdom of heaven. Whosoever therefore shall humble himself as this little child, the same is greatest in the kingdom of heaven."

John 3:5. "Jesus answered, Verily, verily, I say unto thee, Except a man be born of water and of the Spirit, he cannot enter into the kingdom of God."

Mosiah 3:19. "For the natural man is an enemy to God, and has been from the fall of Adam, and will be, forever and ever, unless he yields to the enticings of the Holy Spirit, and putteth off the natural man and becometh a saint through the atonement of Christ the Lord, and becometh as a child, submissive, meek, humble, patient, full of love, willing to submit to all things which the Lord seeth fit to inflict upon him, even as a child doth submit to his father."

Mosiah 5:2. "And they all cried with one voice, saying: Yea, we believe all the words which thou hast spoken unto us; and also, we know of their surety and truth, because of the Spirit of the Lord Omnipotent, which has wrought a mighty change in us, or in our hearts, that we have no more disposition to do evil, but to do good continually."

Mosiah 5:7–8. "And now, because of the covenant which ye have made ye shall be called the children of Christ, his sons, and his daughters; for behold, this day he hath spiritually begotten you; for ye say that your hearts are changed through faith on his name; therefore, ye are born of him and have become his sons and his daughters. And under this head ye are made free, and there is no other head whereby ye can be made free. There is no other name given whereby salvation cometh; therefore, I would that ye should take upon you the name of Christ, all you that have entered into the covenant with God that ye should be obedient unto the end of your lives."

Alma 5:14. "And now behold, I ask of you, my brethren of the church, have ye spiritually been born of God? Have ye received his image in your countenances? Have ye experienced this mighty change in your hearts?"

3 Nephi 9:13–15. "O all ye that are spared because ye were more righteous than they, will ye not now return unto me, and repent of your sins, and be converted, that I may heal you? Yea, verily I say unto you, if ye will come unto me ye shall have eternal life. Behold, mine arm of mercy is extended towards you, and whosoever will come, him will I receive; and blessed are those who come unto me. Behold, I am Jesus Christ the Son of God. I created the heavens and the earth, and all things that in them are. I was with the Father from the beginning. I am in the Father, and the Father in me; and in me hath the Father glorified his name."

Moroni 8:25–26. "And the first fruits of repentance is baptism; and baptism cometh by faith unto the fulfilling the commandments; and the fulfilling the commandments bringeth remission of sins; And the remission of sins bringeth meekness, and lowliness of heart; and because of meekness and lowliness of heart cometh the visitation of the Holy Ghost, which Comforter filleth with hope and perfect love, which love endureth by diligence unto prayer, until the end shall come, when all the saints shall dwell with God."

Moses 6:58–60. "Therefore I give unto you a commandment, to teach these things freely unto your children, saying: That by reason of transgression cometh the fall, which fall bringeth death, and inasmuch as ye were born into the world by water, and blood, and the spirit, which I have made, and so became of dust a living soul, even so ye must be born again into the kingdom of heaven, of water, and of the Spirit, and be cleansed by blood, even the blood of mine Only Begotten; that ye might be sanctified from all sin, and enjoy the words of eternal life in this world, and eternal life in the world to come, even immortal glory; For by the water ye keep the commandment; by the Spirit ye are justified, and by the blood ye are sanctified."

Words of the Prophets | **Joseph Smith on the process of conversion.** "We consider that God has created man with a mind capable of instruction, and a faculty which may be enlarged in proportion to the heed and diligence given to the light communicated from heaven to the intellect; and that the nearer man approaches perfection, the clearer are his views, and the greater his enjoyments, till he has overcome the evils of his life and lost every desire for sin." —Joseph Smith, *Teachings of the Prophet Joseph Smith*, sel. Joseph Fielding Smith (Salt Lake City: Deseret Book, 1976), 51.

Cross reference to "Conversion": see Preach My Gospel, *92–93.*

COVENANTS [555]. Eternal covenants are binding agreements between God and His children. God gives covenants through revelation to His prophets. We, with our moral agency, can agree to and enter into these covenants if we are worthy. There are many covenants and ordinances we can participate in within the Church. The covenants and ordinances of salvation and exaltation are baptism, bestowing the gift of the Holy Ghost, priesthood covenants, and temple covenants and ordinances, which include washings and anointings, the endowment, and temple sealings. These lifesaving covenants, along with other gospel ordinances, provide the means whereby we can receive the blessings of exaltation from our Heavenly Father through obedience and enduring to the end. In ancient times and earlier in this dispensation, the righteous Saints were asked to consecrate everything to the kingdom of God as part of their covenant agreement. Today we consecrate a portion of our substance through tithing, fast offerings, and other contributions.

Isaiah 24:5. "The earth also is defiled under the inhabitants thereof; because they have transgressed the laws, changed the ordinance, broken the everlasting covenant."

Jeremiah 31:31–34. "Behold, the days come, saith the Lord, that I will make a new covenant with the house of Israel, and with the house of Judah: Not according to the covenant that I made with their fathers in the day that I took them by the hand to bring them out of the land of Egypt; which my covenant they brake, although I was an husband unto them, saith the Lord: But this shall be the covenant that I will make with the house of Israel; After those days, saith the Lord, I will put my law in their inward parts, and write it in their hearts; and will be their God, and they shall be my people. And they shall teach no more every man his neighbour, and every man his brother, saying, Know the Lord: for they shall all know me, from the least of them unto the greatest of them, saith the Lord: for I will forgive their iniquity, and I will remember their sin no more."

Mosiah 18:13. "And when he had said these words, the Spirit of the Lord was upon him, and he said: Helam, I baptize thee, having authority from the Almighty God, as a testimony that ye have entered into a covenant to serve him until you are dead as to the mortal body; and may the Spirit of the Lord be poured out upon you; and may he grant unto you eternal life, through the redemption of Christ, whom he has prepared from the foundation of the world." (See also D&C 20:37, 77, 79; 2 Nephi 31:19–20.)

3 Nephi 22:10. "For the mountains shall depart and the hills be removed, but my kindness shall not depart from thee, neither shall the covenant if my peace be removed, saith the Lord that hath mercy on thee."

D&C 52:15–16. "Wherefore he that prayeth, whose spirit is contrite, the same is accepted of me if he obey mine ordinances. He that speaketh, whose spirit is contrite, whose language is meek and edifieth, the same is of God if he obey mine ordinances."

D&C 84:33–40. "For whoso is faithful unto the obtaining these two priesthoods of which I have spoken, and the magnifying their calling, are sanctified by the Spirit unto the renewing of their bodies. They become the sons of Moses and of Aaron and the seed of Abraham, and the church and kingdom, and the elect of God. And also all they who receive this priesthood receive me, saith the Lord; For he that receiveth my servants receiveth me; And he that receiveth me receiveth my Father; And he that receiveth my Father receiveth my Father's kingdom; therefore all that my Father hath shall be given unto him. And this is according to the oath and covenant which belongeth to the priesthood. Therefore, all those who receive the priesthood, receive this oath and covenant of my Father, which he cannot break, neither can it be moved."

D&C 97:8. "Verily I say unto you, all among them who know their hearts are honest, and are broken, and their spirits contrite, and are willing to observe their covenants by sacrifice—yea, every sacrifice which I, the Lord, shall command—they are accepted of me."

D&C 131:1–4. "In the celestial glory there are three heavens or degrees; And in order to obtain the highest, a man must enter into this order of the priesthood [meaning the new and everlasting covenant of marriage]; And if he does not, he cannot obtain it. He may enter into the other, but that is the end of his kingdom; he cannot have an increase."

D&C 132:6–7. "And as pertaining to the new and everlasting covenant, it was instituted for the fulness of my glory; and he that receiveth a fulness thereof must and shall abide the law, or he shall be damned, saith the Lord God. And verily I say unto you, that the conditions of this law are these: All covenants, contracts, bonds, obligations, oaths, vows, performances, connections, associations, or expectations, that are not made and entered into and sealed by the Holy Spirit of promise, of him who is anointed, both as well for time and for all eternity, and that too most holy, by revelation and commandment through the medium of mine anointed, whom I have appointed on the earth to hold this power (and I have appointed unto my servant Joseph to hold this power in the last days, and there is never but one on the earth at a time on whom this power and the keys of this priesthood are conferred), are of no efficacy, virtue, or force in and after the resurrection from the dead; for all contracts that are not made unto this end have an end when men are dead."

D&C 136:2–4. "Let all the people of the Church of Jesus Christ of Latter-day Saints, and those who journey with them, be organized into companies, with a covenant and promise to keep all the commandments and statutes of the Lord our God. Let the companies be organized with captains of hundreds, captains of fifties, and captains of tens, with a president and his two counselors at their head, under the direction of the Twelve Apostles. And this shall be our covenant—that we will walk in all the ordinances of the Lord."

Words of the Prophets | Howard W. Hunter on keeping our covenants. "This question may appear as a play on the words of the Lord when he said this is the true and living church. When I ask, 'Am I a true and living member?' my question is, Am I deeply and fully dedicated to keeping the covenants I have made with the Lord? Am I totally committed to living the gospel and being a doer of the word and not a hearer only? Do I live my religion? Will I remain true? Do I stand firm against Satan's temptations? He is seeking to cause us to lose our way in a storm of derision and a tide of sophistry. We can have victory, however, by responding to that inner voice calling 'Stand firm!'" —Howard W. Hunter, *That We Might Have Joy* (Salt Lake City: Deseret Book, 1994), 149.

Cross reference to "Covenants": see Preach My Gospel, *63, 70.*

CREATION [205]. The earth in all its splendor and beauty has a singular purpose—to be a place for Heavenly Father's children to live, receive mortal bodies, be tested, and receive all requisite preparations to reside in the celestial kingdom if found worthy. This earth was made for us. The Creation provided an environment where agency could prevail for the children of the Almighty. This earth life is therefore a probationary state (Abraham 3:25). Through the sublime knowledge of our divine parentage, we, through this creation, can humbly set our course on the quest to become perfect, even as our Father and His Son are perfect (see Matthew 5:48; 3 Nephi 12:48). The Creation bears the indelible signature of the Creators—the Father of all goodness, and His Son Jesus Christ, who has charge of the heavenly light of life, "which light proceedeth forth from the presence of God to fill the immensity of space" (D&C 88:12). The Creation was perfect; the plan behind it is perfect; the majestic ebb and flow of life attest to the perfection of the Maker.

Genesis 1:1. "In the beginning God created the heaven and the earth."

Genesis 1:26–27. "And God said, Let us make man in our image, after our likeness: and let them have dominion over the fish of the sea, and over the fowl of the air, and over the cattle, and over all the earth, and over every creeping thing that creepeth upon the earth. So God created man in his own image, in the image of God created he him; male and female created he them."

Genesis 2:7. "And the Lord God formed man of the dust of the ground, and breathed into his nostrils the breath of life; and man became a living soul." (See also Abraham 5:7.)

John 1:1–4. "In the beginning was the Word, and the Word was with God, and the Word was God. The same was in the beginning with God. All things were made by him; and without him was not any thing made that was made. In him was life; and the life was the light of men."

Revelation 4:11. "Thou art worthy, O Lord, to receive glory and honour and power: for thou hast created all things, and for thy pleasure they are and were created."

D&C 93:8–10. "Therefore, in the beginning the Word was, for he was the Word, even the messenger of salvation—The light and the Redeemer of the world; the Spirit of truth, who came into the world, because the world was made by him, and in him was the life of men and the light of men. The worlds were made by him; men were made by him; all things were made by him, and through him, and of him."

Moses 2:1. "And it came to pass that the Lord spake unto Moses, saying: Behold, I reveal unto you concerning this heaven, and this earth; write the words which I speak. I am the Beginning and the End, the Almighty God; by mine Only Begotten I created these things; yea, in the beginning I created the heaven, and the earth upon which thou standest."

Abraham 3:24. "And there stood one among them that was like unto God, and he said unto those who were with him: We will go down, for there is space there, and we will take of these materials, and we will make an earth whereon these may dwell."

Words of the Prophets | Ezra Taft Benson on the Creator. "Jesus Christ was and is the Lord God Omnipotent (see Book of Mormon, Mosiah 3:5). He was chosen before He was born. He was the all-powerful Creator of the heavens and the earth. He is the source of life and light to all things. His word is the law by which all things are governed in the universe. All things created and made by Him are subject to His infinite power." —Ezra Taft Benson, *Come unto Christ* (Salt Lake City: Deseret Book, 1983), 128.

Cross reference to "Creation": see Preach My Gospel, *49.*

DEATH [647]. Life is full of situations we may not fully understand. One of the most difficult is death. There are two kinds of death: physical (or temporal) and spiritual. Temporal death is a temporary separation of our body and spirit, for the spirit never dies. Spiritual death is a separation of our being from the presence of God (as in the transition from the premortal existence to the mortal world or the transition from the Garden of Eden to the outer world) or from a state of allegiance to and favor by God to a state of disloyalty and being cut off from God and his blessings (as in the case of those who choose wickedness over righteousness). To our finite mortal minds, temporal death is difficult and seemingly final. The sorrow is deep with the loss of loved ones and their relationships. But death is part of Heavenly Father's plan of happiness because it marks a key transition point along the pathway that guides the faithful toward glory and eternal life. All mortals pass through death so that all can attain immortality through the universal resurrection and—except the sons of perdition (see D&C 76:36–37)—go on to that inheritance of glory that accords with their degree of obedience and righteousness in this life. Those whose lives are marked by complete and enduring covenant valor are perfected in Christ through His mercy and grace (see Moroni 10:32–33) and thereby inherit celestial glory. It was the death of Christ through His willing obedience to the will of the Father that the death of mankind was overcome.

Genesis 2:16–17. "And the Lord God commanded the man, saying, Of every tree of the garden thou mayest freely eat: But of the tree of the knowledge of good and evil, thou shalt not eat of it: for in the day that thou eatest thereof thou shalt surely die." (See also Moses 3:16–17; Abraham 5:12–13.)

Psalm 23:4. "Yea, though I walk through the valley of the shadow of death, I will fear no evil: for thou art with me; thy rod and thy staff they comfort me."

John 11:25–26. "Jesus said unto her [Martha], I am the resurrection, and the life: he that believeth in me, though he were dead, yet shall he live: And whosoever liveth and believeth in me shall never die."

1 Corinthians 15:21–22. "For since by man came death, by man came also the resurrection of the dead. For as in Adam all die, even so in Christ shall all be made alive."

1 Corinthians 15:55–58. "O death, where is thy sting? O grave, where is thy victory? The sting of death is sin; and the strength of sin is the law. But thanks be to God, which giveth us the victory through our Lord Jesus Christ. Therefore, my beloved brethren, be ye stedfast, unmoveable, always abounding in the work of the Lord, forasmuch as ye know that your labour is not in vain in the Lord."

2 Nephi 9:5–7. "Yea, I know that ye know that in the body he shall show himself unto those at Jerusalem, from whence we came; for it is expedient that it should be among them; for it behooveth the great Creator that he suffereth himself to become subject unto man in the flesh, and die for all men, that all men might become subject unto him. For as death hath passed upon all men, to fulfil the merciful plan of the great Creator, there must needs be a power of resurrection, and the resurrection must needs come unto man by reason of the fall; and the fall came by reason of transgression; and because man became fallen they were cut off from the presence of the Lord. Wherefore, it must needs be an infinite atonement—save it should be an infinite atonement this corruption could not put on incorruption. Wherefore, the first judgment which came upon man must needs have remained to an endless duration. And if so, this flesh must have laid down to rot and to crumble to its mother earth, to rise no more."

2 Nephi 9:39. "O, my beloved brethren, remember the awfulness in transgressing against that Holy God, and also the awfulness of yielding to the enticings of that cunning one. Remember, to be carnally-minded is death, and to be spiritually-minded is life eternal." (See also Romans 8:6.)

Alma 7:12. "And he will take upon him death, that he may loose the bands of death which bind his people; and he will take upon him their infirmities, that his bowels may be filled with mercy, according to the flesh, that he may know according to the flesh how to succor his people according to their infirmities."

Alma 12:24. "And we see that death comes upon mankind, yea, the death which has been spoken of by Amulek, which is the temporal death; nevertheless there was a space granted unto man in which he might repent; therefore this life became a probationary state; a time to prepare to meet God; a time to prepare for that endless state which has been spoken of by us, which is after the resurrection of the dead."

Mormon 9:12–13. "Behold, he created Adam, and by Adam came the fall of man. And because of the fall of man came Jesus Christ, even the Father and the Son; and because of Jesus Christ came the redemption of man. And because of the redemption of man, which came by Jesus Christ, they are brought back into the presence of the Lord; yea, this is wherein all men are redeemed, because the death of Christ bringeth to pass the resurrection, which bringeth to pass a redemption from an endless sleep, from which sleep all men shall be awakened by the power of God when the trump shall sound; and they shall come forth, both small and great, and all shall stand before his bar, being redeemed and loosed from this eternal band of death, which death is a temporal death."

D&C 29:40–44. "Wherefore, it came to pass that the devil tempted Adam, and he partook of the forbidden fruit and transgressed the commandment, wherein he became subject to the will of the devil, because he yielded unto temptation. Wherefore, I, the Lord God, caused that he should be cast out from the Garden of Eden, from my presence, because of his transgression, wherein he became spiritually dead, which is the first death, even that same death which is the last death, which is spiritual, which shall be pronounced upon the wicked when I shall say: Depart, ye cursed. But, behold, I say unto you that I, the Lord God, gave unto Adam and unto his seed, that they should not die as to the temporal death, until I, the Lord God, should send forth angels to declare unto them repentance and redemption, through faith on the name of mine Only Begotten Son. And thus did I, the Lord God, appoint unto man the days of his probation—that by his natural death he might be raised in immortality unto eternal life, even as many as would believe; And they that believe not unto eternal damnation; for they cannot be redeemed from their spiritual fall, because they repent not."

D&C 88:15–16. "And the spirit and the body are the soul of man. And the resurrection from the dead is the redemption of the soul."

Words of the Prophets | Joseph Smith on death. "The only difference between the old and young dying is, one lives longer in heaven and eternal light and glory than the other, and is freed a little sooner from this miserable, wicked world. Notwithstanding all this glory, we for a moment lose sight of it, and mourn the loss, but we do not mourn as those without hope. . . . It mattereth not whether we live long or short on the earth after we come to a knowledge of these principles [the principles of the gospel] and obey them unto the end." —Joseph Smith, *HC* 4:554, 555.

DEGREES OF GLORY [0]. The purpose of life is to become like unto our Heavenly Father and His Only Begotten Son, who are exalted Beings of infinite power, knowledge, glory, mercy, and love. The word *exalted* means "elevated to a great height" (from the Latin *ex*, "up or away" and *altus*, "high"). The plan of salvation is a divine design of transformation to lift us upward to the destined level of being truly exalted, receiving the promised fulness of the glory of God, even eternal life. The goal is precise: "Therefore I would that ye should be perfect even as I, or your Father who is in heaven is perfect" (3 Nephi 12:48). And Their work and glory is to "bring to pass the immortality and eternal life of man" (Moses 1:39).

The vision of the kingdoms of glory, when viewed within the framework of the atoning mission of the Savior and Redeemer Jesus Christ, is one of the most compelling and moving vistas bestowed upon latter-day seekers of truth through the restoration of the gospel. The rising hierarchy of kingdoms shown in Doctrine and Covenants 76—beginning with the utter bleakness and spiritual vacuum of outer darkness (world of the sons of perdition) and continuing upward, with the starlike glory of the telestial and the moonlike glory of the terrestrial, until the culmination and pinnacle of the iridescent sunlike glory of the celestial—this picture is indelibly impressed upon the soul of all students of spiritual truth as they seek to confirm their ascent toward the only possible objective of the gospel plan that accords with reason and human potentiality: attaining the highest degree of the celestial kingdom and the unspeakable blessings of immortality, exaltation, and eternal lives. It will be a "state of never-ending happiness" (Mosiah 2:41).

John 14:2. "In my Father's house are many mansions: if it were not so, I would have told you. I go to prepare a place for you."

Romans 8:16–17. "The Spirit itself beareth witness with our spirit, that we are the children of God: And if children, then heirs; heirs of God, and joint-heirs with Christ; if so be that we suffer with him, that we may be also glorified together."

1 Corinthians 15:40–41. "There are also celestial bodies, and bodies terrestrial: but the glory of the celestial is one, and the glory of the terrestrial is another. There is one glory of the sun, and another glory of the moon, and another glory of the stars: for one star differeth from another star in glory."

2 Corinthians 12:1–3. "It is not expedient for me doubtless to glory. I will come to visions and revelations of the Lord. I knew a man in Christ [i.e. Paul, speaking of himself] above fourteen years ago, (whether in the body, I cannot tell; or whether out of the body, I cannot tell: God knoweth;) such an one caught up to the third heaven. And I knew such a man, (whether in the body, or out of the body, I cannot tell: God knoweth)."

2 Nephi 2:25. "Adam fell that men might be; and men are, that they might have joy."

Moroni 10:32–33. "Yea, come unto Christ, and be perfected in him, and deny yourselves of all ungodliness; and if ye shall deny yourselves of all ungodliness, and love God with all your might, mind and strength, then is his grace sufficient for you, that by his grace ye may be perfect in Christ; and if by the grace of God ye are perfect in Christ, ye can in nowise deny the power of God. And again, if ye by the grace of God are perfect in Christ, and deny not his power, then are ye sanctified in Christ by the grace of God, through the shedding of the blood of Christ, which is in the covenant of the Father unto the remission of your sins, that ye become holy, without spot."

D&C 14:6–7. "Seek to bring forth and establish my Zion. Keep my commandments in all things. And, if you keep my commandments and endure to the end you shall have eternal life, which gift is the greatest of all the gifts of God."

D&C 50:41–42. "Fear not, little children, for you are mine, and I have overcome the world, and you are of them that my Father hath given me; And none of them that my Father hath given me shall be lost."

D&C 51:19. "And whoso is found a faithful, a just, and a wise steward shall enter into the joy of his Lord, and shall inherit eternal life."

D&C 76:41–43. "That he came into the world, even Jesus, to be crucified for the world, and to bear the sins of the world, and to sanctify the world, and to cleanse it from all unrighteousness; That through him all might be saved whom the Father had put into his power and made by him; Who glorifies the Father, and saves all the works of his hands, except those sons of perdition who deny the Son after the Father has revealed him."

D&C 88:49–50. "The light shineth in darkness, and the darkness comprehendeth it not; nevertheless, the day shall come when you shall comprehend even God, being quickened in him and by him. Then shall ye know that ye have seen me, that I am, and that I am the true light that is in you, and that you are in me; otherwise ye could not abound."

D&C 101:65. "Therefore, I must gather together my people, according to the parable of the wheat and the tares, that the wheat may be secured in the garners to possess eternal life, and be crowned with celestial glory, when I shall come in the kingdom of my Father to reward every man according as his work shall be."

Moses 6:59. "That by reason of transgression cometh the fall, which fall bringeth death, and inasmuch as ye were born into the world by water, and blood, and the spirit, which I have made, and so became of dust a living soul, even so ye must be born again into the kingdom of heaven, of water, and of the Spirit, and be cleansed by blood, even the blood of mine Only Begotten; that ye might be sanctified from all sin, and enjoy the words of eternal life in this world, and eternal life in the world to come, even immortal glory."

Words of the Prophets | Joseph Smith on becoming as God is. "God himself was once as we are now, and is an exalted man, and sits enthroned in yonder heavens! That is the great secret. If the veil were rent today, and the great God who holds this world in its orbit, and who upholds all worlds and all things by His power, was to make himself visible,—I say, if you were to see him today, you would see him like a man in form—like yourselves in all the person, image, and very form as a man; for Adam was created in the very fashion, image and likeness of God, and received instruction from, and walked, talked and conversed with Him, as one man talks and communes with another. . . . Here, then, is eternal life—to know the only wise and true God; and you have got to learn how to be gods yourselves, and to be kings

and priests to God, the same as all gods have done before you, namely, by going from one small degree to another, and from a small capacity to a great one; from grace to grace, from exaltation to exaltation." —Joseph Smith, *HC* 6:305–306.
Cross reference to "Degrees of Glory": see Preach My Gospel, *53, 58, 85.*

What are the admission qualifications for outer darkness and each of the three degrees of glory?

Outer darkness. D&C 76:31. "Thus saith the Lord concerning all those who know my power, and have been made partakers thereof, and suffered themselves through the power of the devil to be overcome, and to deny the truth and defy my power—They are they who are the sons of perdition, of whom I say that it had been better for them never to have been born; For they are vessels of wrath, doomed to suffer the wrath of God, with the devil and his angels in eternity; Concerning whom I have said there is no forgiveness in this world nor in the world to come—Having denied the Holy Spirit after having received it, and having denied the Only Begotten Son of the Father, having crucified him unto themselves and put him to an open shame. These are they who shall go away into the lake of fire and brimstone, with the devil and his angels—And the only ones on whom the second death shall have any power; Yea, verily, the only ones who shall not be redeemed in the due time of the Lord, after the sufferings of his wrath." (See also Matthew 12:31; 2 Peter 2:4; Jude 1:6; D&C 88:32–33.)

Telestial kingdom. D&C 76:82–86. "These are they who received not the gospel of Christ, neither the testimony of Jesus. These are they who deny not the Holy Spirit. These are they who are thrust down to hell. These are they who shall not be redeemed from the devil until the last resurrection, until the Lord, even Christ the Lamb, shall have finished his work. These are they who receive not of his fulness in the eternal world, but of the Holy Spirit through the ministration of the terrestrial." (See also D&C 76:81, 89, 98; 100–106.)

Terrestrial kingdom. D&C 76:72–77, 79. "Behold, these are they who died without law; And also they who are the spirits of men kept in prison, whom the Son visited, and preached the gospel unto them, that they might be judged according to men in the flesh; Who received not the testimony of Jesus in the flesh, but afterwards received it. These are they who are honorable men of the earth, who were blinded by the craftiness of men. These are they who receive of his glory, but not of his fulness. These are they who receive of the presence of the Son, but not of the fulness of the Father. . . . These are they who are not valiant in the testimony of Jesus; wherefore, they obtain not the crown over the kingdom of our God." (See also D&C 76: 71, 78, 97.)

Celestial kingdom. D&C 76:51–58, 62–65, 68–69. "They are they who received the testimony of Jesus, and believed on his name and were baptized after the manner of his burial, being buried in the water in his name, and this according to the commandment which he has given—That by keeping the commandments they might be washed and cleansed from all their sins, and receive the Holy Spirit by the laying on of the hands of him who is ordained and sealed unto this power; And who overcome by faith, and are sealed by the Holy Spirit of promise, which the Father sheds forth upon all those who are just and true. They are they who are the church of the Firstborn. They are they into whose hands the Father has given all things—They are they who are priests and kings, who have received of his fulness, and of his glory; And are priests of the Most High, after the order of Melchizedek, which was after the order of Enoch, which was after the order of the Only Begotten Son. Wherefore, as it is written, they are gods, even the sons of God. . . . These shall dwell in the presence of God and his Christ forever and ever. These are they whom he shall bring with him, when he shall come in the clouds of heaven to reign on the earth over his people. These are they who shall have part in the first resurrection. These are they who shall come forth in the resurrection of the just. . . . These are they whose names are written in heaven, where God and Christ are the judge of all. These are they who are just men made perfect through Jesus the mediator of the new covenant, who wrought out this perfect atonement through the shedding of his own blood." (See also D&C 76:70, 96; 131:1–4.)

DISCIPLESHIP [353]. The word *disciple* derives from a Latin term meaning "one who learns." As baptized members and followers of the Lord Jesus Christ, we become His disciples, with a commitment to learn and share the principles of salvation and exaltation. The Lord referred to His chosen leaders as "disciples," but He also applied the term generally to all of His valiant followers. As such, we can be grateful that we have a belief and testimony of the doctrines and teachings of the gospel of Jesus Christ and of the Church and kingdom of God here upon the earth. We seek to be obedient to the commandments, to stand as witnesses at all times and in all places (see Mosiah 18:8–9), and to share the gospel with all mankind (see Mormon 9:22). We seek to become like Him (see 3 Nephi 27:27). We truly become His disciples as we love and serve our fellowman and seek to do the will of God in all things.

Isaiah 8:16. "Bind up the testimony, seal the law among my disciples." (See also D&C 20:69; 88:84; 133:71.) (Note: The image suggests rolling up a parchment and sealing it that it may be rendered complete and final—representing figuratively the planting of the sacred testimony of truth in the hearts of the Lord's missionaries as they preserve their witness of how the people receive the word of God.)

John 13:34–35. "A new commandment I give unto you, That ye love one another; as I have loved you, that ye also love one another. By this shall all men know that ye are my disciples, if ye have love one to another."

Acts 11:26. "And the disciples were called Christians first in Antioch."

Mormon 9:22. "For behold, thus said Jesus Christ, the Son of God, unto his disciples who should tarry, yea, and also to all his disciples, in the hearing of the multitude: Go ye into all the world, and preach the gospel to every creature."

D&C 6:32. "Verily, verily, I say unto you, as I said unto my disciples, where two or three are gathered together in my name, as touching one thing, behold, there will I be in the midst of them—even so am I in the midst of you." (See also Matthew 18:19–20.)

D&C 41:5. "He that receiveth my law and doeth it, the same is my disciple; and he that saith he receiveth it and doeth it not, the same is not my disciple, and shall be cast out from among you."

D&C 103:28. "And whoso is not willing to lay down his life for my sake is not my disciple."

Words of the Prophets | Bruce R. McConkie on true discipleship. "Scriptural tests establishing true discipleship include: 1. Believing the true doctrines of Christ (Ether 4:10–12); 2. Obeying the principles of the gospel (John 8:31); 3. Having 'love one to another' (John 13:35); 4. Accepting the message and aiding the work of the missionaries (D&C 84:87–91); and 5. Bringing forth works of righteousness (John 15:4–8.)." —Bruce R. McConkie, *Mormon Doctrine*, 2d ed. (Salt Lake City: Bookcraft, 1966), 198.

DISPENSATION [21]. The word *dispensation* implies the dispensing, revealing, or restoring of essential powers, keys, and doctrines pertaining to salvation and exaltation. A period of time in which such powers and authorities are established on earth, allowing the kingdom of God to be unfolding for the benefit of God's children, is known as a "dispensation." When wickedness abounds to the degree that the continuation of such powers and authorities from one generation to the next is interrupted (in an apostasy), then a restoration from heaven is needed so the work of the Lord can go forward. In general, we speak of the dispensations of Adam, Enoch, Noah, Abraham, Moses, the Lord in the meridian of time, and the Restoration under Joseph Smith. In addition, there were dispensations recorded in the Book of Mormon, as with the Jaredites, the Nephites, and the Saints at the time of Christ's ministry in the New World. There have likely also been other dispensations about which we know little at this time, as with the visit of the resurrected Lord among the Ten Tribes.

Dispensations in general. Romans 1:16–17. "For I am not ashamed of the gospel of Christ: for it is the power of God unto salvation to every one that believeth; to the Jew first, and also to the Greek. For therein is the righteousness of God revealed from faith to faith [i.e., from dispensation to dispensation]: as it is written, The just shall live by faith [on his name—JST]."

Adam. Moses 5:58–59. "And thus the Gospel began to be preached, from the beginning, being declared by holy angels sent forth from the presence of God, and by his own voice, and by the gift of the Holy Ghost. And thus all things were confirmed unto Adam, by an holy ordinance, and the Gospel preached, and a decree sent forth, that it should be in the world, until the end thereof; and thus it was."

Noah. Moses 8:16, 19–20, 23–24. "And it came to pass that Noah prophesied, and taught the things of God, even as it was in the beginning. . . . And the Lord ordained Noah after his own order, and commanded him that he should go forth and declare his Gospel unto the children of men, even as it was given unto Enoch. And it came to pass that Noah called upon the children of men that they should repent; but they hearkened not unto his words. . . . And it came to pass that Noah continued his preaching unto the people, saying: Hearken, and give heed unto my words; Believe and repent of your sins and be baptized in the name of Jesus Christ, the Son of God, even as our fathers, and ye shall receive the Holy Ghost, that ye may have all things made manifest; and if ye do not this, the floods will come in upon you; nevertheless they hearkened not." (See also all of Moses 8.)

Abraham. Abraham 2:8–11. "My name is Jehovah, and I know the end from the beginning; therefore my hand shall be over thee. And I will make of thee a great nation, and I will bless thee above measure, and make thy name great among all nations, and thou shalt be a blessing unto thy seed after thee, that in their hands they shall bear this ministry and Priesthood unto all nations; And I will bless them through thy name; for as many as receive this Gospel shall be called after thy name, and shall be accounted thy seed, and shall rise up and bless thee, as their father; And I will bless them that bless thee, and curse them that curse thee; and in thee (that is, in thy Priesthood) and in thy seed (that is, thy Priesthood), for I give unto thee a promise that this right shall continue in thee, and in thy seed after thee (that is to say, the literal seed, or the seed of the body) shall all the families of the earth be blessed, even with the blessings of the Gospel, which are the blessings of salvation, even of life eternal." (See also Galatians 3:6–8.)

Moses. D&C 84:17–25. "Which priesthood continueth in the church of God in all generations, and is without beginning of days or end of years. And the Lord confirmed a priesthood also upon Aaron and his seed, throughout all their generations, which priesthood also continueth and abideth forever with the priesthood which is after the holiest order of God. And this greater priesthood administereth the gospel and holdeth the key of the mysteries of the kingdom, even the key of the knowledge of God. Therefore, in the ordinances thereof, the power of godliness is manifest. And without the ordinances thereof, and the authority of the priesthood, the power of godliness is not manifest unto men in the flesh; For without this no man can see the face of God, even the Father, and live. Now this Moses plainly taught to the children of Israel in the wilderness, and sought diligently to sanctify his people that they might behold the face of God; But they hardened their hearts and could not endure his presence; therefore, the Lord in his wrath, for his anger was kindled against them, swore that they should not enter into his rest while in the wilderness, which rest is the fulness of his glory. Therefore, he took Moses out of their midst, and the Holy Priesthood also."

Apostles in the meridian of time. Matthew 16:18–19. "And I say also unto thee, That thou art Peter, and upon this rock [i.e., the rock of revelation as empowered through Jesus Christ as the governing Lord] I will build my church; and the gates of hell shall not prevail against it. And I will give unto thee the keys of the kingdom of heaven: and whatsoever thou shalt bind on earth shall be bound in heaven: and whatsoever thou shalt loose on earth shall be loosed in heaven." (See also Matthew 18: 8.)

Jaredites. Ether 1:41–43. "Go to and gather together thy flocks, both male and female, of every kind; and also of the seed of the earth of every kind; and thy families; and also Jared thy brother and his family; and also thy friends and their families, and the friends of Jared and their families. And when thou hast done this thou shalt go at the head of them down into the valley which is northward. And there will I meet thee, and I will go before thee into a land which is choice above all the lands of the earth. And there will I bless thee and thy seed, and raise up unto me of thy seed, and of the seed of thy brother, and they who shall go with thee, a great nation. And there shall be none greater than the nation which I will raise up unto me of thy seed, upon all the face of the earth. And thus I will do unto thee because this long time ye have cried unto me." (See also the entire book of Ether.)

Nephites. 1 Nephi 2:1–3. "For behold, it came to pass that the Lord spake unto my father, yea, even in a dream, and said unto him: Blessed art thou Lehi, because of the things which thou hast done; and because thou hast been faithful and declared unto this people the things which I commanded thee, behold, they seek to take away thy life. And it came to pass that the Lord commanded my father, even in a dream, that he should take his family and depart into the wilderness. And it came to pass that he was obedient unto the word of the Lord, wherefore he did as the Lord commanded him." (See also the various books of the Book of Mormon down to the time of Christ's visit in the New World.)

The resurrected Lord in the New World. 3 Nephi 9:15–18. "Behold, I am Jesus Christ the Son of God. I created the heavens and the earth, and all things that in them are. I was with the Father from the beginning. I am in the Father, and the Father in me; and in me hath the Father glorified his name. I came unto my own, and my own received me not. And the scriptures concerning my coming are fulfilled. And as many as have received me, to them have I given to become the sons of God; and even so will I to as many as shall believe on my name, for behold, by me redemption cometh, and in me is the law of Moses fulfilled. I am the light and the life of the world. I am Alpha and Omega, the beginning and the end." (See also 3 Nephi 11:7, 21–22; 18:36–37.)

The Ten Tribes. 2 Nephi 29:12–14. "For behold, I shall speak unto the Jews and they shall write it; and I shall also speak unto the Nephites and they shall write it; and I shall also speak unto the other tribes of the house of Israel, which I have led away, and they shall write it; and I shall also speak unto all nations of the earth and they shall write it. And it shall come to pass that the Jews shall have the words of the Nephites, and the Nephites shall have the words of the Jews; and the Nephites and the Jews shall have the words of the lost tribes of Israel; and the lost tribes of Israel shall have the words of the Nephites and the Jews. And it shall come to pass that my people, which are of the house of Israel, shall be gathered home unto the lands of their possessions; and my word also shall be gathered in one. And I will show unto them that fight against my word and against my people, who are of the house of Israel, that I am God, and that I covenanted with Abraham that I would remember his seed forever." (See also 3 Nephi 16:1–4.)

Restoration through Joseph Smith (dispensation of the fulness of times). D&C 128:20. "And again, what do we hear? Glad tidings from Cumorah! Moroni, an angel from heaven, declaring the fulfilment of the prophets—the book to be revealed. A voice of the Lord in the wilderness of Fayette, Seneca county, declaring the three witnesses to bear record of the book! The voice of Michael on the banks of the Susquehanna, detecting the devil when he appeared as an angel of light! The voice of Peter, James, and John in the wilderness between Harmony, Susquehanna county, and Colesville, Broome county, on the Susquehanna river, declaring themselves as possessing the keys of the kingdom, and of the dispensation of the fulness of times!" (See also D&C 13:1; 27:12–13; 110:11–16; 112:14–32).

Cross reference to "Dispensations": see Preach My Gospel, *32–34.*

ELIAS [122]. The name *Elias* has four distinct applications in the scriptures: (1) a title designating an individual who acts in the office of forerunner (preparer); (2) a title designating an individual who acts in the office of a restorer (completer); (3) the Greek form of the Hebrew name Elijah, the prophet; (4) a prophet who lived apparently during the time of Abraham. The following material illustrates these various usages:

Title of a forerunner (preparer). Matthew 11:10–14. "For this is he, of whom it is written, Behold, I send my messenger before thy face, which shall prepare thy way before thee. Verily I say unto you, Among them that are born of women there hath not risen a greater than John the Baptist: notwithstanding he that is least in the kingdom of heaven is greater than he. And from the days of John the Baptist until now the kingdom of heaven suffereth violence, and the violent take it by force. For all the prophets and the law prophesied until John. And if ye will receive it, this is Elias, which was for to come." (See also Luke 1:11–17; D&C 27:7; JST Matthew 11:13–15.)

Title of a restorer (completer). JST John 1:19–28. "And no man hath seen God at any time, except he hath borne record of the Son; for except it is through him no man can be saved. And this is the record of John, when the Jews sent priests and Levites from Jerusalem, to ask him; Who art thou? And he confessed, and denied not that he was Elias; but confessed, saying; I am not the Christ. And they asked him, saying; How then art thou Elias? And he said, I am not that Elias who was to restore all things. And they asked him, saying, Art thou that prophet? And he answered, No. Then said they unto him, Who art thou? that we may give an answer to them that sent us. What sayest thou of thyself? He said, I am the voice of one crying in the wilderness, Make straight the way of the Lord, as saith the prophet Esaias. And they who were sent were of the Pharisees. And they asked him, and said unto him, Why baptizest thou then, if thou be not the Christ, nor Elias who was to restore all things, neither that prophet? John answered them, saying, I baptize with water, but there standeth one among you, whom ye know not; He it is of whom I bear record. He is that prophet, even Elias, who, coming after me, is preferred before me, whose shoe's latchet I am not worthy to unloose, or whose place I am not able to fill; for he shall baptize, not only with water, but with fire, and with the Holy Ghost." (See also John 1:18–27.)

Equivalent of Elijah. Matthew 17:1–3. "And after six days Jesus taketh Peter, James, and John his brother, and bringeth them up into an high mountain apart, And was transfigured before them: and his face did shine as the sun, and his raiment was white as the light. And, behold, there appeared unto them Moses and Elias [i.e., Elijah] talking with him." (See also JST Mark 9:1–3; D&C 110:12.)

ADDITIONAL INFORMATION—**Who was the prophet Elias?** Elias is both an individual prophet as well as a title. Along with other heavenly ministrants who came to restore their several keys, Elias the individual appeared to Joseph Smith and Oliver Cowdery in the Kirtland Temple on April 3, 1836, "and committed the dispensation of the gospel of Abraham, saying that in us and our seed all generations after us should be blessed" (D&C 110:12). President Joseph Fielding Smith taught that Elias, in this extraordinary appearance, was Noah, also known as the Angel Gabriel (see Joseph Fielding Smith, *Answers to Gospel Questions*, 5 vols. [Salt Lake City: Deseret Book, 1957, 1958, 1960, 1963, 1966], 3:138–141). Elder Bruce R. McConkie says in this context only that "we have no information, at this time, as to the mortal life or ministry of Elias. Apparently he lived in the days of Abraham, but whether he was Abraham, or Melchizedek, or some other prophet, we do not know" (*Mormon Doctrine*, 2nd ed. [Salt Lake City: Bookcraft, 1966], 220). It is of interest that the ancient prophet Noah may have still been alive, in his very senior years, during the time of Abraham (see Genesis 9:28–29).

ENDURING TO THE END [enduring: 143; enduring to the end: 18]. Enduring to the end is the process of continuing on the straight and narrow course, serving God and our fellowmen to the end of our mortal lives. It means being persistent in doing our duty and keeping the commandments with unwavering steadfastness. Enduring to the end is proof of our faith and confirmation of the depth of our conversion to the gospel of Jesus Christ.

Matthew 24:13. "But he that shall endure unto the end, the same shall be saved."

2 Nephi 31:20. "Wherefore, ye must press forward with a steadfastness in Christ, having a perfect brightness of hope, and a love of God and of all men. Wherefore, if ye shall press forward, feasting upon the word of Christ, and endure to the end, behold, thus saith the Father: Ye shall have eternal life."

3 Nephi 15:9. "Look unto me, and endure to the end, and ye shall live; for unto him that endureth to the end will I give eternal life."

3 Nephi 27:15–17. "And for this cause have I been lifted up; therefore, according to the power of the Father I will draw all men unto me, that they may be judged according to their works. And it shall come to pass, that whoso repenteth and is baptized in my name shall be filled; and if he endureth to the end, behold, him will I hold guiltless before my Father at that day when I shall stand to judge the world. And he that endureth not unto the end, the same is he that is also hewn down and cast into the fire, from whence they can no more return, because of the justice of the Father."

D&C 14:7. "And, if you keep my commandments and endure to the end you shall have eternal life, which gift is the greatest of all the gifts of God."

D&C 20:29. "And we know that all men must repent and believe on the name of Jesus Christ, and worship the Father in his name, and endure in faith on his name to the end, or they cannot be saved in the kingdom of God."

Words of the Prophets | **Howard W. Hunter on enduring to the end.** "If you endure to the end, and if you are valiant in the testimony of Jesus, you will achieve true greatness and will live in the presence of our Father in Heaven." —Howard W. Hunter, "True Greatness," *Ensign*, May 1982, 19-20. *The Teachings of Howard W. Hunter*, edited by Clyde J. Williams (Salt Lake City: Bookcraft, 1997), 72.

ETERNAL PROGRESSION/EXALTATION [eternal: 271; progress: 6; eternal progression: 0]. The purpose of life is to become like unto our Heavenly Father and His Only Begotten Son, who are exalted Beings of infinite power, knowledge, glory, mercy, and love. The plan of salvation is a plan of eternal progression, divine design of transformation to lift us upward to the destined level of being truly exalted, receiving the promised fulness of the glory of God, even eternal life. The goal is precise: "Therefore I would that ye should be perfect even as I, or your Father who is in heaven is perfect" (3 Nephi 12:48). As we strive to take on the divine nature and fulfill our destiny, we bring glory to our Heavenly Father and His Son. Their ultimate goal is to receive us unto Themselves forever in the celestial kingdom, having endowed us with saving knowledge, guided us by the Spirit, given us an abundance of temporal strength and spiritual power, prepared and sealed us through sacred covenant ordinances, and granted unto us the capacity to endure to the end—throughout our endless struggles and devoted labors—by honoring gospel principles and meriting the sublime blessings of the Atonement of Jesus Christ.

Genesis 1:26. "And God said, Let us make man in our image, after our likeness: and let them have dominion over the fish of the sea, and over the fowl of the air, and over the cattle, and over all the earth, and over every creeping thing that creepeth upon the earth. So God created man in his own image, in the image of God created he him; male and female created he them." (See also Moses 2:26–27.)

Psalm 82:6. "I have said, Ye are gods; and all of you are children of the most High."

Job 36:22. "Behold, God exalteth by his power: who teacheth like him?"

Isaiah 2:2. "And it shall come to pass in the last days, that the mountain of the Lord's house shall be established in the top of the mountains, and shall be exalted above the hills; and all nations shall flow unto it." (See also Micah 4:1; 2 Nephi 12:2.)

Matthew 5:48. "Be ye therefore perfect, even as your Father which is in heaven is perfect." (See also 3 Nephi 12:48.)

Acts 5:31. "Him hath God exalted with his right hand to be a Prince and a Saviour, for to give repentance to Israel, and forgiveness of sins."

1 Peter 5:6. "Humble yourselves therefore under the mighty hand of God, that he may exalt you in due time."

2 Nephi 31:19–20. "And now, my beloved brethren, after ye have gotten into this strait and narrow path, I would ask if all is done? Behold, I say unto you, Nay; for ye have not come thus far save it were by the word of Christ with unshaken faith in him, relying wholly upon the merits of him who is mighty to save. Wherefore, ye must press forward with a steadfastness in Christ, having a perfect brightness of hope, and a love of God and of all men. Wherefore, if ye shall press forward, feasting upon the word of Christ, and endure to the end, behold, thus saith the Father: Ye shall have eternal life."

D&C 14:7. "And, if you keep my commandments and endure to the end you shall have eternal life, which gift is the greatest of all the gifts of God."

D&C 76:58–60. "Wherefore, as it is written, they are gods, even the sons of God— Wherefore, all things are theirs, whether life or death, or things present, or things to come, all are theirs and they are Christ's, and Christ is God's. And they shall overcome all things."

D&C 121:8. "And then, if thou endure it well, God shall exalt thee on high; thou shalt triumph over all thy foes."

D&C 132:22–23. "For strait is the gate, and narrow the way that leadeth unto the exaltation and continuation of the lives, and few there be that find it, because ye receive me not in the world neither do ye know me. But if ye receive me in the world, then shall ye know me, and shall receive your exaltation; that where I am ye shall be also."

Moses 1:39. "For behold, this is my work and my glory—to bring to pass the immortality and eternal life of man."

Words of the Prophets | Joseph Smith on eternal progression. "Could you gaze into heaven five minutes, you would know more than you would by reading all that ever was written on the subject. . . . God himself was once as we are now, and is an exalted man, and sits enthroned in yonder heavens! That is the great secret. . . . Here, then, is eternal life—to know the only wise and true God; and you have got to learn how to be gods yourselves, and to be kings and priests to God, the same as all gods have done before you, namely, by going from one small degree to another, and from a small capacity to a great one; from grace to grace, from exaltation to exaltation..." —Joseph Smith, *HC* 6:50; 305–306.

FAITH [627]. Faith is the first principle of the gospel of Jesus Christ and the governing principle in applying the Atonement to our lives. We learn that it is impossible to please God without faith (see Hebrews 11:6), for through faith we are enabled to do the will of the Lord while in this world and thus gain eternal life in the world to come. Faith is something true that we hope for but do not see (see Hebrews 11:1; Alma 32:21; Lectures on Faith 1:7–8)—but its role in the gospel plan extends beyond this, as the Prophet Joseph Smith confirmed: "Faith is the moving cause of all action in temporal things" (Lectures on Faith 1:12) and the principle and source of saving power (see Lectures on Faith 1:15). He summarizes: "Faith, then, is the first great governing principle which has power, dominion, and authority over all things; by it they exist, by it they are upheld, by it they are changed, or by it they remain, agreeable to the will of God" (Lectures on Faith 1:24).

Ephesians 4:5. "One Lord, one faith, one baptism."

Hebrews 11:1. "Now faith is the substance of things hoped for, the evidence of things not seen."

Hebrews 11:6. "But without faith it is impossible to please him: for he that cometh to God must believe that he is, and that he is a rewarder of them that diligently seek him."

2 Nephi 9:23. "And he commandeth all men that they must repent, and be baptized in his name, having perfect faith in the Holy One of Israel, or they cannot be saved in the kingdom of God."

2 Nephi 26:13. "He manifesteth himself unto all those who believe in him, by the power of the Holy Ghost; yea, unto every nation, kindred, tongue, and people, working mighty miracles, signs, and wonders, among the children of men according to their faith."

Mosiah 18:20. "Yea, even he [Alma] commanded them that they should preach nothing save it were repentance and faith on the Lord, who had redeemed his people." (See also Mosiah 25:22.)

Alma 32:21. "And now as I said concerning faith—faith is not to have a perfect knowledge of things; therefore if ye have faith ye hope for things which are not seen, which are true."

Alma 34:15. "And thus he shall bring salvation to all those who shall believe on his name; this being the intent of this last sacrifice, to bring about the bowels of mercy, which overpowereth justice, and bringeth about means unto men that they may have faith unto repentance."

Ether 12:3–4. "For he [Ether] did cry from the morning, even until the going down of the sun, exhorting the people to believe in God unto repentance lest they should be destroyed, saying unto them that by faith all things are fulfilled—Wherefore, whoso believeth in God might with surety hope for a better world, yea, even a place at the right hand of God, which hope cometh of faith, maketh an anchor to the souls of men, which would make them sure and steadfast, always abounding in good works, being led to glorify God."

Ether 12:6. "And now, I, Moroni, would speak somewhat concerning these things; I would show unto the world that faith is things which are hoped for and not seen; wherefore, dispute not because ye see not, for ye receive no witness until after the trial of your faith."

Ether 12:12. "For if there be no faith among the children of men God can do no miracle among them; wherefore, he showed not himself until after their faith."

Moroni 7:33. "And Christ hath said: If ye will have faith in me ye shall have power to do whatsoever thing is expedient in me."

Moroni 7:37–38. "Behold I say unto you, Nay; for it is by faith that miracles are wrought; and it is by faith that angels appear and minister unto men; wherefore, if these things have ceased wo be unto the children of men, for it is because of unbelief, and all is vain. For no man can be saved, according to the words of Christ, save they shall have faith in his name; wherefore, if these things have ceased, then has faith ceased also; and awful is the state of man, for they are as though there had been no redemption made."

D&C 8:10. "Remember that without faith you can do nothing; therefore ask in faith." (See also D&C 18:19.)

D&C 29:6. "Whatsoever ye shall ask in faith, being united in prayer according to my command, ye shall receive."

D&C 42:49–52. "He who hath faith to see shall see. He who hath faith to hear shall hear. The lame who hath faith to leap shall leap. And they who have not faith to do these things, but believe in me, have power to become my sons; and inasmuch as they break not my laws thou shalt bear their infirmities."

Faith or Works?

Romans 3:27–28. "Where is boasting then? It is excluded. By what law? of works? Nay: but by the law of faith. Therefore we conclude that a man is justified by faith without the deeds of the law."

Galatians 2:16. "Knowing that a man is not justified by the works of the law, but by the faith of Jesus Christ, even we have believed in Jesus Christ, that we might be justified by the faith of Christ, and not by the works of the law: for by the works of the law shall no flesh be justified."

Ephesians 2:8–9. "For by grace are ye saved through faith; and that not of yourselves: it is the gift of God: Not of works, lest any man should boast." (See also Romans 3:28.)

James 2:14, 17–18, 22, 24, 26. "What doth it profit, my brethren, though a man say he hath faith, and have not works? can faith save him?. . . Even so faith, if it hath not works, is dead, being alone. Yea, a man may say, Thou hast faith, and I have works: shew me thy faith without thy works, and I will shew thee my faith by my works . . . Seest thou how faith wrought with his works, and by works was faith made perfect? . . . Ye see then how that by works a man is justified, and not by faith only . . . For as the body without the spirit is dead, so faith without works is dead also."

WORDS OF THE PROPHETS | **Gordon B. Hinckley on faith helping us to be humble.** "If there is any one thing you and I need in this world it is faith, that dynamic, powerful,

marvelous element by which, as Paul declared, the very worlds were framed (Hebrews 11:3) . . . faith—the kind of faith that moves one to get on his knees and plead with the Lord and then get on his feet and go to work—is an asset beyond compare, even in the acquisition of secular knowledge." —Gordon B. Hinckley, "God Shall Give unto You Knowledge by His Holy Spirit," *BYU Speeches of the Year*, September 25, 1973, 109.
Cross-reference to "Faith": see Preach My Gospel, *61–62, 93–95, 116–117.*

FALL [959]. The Lord anticipated the Fall of mankind as a necessary part of man's journey toward immortality and eternal life (see Moses 4:28). Prior to the Fall, Adam and Eve were in a state of innocence. They were in the presence of God, but did not know good from evil and were not subject to death (see 2 Nephi 2:22–26). They were commanded to multiply and replenish the earth, and they were also commanded not to partake of the forbidden fruit—yet they had the power to choose (see Moses 3:15–17)—and Eve, beguiled by Satan, partook of the forbidden fruit (see Moses 4:7–13). Consequently, knowing good from evil, she realized that she would be cast out from the Garden of Eden and, being separated from Adam, would be unable to have children (see Moses 5:11). Adam, now aware of this state of affairs, made the choice, knowingly partaking of the fruit (2 Nephi 2:25), and then Adam and Eve together were sent forth on their mortal journey (see Moses 4:23–25, 28–31; see also Genesis 3:22–24). The results of the Fall proved to be a blessing for all mankind; because of the Fall, we have mortal tabernacles and a chance to grow and be tested and to prove ourselves worthy of returning to our Father's presence. The mortal experience, brought about by the Fall, opens the gateway to salvation, exaltation, and eternal life through the Atonement of Jesus Christ. Though trials many and tribulations not a few may confront us along the pathway forward, the light of Christ illuminates our way toward peace, glory, and eternal joy. In the strength of the Lord we will prevail. The designs of the Almighty will be accomplished.

Genesis 3:22–24. "And the Lord God said, Behold, the man is become as one of us, to know good and evil: and now, lest he put forth his hand, and take also of the tree of life, and eat, and live for ever: Therefore the Lord God sent him forth from the garden of Eden, to till the ground from whence he was taken. So he drove out the man; and he placed at the east of the garden of Eden Cherubims, and a flaming sword which turned every way, to keep the way of the tree of life." (See also Genesis 2:17; 3:6–7; Moses 3:17; 4:12.)

Romans 5:12. "Wherefore, as by one man sin entered into the world, and death by sin; and so death passed upon all men, for that all have sinned."

1 Corinthians 15:22. "For as in Adam all die, even so in Christ shall all be made alive."

D&C 29:39–43. "And it must needs be that the devil should tempt the children of men, or they could not be agents unto themselves; for if they never should have bitter they could not know the sweet—Wherefore, it came to pass that the devil tempted Adam, and he partook of the forbidden fruit and transgressed the commandment, wherein he became subject to the will of the devil, because he yielded unto temptation. Wherefore, I, the Lord God, caused that he should be cast out from the Garden of Eden, from my presence, because of his transgression, wherein he became spiritually dead, which is the first death, even that same death which is the last death, which is spiritual, which shall be pronounced upon the wicked when I shall say: Depart, ye cursed. But, behold, I say unto you that I, the Lord God, gave unto Adam and unto his seed, that they should not die as to the temporal death, until I, the Lord God, should send forth angels to declare unto them repentance and redemption, through faith on the name of mine Only Begotten Son. And thus did I, the Lord God, appoint unto man the days of his probation—that by his natural death he might be raised in immortality unto eternal life, even as many as would believe."

Moses 4:25–32. "By the sweat of thy face shalt thou eat bread, until thou shalt return unto the ground—for thou shalt surely die—for out of it wast thou taken: for dust thou wast, and unto dust shalt thou return. And Adam called his wife's name Eve, because she was the mother of all living; for thus have I, the Lord God, called the first of all women, which are many. Unto Adam, and also unto his wife, did I, the Lord God, make coats of skins, and clothed them. And I, the Lord God, said unto mine Only Begotten: Behold, the man is become as one of us to know good and evil; and now lest he put forth his hand and partake also of the tree of life, and eat and live forever, Therefore I, the Lord God, will send him forth from the Garden of Eden, to till the ground from whence he was taken; For as I, the Lord God, liveth, even so my words cannot return void, for as they go forth out of my mouth they must be fulfilled. So I drove out the man, and I placed at the east of the Garden of Eden, cherubim and a flaming sword, which turned every way to keep the way of the tree of life. (And these are the words which I spake unto my servant Moses, and they are true even as I will; and I have spoken them unto you. See thou show them unto no man, until I command you, except to them that believe. Amen.)."

Moses 5:10–12. "And in that day Adam blessed God and was filled, and began to prophesy concerning all the families of the earth, saying: Blessed be the name of God, for because of my transgression my eyes are opened, and in this life I shall have joy, and again in the flesh I shall see God. And Eve, his wife, heard all these things and was glad, saying: Were it not for our transgression we never should have had seed, and never should have known good and evil, and the joy of our redemption, and the eternal life which God giveth unto all the obedient. And Adam and Eve blessed the name of God, and they made all things known unto their sons and their daughters."

Second Article of Faith. "We believe that men will be punished for their own sins, and not for Adam's transgression."

WORDS OF THE PROPHETS | **Bruce R. McConkie on the three pillars of eternity.** "God himself, the Father of us all, established a plan of salvation whereby his spirit children might progress and become like him. It is the gospel of God, the plan of Eternal Elohim, the system that saves and exalts, and it consists of three things. These three are the very pillars of eternity itself. They are the most important events that ever have or will occur in all eternity. They are the Creation, the Fall, and the Atonement." —Bruce R. McConkie, "Christ and the Creation," *Tambuli*, Sept. 1983, 22.

FAMILIES CAN BE FOREVER [family 404]. The family is an eternal institution, extending from the premortal existence (where the spirit children of Heavenly Father were associated within His vast family circle) to the mortal world, where family units are to be organized according to the pattern of enduring relationships, and extending into the postmortal sphere, where eternal families have the cherished opportunity to be together forever through the sealing keys and powers of the priesthood. The rise and unfolding of families of covenant valor has been decreed by God. His covenant is once again restored to the earth, with all the rights, privileges, powers, and keys needed to secure and nurture the eternal family.

Family life is the proper place for the gospel to be taught and practiced. The home is a refuge from the world. We are to do all that we can to maintain a strong marriage and happy families by living the gospel of Jesus Christ and by participating in the covenants and ordinances of exaltation. The greatest commission from God to us as His children is to raise up our families in righteousness and truth, looking forward to the eternal world, where families can be together forever. The uniting of families forever through the blessings of the sealing covenants is a choice and magnificent framework for the work of the ministry of God and the building up of His kingdom in the latter days.

Genesis 1:27–28. "So God created man in his own image, in the image of God created he him; male and female created he them. And God blessed them, and God said unto them, Be fruitful, and multiply, and replenish the earth, and subdue it: and have dominion over the fish of the sea, and over the fowl of the air, and over every living thing that moveth upon the earth." (See also Moses 2:27–28.)

Genesis 2:18, 24. "And the Lord God said, It is not good that the man should be alone; I will make him an help meet for him. . . .Therefore shall a man leave his father and his mother, and shall cleave unto his wife: and they shall be one flesh." (See also Moses 3:18, 24.)

1 Corinthians 11:11. "Nevertheless neither is the man without the woman, neither the woman without the man, in the Lord."

D&C 66:2. "Verily I say unto you, blessed are you for receiving mine everlasting covenant, even the fulness of my gospel, sent forth unto the children of men, that they might have life and be made partakers of the glories which are to be revealed in the last days, as it was written by the prophets and apostles in days of old."

D&C 130:2. "And that same sociality which exists among us here will exist among us there, only it will be coupled with eternal glory, which glory we do not now enjoy."

D&C 131:1–4. "In the celestial glory there are three heavens or degrees; And in order to obtain the highest, a man must enter into this order of the priesthood [meaning the new and everlasting covenant of marriage]; And if he does not, he cannot obtain it. He may enter into the other, but that is the end of his kingdom; he cannot have an increase."

D&C 132:19–20. "And again, verily I say unto you, if a man marry a wife by my word, which is my law, and by the new and everlasting covenant, and it is sealed unto them by the Holy Spirit of promise, by him who is anointed, unto whom I have appointed this power and the keys of this priesthood; . . . Then shall they be gods, because they have no end; therefore shall they be from everlasting to everlasting, because they continue; then shall they be above all, because all things are subject unto them."

Moses 5:11. "And Eve, his wife, heard all these things and was glad, saying: Were it not for our transgression we never should have had seed, and never should have known good and evil, and the joy of our redemption, and the eternal life which God giveth unto all the obedient."

Abraham 2:11. "And I will bless them that bless thee, and curse them that curse thee; and in thee (that is, in thy Priesthood) and in thy seed (that is, thy Priesthood), for I give unto thee a promise that this right shall continue in thee, and in thy seed after thee (that is to say, the literal seed, or the seed of the body) shall all the families of the earth be blessed, even with the blessings of the Gospel, which are the blessings of salvation, even of life eternal."

What qualities define and characterize enduring relationships within a forever family?

Charity. Moroni 7:45. "And charity suffereth long, and is kind, and envieth not, and is not puffed up, seeketh not her own, is not easily provoked, thinketh no evil, and rejoiceth not in iniquity but rejoiceth in the truth, beareth all things, believeth all things, hopeth all things, endureth all things."

Delight in one's spouse. D&C 25:14. "Let thy soul delight in thy husband, and the glory which shall come upon him."

Gratitude for children. Genesis 46:29–30. "And Joseph made ready his chariot, and went up to meet Israel his father, to Goshen, and presented himself unto him; and he fell on his neck, and wept on his neck a good while. And Israel [Jacob] said unto Joseph, Now let me die, since I have seen thy face, because thou art yet alive." (See also 1 Samuel 1:27–28; Psalm 127:3.)

Informed trust. Mosiah 23:14. "And also trust no one to be your teacher nor your minister, except he be a man of God, walking in his ways and keeping his commandments."

Leadership. 1 Timothy 3:4–5. "One that ruleth well his own house, having his children in subjection with all gravity; (For if a man know not how to rule his own house, how shall he take care of the church of God?)."

Love. Genesis 29:20. "And Jacob served seven years for Rachel; and they seemed unto him but a few days, for the love he had to her." (See also Ephesians 5:25, 28, 33.)

Nurture. Ephesians 6:4. "And, ye fathers, provoke not your children to wrath: but bring them up in the nurture and admonition of the Lord."

Obedience. Colossians 3:20. "Children, obey your parents in all things: for this is well pleasing unto the Lord."

Patience. Luke 21:19. "In your patience possess ye your souls." (See also D&C 101:38.)

Prayer. 3 Nephi 18:21. "Pray in your families unto the Father, always in my name, that your wives and your children may be blessed." (See also D&C 42:14.)

Providence. D&C 75:28. "And again, verily I say unto you, that every man who is obliged to provide for his own family, let him provide, and he shall in nowise lose his crown; and let him labor in the church."

Reverence for God. Hebrews 12:9. "Furthermore we have had fathers of our flesh which corrected us, and we gave them reverence: shall we not much rather be in subjection unto the Father of spirits, and live?"

Words of the Prophets | **Gordon B. Hinckley on family members caring for each other.** "We are a church which bears testimony of the importance of the family—the father, the mother, the children—and of the fact that we are all children of God our Eternal Father. Parents who bring children into the world have a responsibility to love those children, to nurture them and care for them, to teach them those values which would bless their lives so that they will grow to become good citizens. If there is less trouble in the homes, there will be less trouble in the nations. I want to emphasize that which is already familiar to you, and that is the importance of binding our families together with love and kindness, with appreciation and respect, and with teaching the ways of the Lord so that your children will grow in righteousness and avoid the tragedies which are overcoming so many families across the world." —Gordon B. Hinckley, *Teachings of Gordon B. Hinckley* (Salt Lake City: Deseret Book, 1997), 208.
Cross reference to "Families Can Be Forever": see Preach My Gospel, *3, 32, 85, 159–160.*

FAST/FASTING [172]. Some applications of the word *fast* in the scriptures relate to the speed or quickness of something taking place, as in these examples (see Mosiah 4:27; D&C 10:4). Other uses of the word *fast* reflect the meaning of being firmly fixed or secure in commitment or loyal to a cause. Fasting, as in the abstinence from food, is associated with the desire to increase personal spirituality and act for the welfare of others. Fasting is never complete without prayer, hence the phrase "fasting and prayer" (D&C 59:14) is commonly used in relation to this principle. We are counseled always to align our fast with a spiritual purpose. When we pay our fast offerings abundantly, we practice the great commandment of love.

Psalm 89:28. "My mercy will I keep for him for evermore, and my covenant shall stand fast with him."

Galatians 5:1. "Stand fast therefore in the liberty wherewith Christ hath made us free, and be not entangled again with the yoke of bondage." (See also Mosiah 23:13; Alma 58:40; 61:9, 21.)

1 Thessalonians 5:21. "Prove all things; hold fast that which is good."

1 Nephi 8:30. "But, to be short in writing, behold, he saw other multitudes pressing forward; and they came and caught hold of the end of the rod of iron; and they did press their way forward, continually holding fast to the rod of iron, until they came forth and fell down and partook of the fruit of the tree."

Alma 1:25. "Now this was a great trial to those that did stand fast in the faith; nevertheless, they were steadfast and immovable in keeping the commandments of God, and they bore with patience the persecution which was heaped upon them." (See also Alma 46:27.)

D&C 9:14. "Stand fast in the work wherewith I have called you, and a hair of your head shall not be lost, and you shall be lifted up at the last day."

How is the term fast, or fasting, used in the scriptures to indicate abstinence from food or drink for spiritual reasons?

Judges 20:26. "Then all the children of Israel, and all the people, went up, and came unto the house of God, and wept, and sat there before the Lord, and fasted that day until even, and offered burnt offerings and peace offerings before the Lord."

Isaiah 58: 6–7. "Is not this the fast that I have chosen? to loose the bands of wickedness, to undo the heavy burdens, and to let the oppressed go free, and that ye break every yoke? Is it not to deal thy bread to the hungry, and that thou bring the poor that are cast out to thy house? when thou seest the naked, that thou cover him; and that thou hide not thyself from thine own flesh?"

Matthew 4:1–2. "Then was Jesus led up of the Spirit into the wilderness to be tempted of the devil. And when he had fasted forty days and forty nights, he was afterward an hungred."

Matthew 9:14–15. "Then came to him the disciples of John, saying, Why do we and the Pharisees fast oft, but thy disciples fast not? And Jesus said unto them, Can the children of the bridechamber mourn, as long as the bridegroom is with them? but the days will come, when the bridegroom shall be taken from them, and then shall they fast." (See also Mark 2:18–20; Luke 5:33–35.)

Luke 2:36–37. "And there was one Anna, a prophetess, the daughter of Phanuel, of the tribe of Aser: she was of a great age, and had lived with an husband seven years from her virginity; And she was a widow of about fourscore and four years, which departed not from the temple, but served God with fastings and prayers night and day."

Acts 10:30. "And Cornelius said, Four days ago I was fasting until this hour; and at the ninth hour I prayed in my house, and, behold, a man stood before me in bright clothing."

Omni 1:26. "And now, my beloved brethren, I would that ye should come unto Christ, who is the Holy One of Israel, and partake of his salvation, and the power of his redemption. Yea, come unto him, and offer your whole souls as an offering unto him, and continue in fasting and praying, and endure to the end; and as the Lord liveth ye will be saved."

D&C 88:119. "Organize yourselves; prepare every needful thing; and establish a house, even a house of prayer, a house of fasting, a house of faith, a house of learning, a house of glory, a house of order, a house of God." (See also D&C 109:8, 16.)

Words of the prophets | Joseph Smith on the principle of fasting. "Let this be an ensample to all saints, and there will never be any lack for bread: When the poor are starving, let those who have, fast one day and give what they otherwise would have eaten to the bishops for the poor, and every one will abound for a long time; and this is one great and important principle of fasts approved of the Lord. And so long as the saints will all live to this principle with glad hearts and cheerful countenances they will always have an abundance." —Joseph Smith, *HC* 7:413.

FATHER IN HEAVEN [188]. Our Father in Heaven—as presented in holy writ and confirmed to the devout and faithful through the Holy Ghost—is the Supreme Lord and God of all Creation, the eternal Source of light and truth, the benevolent and ever-loving Father of our spirits (see Hebrews 12:9; 1 John 4:7–8), the Author of the glorious gospel plan of happiness (see Abraham 3:23, 27), the Exemplar of the pattern for all holiness and perfection, the merciful Grantor of agency unto His children, and the Benefactor of all mankind through the gift of His Only Begotten Son, whose atoning sacrifice empowers the process for achieving immortality and exaltation (see John 3:16). It is to our Father in Heaven that we pray, in the name of Jesus Christ, as directed by Jesus Christ Himself (Matthew 6:9; 19:6–7; Luke 11:2; John 20:17; 2 Nephi 32:9; 3 Nephi 13:9; 18:19–23, 30; 19:6–7; 20:31; D&C 20:77, 79).

Our Heavenly Father loves us. We are His children. We recognize His surpassing power and perfection. We are thankful to our Father in Heaven for the divine qualities and supernal causes He represents: mercy, goodness, lovingkindness, righteous judgments, understanding, victorious plan of happiness, mighty deeds, and wondrous works. He is willing to answer our prayers and keep His covenants, and He is mindful of all peoples. He is all-powerful, as the brother of Jared confirmed (see Ether 3:4). He is all-knowing, as Jacob testified (see 2 Nephi 9:20). He is in and through all things (see D&C 88:41). Thus we see that our Father in Heaven is the embodiment of perfection, being omnipotent, omniscient, and (through His divine and pervasive influence) truly omnipresent. The Doctrine and Covenants teaches us: "By these things [His restored word and covenants] we know that there is a God in heaven, who is infinite and eternal, from everlasting to everlasting the same unchangeable God, the framer of heaven and earth, and all things which are in them" (D&C 20:17).

Life eternal is to know the Father and Son. John 17:3. "And this is life eternal, that they might know thee the only true God, and Jesus Christ, whom thou hast sent." (See also D&C 132:24.)

Love of the Father. John 3:16. "God so loved the world, that he gave his only begotten Son, that whosoever believeth in him should not perish, but have everlasting life."

Perfection of the Father. Matthew 5:48. "Be ye therefore perfect, even as your Father which is in heaven is perfect." (See also 3 Nephi 12:48.)

Destiny of man as a child of God. John 1:12. "But as many as received him, to them gave he power to become the sons of God, even to them that believe on his name." (See also 2 Nephi 25:23; Moroni 10:32; Moses 1:39.)

The Father as an individual and distinct Being. Matthew 3:16–17. "And Jesus, when he was baptized, went up straightway out of the water: and, lo, the heavens were opened unto him, and he saw the Spirit of God descending like a dove, and lighting upon him: And lo a voice from heaven, saying, This is my beloved Son, in whom I am well pleased." (See also Matthew 17:5; Mark 1:9–11; Luke 3:21–22; John 1:32–34; Acts 7:55–56; 2 Nephi 31:14–15; 3 Nephi 11:6–7; D&C 76:22–24; 93:15–16; 137:2–3; JS—H 1:17).

The Father as a corporeal Being. D&C 130:22. "The Father has a body of flesh and bones as tangible as man's; the Son also; but the Holy Ghost has not a body of flesh and bones, but is a personage of Spirit. Were it not so, the Holy Ghost could not dwell in us."

How the Father, though a distinct corporeal Being, is omnipresent through His influence. D&C 88:11–13, 41. "And the light which shineth, which giveth you light, is through him who enlighteneth your eyes, which is the same light that quickeneth your understandings; Which light proceedeth forth from the presence of God to fill the immensity of space— The light which is in all things, which giveth life to all things, which is the law by which all things are governed, even the power of God who sitteth upon his throne, *who is in the bosom of eternity, who is in the midst of all things*. . . . He comprehendeth all things, and *all things are before him, and all things are round about him; and he is above all things, and in all things, and is through all things, and is round about all things*; and all things are by him, and of him, even God, forever and ever" (emphasis added). (See also D&C 130:7–8; Moses 1:6.)

WORDS OF THE PROPHETS | **Brigham Young on God's role.** "He is our Heavenly Father; He is also our God, and the Maker and upholder of all things in heaven and on earth. He sends forth His counsels and extends His providences to all living. He is the Supreme Controller of the universe." —Brigham Young (*Journal of Discourses* 11:41, January 8, 1865).

ADDITIONAL INFORMATION—**"I've a mother there."** There is a memorable passage included in the inspiring hymn, "O My Father," written by Eliza R. Snow: "In the heav'ns are parents single? / No, the thought makes reason stare! Truth is reason; truth eternal / Tells me I've a mother there" (*Hymns* no. 292). Joseph Fielding Smith stated: "If we had a Father, which we did, for all of these records speak of him, then does not good common sense tell us that we must have had a mother there also?" (*Answers to Gospel Questions*, vol. 3. [Salt Lake City: Deseret Book, 1960], 142; see also Elaine Anderson Cannon, "Mother in Heaven," *Encyclopedia of Mormonism*, ed. Daniel Ludlow, 4 vols. [New York: Macmillan, 1992, 961).

FIRST PRINCIPLES AND ORDINANCES OF THE GOSPEL [Principles 24; Ordinances 111]. The first principles and ordinances of the gospel—faith, repentance, baptism, and bestowal of the gift of the Holy Ghost by the laying of hands—constitute the founding truths and ordinances of salvation and the preparatory actions for authorized admittance into the Church and kingdom of God. These principles and ordinances are explained pervasively throughout the scriptures—whether one after another, line upon line and precept upon precept, or blended together according to the record of the prophets. There are only four passages where all four principles and ordinances are combined in a single verse:

D&C 19:31–32. "And of tenets thou shalt not talk, but thou shalt declare repentance and faith on the Savior, and remission of sins by baptism, and by fire, yea, even the Holy Ghost. Behold, this is a great and the last commandment which I shall give unto you concerning this matter; for this shall suffice for thy daily walk, even unto the end of thy life."

D&C 68:25. "And again, inasmuch as parents have children in Zion, or in any of her stakes which are organized, that teach them not to understand the doctrine of repentance, faith in Christ the Son of the living God, and of baptism and the gift of the Holy Ghost by the laying on of the hands, when eight years old, the sin be upon the heads of the parents."

D&C 138:33–34. "These were taught faith in God, repentance from sin, vicarious baptism for the remission of sins, the gift of the Holy Ghost by the laying on of hands. And all other principles of the gospel that were necessary for them to know in order to qualify themselves that they might be judged according to men in the flesh, but live according to God in the spirit."

Fourth Article of Faith. "We believe that the first principles and ordinances of the Gospel are: first, Faith in the Lord Jesus Christ; second, Repentance; third, Baptism by immersion for the remission of sins; fourth, Laying on of hands for the gift of the Holy Ghost."

Words of the Prophets | Joseph Smith on the first principles of the gospel. "Declare the first principles, and let mysteries alone, lest ye be overthrown." Joseph Smith, *HC* 5:344.

FORGIVENESS [208]. The capacity to forgive is one of the most divine attributes one can possess. It is a commandment of God (see Matthew 6:14–15). It is a quality that will bring peace to one's soul and allow others to find peace. True forgiveness is without a doubt the most difficult aspect of all human behavior to express. It is an expression of godliness. The divine Exemplars of forgiveness are our Father in Heaven and His Son Jesus Christ. We are to become as They are with respect to the capacity to forgive and forget. It is also important to seek forgiveness. When we have done something wrong, we must also humble ourselves enough to ask the Father and those we have wronged for forgiveness.

Psalm 32:1. "Blessed is he whose transgression is forgiven, whose sin is covered." (See also Romans 4:7.)

Isaiah 1:18. "Come now, and let us reason together, saith the Lord: though your sins be as scarlet, they shall be as white as snow; though they be red like crimson, they shall be as wool."

Matthew 11:28–30. "Come unto me, all ye that labour and are heavy laden, and I will give you rest. Take my yoke upon you, and learn of me; for I am meek and lowly in heart: and ye shall find rest unto your souls. For my yoke is easy, and my burden is light."

D&C 1:31–32. "For I the Lord cannot look upon sin with the least degree of allowance; Nevertheless, he that repents and does the commandments of the Lord shall be forgiven."

D&C 64:9–10. "Wherefore, I say unto you, that ye ought to forgive one another; for he that forgiveth not his brother his trespasses standeth condemned before the Lord; for there remaineth in him the greater sin. I, the Lord, will forgive whom I will forgive, but of you it is required to forgive all men."

D&C 95:1. "Verily, thus saith the Lord unto you whom I love, and whom I love I also chasten that their sins may be forgiven, for with the chastisement I prepare a way for their deliverance in all things out of temptation, and I have loved you."

Words of the Prophets | Spencer W. Kimball on forgetting once we've forgiven. "The Lord forgets when he has forgiven, and certainly must we. . . . No bitterness of past frictions can be held in memory if we forgive with all our hearts." —Spencer W. Kimball, *Faith Precedes the Miracle* (Salt Lake City: Deseret Book, 1972), 194.

GATHERING [725]. According to the dynamics of the grand covenant design, the Lord scatters and gathers His people for the ultimate blessing of mankind. The scattering process may serve to protect, correct, or connect—to protect (as with Lehi's family being guided away from Jerusalem in the wake of torment and abuse), correct (because of iniquity or wickedness, as in the scattering of the Ten Tribes by the Assyrians around 721 BC or the dispersal of the Jewish people by the Babylonians around 587 BC), or connect (as with the modern-day dispatching of missionaries throughout the world to spread the gospel message among the honest at heart). The gathering process is much the same: to protect the Saints by bringing them to holy places of refuge within the stakes of Zion, where houses of the Lord abound (sacred temples as well as chapels and righteous homes); to correct the Saints in a continual way through inspired instruction by the prophets of God to the assembled congregations of Zion; and to connect the Saints one with another and with the Holy Spirit through the unifying and purifying process of daily gospel living that leads to blessings of salvation and exaltation.

When the "children of the covenant" (3 Nephi 20:26) obey and follow the will of the Lord, wherever it might take them, they are blessed with safety under His protecting hand. When they rebel and take counsel from their pride, the Lord, at times, scatters them for correction and to dispel their prideful ambitions. The object is for us to be found worthy to bear the name of His Son Jesus Christ, in whose name alone we can ultimately be gathered home, in company of our loved ones, forever secure in the rest of the Lord. The gathering is a manifestation of the fulfillment of the Abrahamic covenant (see Abraham 2:11).

Isaiah 2:2–3. "And it shall come to pass in the last days, that the mountain of the Lord's house shall be established in the top of the mountains, and shall be exalted above the hills; and all nations shall flow unto it. And many people shall go and say, Come ye, and let us go up to the mountain of the Lord, to the house of the God of Jacob; and he will teach us of his ways, and we will walk in his paths: for out of Zion shall go forth the law, and the word of the Lord from Jerusalem." (See also Micah 4:1–2; 2 Nephi 12:2–3.)

Hosea 14:1. "O Israel, return unto the Lord thy God."

Luke 18:22. "Come, follow me." (See also Matthew 4:19; 8:22; 9:9; 16:24; 19:21; Mark 2:14; 8:34; 10:21; Luke 5:27; 9:23, 59; John 1:43; 10:27; 12:26; 13:36; 21:19.)

Ephesians 1:10. "That in the dispensation of the fulness of times he might gather together in one all things in Christ, both which are in heaven, and which are on earth; even in him."

2 Nephi 10:7–8. "But behold, thus saith the Lord God: When the day cometh that they shall believe in me, that I am Christ, then have I covenanted with their fathers that they shall be restored in the flesh, upon the earth, unto the lands of their inheritance. And it shall come to pass that they shall be gathered in from their long dispersion, from the isles of the sea, and from the four parts of the earth; and the nations of the Gentiles shall be great in the eyes of me, saith God, in carrying them forth to the lands of their inheritance."

2 Nephi 29:14. "And it shall come to pass that my people, which are of the house of Israel, shall be gathered home unto the lands of their possessions; and my word also shall be gathered in one. And I will show unto them that fight against my word and against my people, who are of the house of Israel, that I am God, and that I covenanted with Abraham that I would remember his seed forever." (See also Isaiah 29; Ezekiel 37:15–17; D&C 10:59–62.)

3 Nephi 22:2. "Enlarge the place of thy tent, and let them stretch forth the curtains of thy habitations; spare not, lengthen thy cords and strengthen thy stakes." (See also Isaiah 54:2.)

D&C 33:5–6. "And verily, verily, I say unto you, that this church have I established and called forth out of the wilderness. And even so will I gather mine elect from the four quarters of the earth, even as many as will believe in me, and hearken unto my voice."

D&C 87:8. "Wherefore, stand ye in holy places, and be not moved, until the day of the Lord come; for behold, it cometh quickly, saith the Lord." (See also D&C 45:32).

D&C 101:22. "Behold, it is my will, that all they who call on my name, and worship me according to mine everlasting gospel, should gather together, and stand in holy places."

Abraham 2:8–11. "My name is Jehovah, and I know the end from the beginning; therefore my hand shall be over thee. And I will make of thee a great nation, and I will bless thee above measure, and make thy name great among all nations, and thou shalt be a blessing unto thy seed after thee, that in their hands they shall bear this ministry and Priesthood unto all nations; And I will bless them through thy name; for as many as receive this Gospel shall be called after thy name, and shall be accounted thy seed, and shall rise up and bless thee, as their father; And I will bless them that bless thee, and curse them that curse thee; and in thee (that is, in thy Priesthood) and in thy seed (that is, thy Priesthood), for I give unto thee a promise that this right shall continue in thee, and in thy seed after thee (that is to say, the literal seed, or the seed of the body) shall all the families of the earth be blessed, even with the blessings of the Gospel, which are the blessings of salvation, even of life eternal." (See also Genesis 17:6–7; 22:15–18; D&C 84:34.)

Tenth Article of Faith. "We believe in the literal gathering of Israel and in the restoration of the Ten Tribes; that Zion (the New Jerusalem) will be built upon the American continent; that Christ will reign personally upon the earth; and, that the earth will be renewed and receive its paradisiacal glory."

Words of the Prophets | Joseph F. Smith on missionary work. "You and I live in a day in which the Lord our God has set his hand for the last time, to gather out the righteous and to prepare a people to reign on this earth,—a people who will be purified by good works, who will abide the faith of the living God and be ready to meet the Bridegroom when he comes to reign over the earth, even Jesus Christ . . . and be prepared for that glorious event—the coming of the Son of Man—which I believe will not be at any great distant day." —Joseph F. Smith, *Millennial Star* 36:220.

GODHEAD [3]. The Godhead comprises the Father, the Son, and the Holy Ghost—the divine governing council of the eternities—three separate Personages of glory unified in purpose and mission (see Moses 1:39). We need all three to make it back to the presence of the Father. From the Father flows the supernal design of all creation, including the plan of redemption and happiness. From the Son, Creator under the direction of the Father, flows the power and efficacy of the Atonement as the key to salvation. From the Holy Ghost flows the witnessing light of truth and revelation to illuminate the hearts and minds of those who accept the gospel and press forward in valor to become as their Exemplar, even Jesus Christ—the Holy Ghost being the messenger of both the Father and the Son. From all three members of the Godhead flow love and mercy—the love that empowers the gathering of the Saints unto the fold of Christ and the mercy that enables the faithful to return once again to their heavenly home.

Acts 17:28–29. "For in him we live, and move, and have our being; as certain also of your own poets have said, For we are also his offspring. Forasmuch then as we are the offspring of God, we ought not to think that the Godhead is like unto gold, or silver, or stone, graven by art and man's device."

Romans 1:20. "For the invisible things of him from the creation of the world are clearly seen, being understood by the things that are made, even his eternal power and Godhead; so that they are without excuse."

Colossians 2:8–9. "Beware lest any man spoil you through philosophy and vain deceit, after the tradition of men, after the rudiments of the world, and not after Christ. For in him dwelleth all the fulness of the Godhead bodily."

Mormon 7:7. "And he hath brought to pass the redemption of the world, whereby he that is found guiltless before him at the judgment day hath it given unto him to dwell in the presence of God in his kingdom, to sing ceaseless praises with the choirs above, unto the Father, and unto the Son, and unto the Holy Ghost, which are one God, in a state of happiness which hath no end."

D&C 130:22. "The Father has a body of flesh and bones as tangible as man's; the Son also; but the Holy Ghost has not a body of flesh and bones, but is a personage of Spirit. Were it not so, the Holy Ghost could not dwell in us."

First Article of Faith. "We believe in God, the Eternal Father, and in His Son, Jesus Christ, and in the Holy Ghost."

What are the two main themes that are presented where the Father and the Son and the Holy Ghost are mentioned in the same passage?

The divine commission to baptize. Matthew 28:19–20. "Go ye therefore, and teach all nations, baptizing them in the name of the Father, and of the Son, and of the Holy Ghost: Teaching them to observe all things whatsoever I have commanded you: and, lo, I am with you alway, even unto the end of the world. Amen." (See also 2 Nephi 31:11–21; 3 Nephi 11:23; D&C 20:72–73; 68:8–9; Moses 6:64–66; 7:11; 8:23–24.)

The Godhead as witnesses of One Another and of the truth. Ether 5:4. "And in the mouth of three witnesses shall these things be established; and the testimony of three, and this work, in the which shall be shown forth the power of God and also his word, of which the Father, and the Son, and the Holy Ghost bear record—and all this shall stand as a testimony against the world at the last day."(See also D&C 20:27–28; Moses 1:24; 5:9; 7:27.)

GODLINESS [22]. The quality of godliness is a manifestation of the divine nature as exemplified in our Heavenly Father and His Son Jesus Christ. When we follow the example of the Father and Son, we strive to imbue our lives with a growing measure of godliness in keeping with the exhortation: "Therefore I would that ye should be perfect even as I, or your Father who is in heaven is perfect" (3 Nephi 12:48).

1 Timothy 3:16. "And without controversy great is the mystery of godliness: God was manifest in the flesh, justified in the Spirit, seen of angels, preached unto the Gentiles, believed on in the world, received up into glory."

2 Peter 1:3–8. "According as his divine power hath given unto us all things that pertain unto life and godliness, through the knowledge of him that hath called us to glory and virtue: Whereby are given unto us exceeding great and precious promises: that by these ye might be partakers of the divine nature, having escaped the corruption that is in the world through lust. And beside this, giving all diligence, add to your faith virtue; and to virtue knowledge; And to knowledge temperance; and to temperance patience; and to patience godliness; And to godliness brotherly kindness; and to brotherly kindness charity. For if these things be in you, and abound, they make you that ye shall neither be barren nor unfruitful in the knowledge of our Lord Jesus Christ."

D&C 4:6. "Remember faith, virtue, knowledge, temperance, patience, brotherly kindness, godliness, charity, humility, diligence."

D&C 19:9–10. "I speak unto you that are chosen in this thing, even as one, that you may enter into my rest. For, behold, the mystery of godliness, how great is it! For, behold, I am endless, and the punishment which is given from my hand is endless punishment, for Endless is my name."

D&C 84:19–21. "And this greater priesthood administereth the gospel and holdeth the key of the mysteries of the kingdom, even the key of the knowledge of God. Therefore, in the ordinances thereof, the power of godliness is manifest. And without the ordinances thereof, and the authority of the priesthood, the power of godliness is not manifest unto men in the flesh."

GOSPEL OF JESUS CHRIST [313]. The gospel or "good news" is the divine plan of salvation and exaltation designed to "bring to pass the immortality and eternal life of man" (Moses 1:39). The message of the gospel is one of hope and joy because it announces to the world the doctrine of Christ, encompassing all of the principles and ordinances essential for the sons and daughters of God to rise to their potential through the power of the Atonement and return home again to the Father and the Son. The fulness of the gospel was restored in these the latter days. The gospel of Jesus Christ is the foundation of the Church and kingdom of God. We live the gospel as we practice the first four principles and ordinances thereof: faith (in Jesus Christ), repentance (through Jesus Christ), baptism (in which we take upon us the name of Jesus Christ), and then receiving the gift of the Holy Ghost (because of Jesus Christ)—and enduring to the end.

Mark 16:15–16. "And he said unto them [the Apostles], Go ye into all the world, and preach the gospel to every creature. He that believeth and is baptized shall be saved; but he that believeth not shall be damned." (See also Matthew 28:19–20 and Mormon 9:22–23; also Matthew 24:14 and D&C 18:28.)

Romans 1:16. "For I am not ashamed of the gospel of Christ: for it is the power of God unto salvation to every one that believeth; to the Jew first, and also to the Greek."

Revelation 14:6–7. "And I saw another angel fly in the midst of heaven, having the everlasting gospel to preach unto them that dwell on the earth, and to every nation, and kindred, and tongue, and people, Saying with a loud voice, Fear God, and give glory to him; for the hour of his judgment is come: and worship him that made heaven, and earth, and the sea, and the fountains of waters."

3 Nephi 27:13–15. "Behold I have given unto you my gospel, and this is the gospel which I have given unto you—that I came into the world to do the will of my Father, because my Father sent me. And my Father sent me that I might be lifted up upon the cross; and after that I had been lifted up upon the cross, that I might draw all men unto me, that as I have been lifted up by men even so should men be lifted up by the Father, to stand before me, to be judged of their works, whether they be good or whether they be evil—And for this cause have I been lifted up; therefore, according to the power of the Father I will draw all men unto me, that they may be judged according to their works."

D&C 11:24. "Build upon my rock, which is my gospel." (See also D&C 18:3–5, 17; D&C 33:13; D&C 66:2.)

D&C 25:1. "Verily I say unto you, all those who receive my gospel are sons and daughters in my kingdom."

D&C 39:5–6. "And verily, verily, I say unto you, he that receiveth my gospel receiveth me; and he that receiveth not my gospel receiveth not me. And this is my gospel—repentance and baptism by water, and then cometh the baptism of fire and the Holy Ghost, even the Comforter, which showeth all things, and teacheth the peaceable things of the kingdom."

D&C 65:2. "The keys of the kingdom of God are committed unto man on the earth, and from thence shall the gospel roll forth unto the ends of the earth, as the stone which is cut out of the mountain without hands shall roll forth, until it has filled the whole earth." (See also Daniel 2:34–35, 45.)

D&C 101:22. "Behold, it is my will, that all they who call on my name, and worship me according to mine everlasting gospel, should gather together, and stand in holy places."

D&C 101:38–39. "And seek the face of the Lord always, that in patience ye may possess your souls, and ye shall have eternal life. When men are called unto mine everlasting gospel, and covenant with an everlasting covenant, they are accounted as the salt of the earth and the savor of men."

Third Article of Faith. "We believe that through the Atonement of Christ, all mankind may be saved, by obedience to the laws and ordinances of the Gospel."

Fourth Article of Faith. "We believe that the first principles and ordinances of the Gospel are: first, Faith in the Lord Jesus Christ; second, Repentance; third, Baptism by immersion for the remission of sins; fourth, Laying on of hands for the gift of the Holy Ghost."

Fifth Article of Faith. "We believe that a man must be called of God, by prophecy, and by the laying on of hands by those who are in authority, to preach the Gospel and administer in the ordinances thereof."

How do the scriptures confirm that the gospel plan is universal?

All mankind may be saved. Third Article of Faith. "We believe that through the Atonement of Christ, all mankind may be saved, by obedience to the laws and ordinances of the Gospel."

Every man to hear the fulness of the gospel in his native tongue. D&C 90:10–11. "And then cometh the day when the arm of the Lord shall be revealed in power in convincing the nations, the heathen nations, the house of Joseph, of the gospel of their salvation. For it shall come to pass in that day, that every man shall hear the fulness of the gospel in his own tongue, and in his own language, through those who are ordained unto this power, by the administration of the Comforter, shed forth upon them for the revelation of Jesus Christ."

From the beginning of the world to the end thereof. Moses 5:58–59. "And thus the Gospel began to be preached, from the beginning, being declared by holy angels sent forth from the presence of God, and by his own voice, and by the gift of the Holy Ghost. And thus all things were confirmed unto Adam, by an holy ordinance, and the Gospel preached, and a decree sent forth, that it should be in the world, until the end thereof; and thus it was." (See also Moses 8:19.)

Preached unto every creature. Mormon 9:22. "For behold, thus said Jesus Christ, the Son of God, unto his disciples who should tarry, yea, and also to all his disciples, in the hearing of the multitude: Go ye into all the world, and preach the gospel to every creature." (See also Mark 16:15, D&C 58:64, 68:8–9; 112:28.)

Unto all nations, kindreds, tongues, and people. D&C 88:103–104. "And another trump shall sound, which is the fifth trump, which is the fifth angel who committeth the everlasting gospel—flying through the midst of heaven, unto all nations, kindreds, tongues, and people; And this shall be the sound of his trump, saying to all people, both in heaven and in earth, and that are under the earth—for every ear shall hear it, and every knee shall bow, and every tongue shall confess, while they hear the sound of the trump, saying: Fear God, and give glory to him who sitteth upon the throne, forever and ever; for the hour of his judgment is come." (See also D&C 133:36–37.)

What are the blessings of living the gospel?

Accounted as the salt of the earth. D&C 101:38–39. "And seek the face of the Lord always, that in patience ye may possess your souls, and ye shall have eternal life. When men are called unto mine everlasting gospel, and covenant with an everlasting covenant, they are accounted as the salt of the earth and the savor of men."

All to be revealed. D&C 121:28–29. "A time to come in the which nothing shall be withheld, whether there be one God or many gods, they shall be manifest. All thrones and dominions, principalities and powers, shall be revealed and set forth upon all who have endured valiantly for the gospel of Jesus Christ." (See also D&C 25:1; 133:57–58.)

Becoming sons and daughters in the kingdom. D&C 25:1. "Verily I say unto you, all those who receive my gospel are sons and daughters in my kingdom."

Escape the judgment of God. D&C 39:17–18. "Wherefore lay to with your might and call faithful laborers into my vineyard, that it may be pruned for the last time. And inasmuch as they do repent and receive the fulness of my gospel, and become sanctified, I will stay mine hand in judgment."

Fortification against the forces of evil. D&C 18:3–5. "And if you know that they are true, behold, I give unto you a commandment, that you rely upon the things which are written; For in them are all things written concerning the foundation of my church, my gospel, and my rock. Wherefore, if you shall build up my church, upon the foundation of my gospel and my rock, the gates of hell shall not prevail against you."

Large progeny, land of inheritance, and eternal life. Mark 10:29–30. "And Jesus answered and said, Verily I say unto you, There is no man that hath left house, or brethren, or sisters, or father, or mother, or wife, or children, or lands, for my sake, and the gospel's, But he shall receive an hundredfold now in this time, houses, and brethren, and sisters, and mothers, and children, and lands, with persecutions; and in the world to come eternal life."

Life and immortality. 2 Timothy 1:9–11. "Who hath saved us, and called us with an holy calling, not according to our works, but according to his own purpose and grace, which was given us in Christ Jesus before the world began, But is now made manifest by the appearing of our Saviour Jesus Christ, who hath abolished death, and hath brought life and immortality to light through the gospel: Whereunto I am appointed a preacher, and an apostle, and a teacher of the Gentiles."

Peace, rather than contention. D&C 10:62–63. "Yea, and I will also bring to light my gospel which was ministered unto them, and, behold, they shall not deny that which you have received, but they shall build it up, and shall bring to light the true points of my doctrine, yea, and the only doctrine which is in me. And this I do that I may establish my gospel, that there may not be so much contention; yea, Satan doth stir up the hearts of the people to contention concerning the points of my doctrine; and in these things they do err, for they do wrest the scriptures and do not understand them."

Revelation. Ephesians 3:4–6. "Whereby, when ye read, ye may understand my knowledge in the mystery of Christ[,] which in other ages was not made known unto the sons of men, as it is now revealed unto his holy apostles and prophets by the Spirit; That the Gentiles should be fellowheirs, and of the same body, and partakers of his promise in Christ by the gospel." (See also D&C 39:5–6; 59:3–4; 66:2.)

Salvation. Ephesians 1:12–13. "That we should be to the praise of his glory, who first trusted in Christ. In whom ye also trusted, after that ye heard the word of truth, the gospel of your salvation: in whom also after that ye believed, ye were sealed with that holy Spirit of promise." (See also Romans 1:16; Ether 4:17–19.)

How is the gospel preached also in the spirit world?

Christ inaugurated gospel teaching in the spirit world. 1 Peter 3:18–20. "For Christ also hath once suffered for sins, the just for the unjust, that he might bring us to God, being put to death in the flesh, but quickened by the Spirit: By which also he went and preached unto the spirits in prison; Which sometime were disobedient, when once the longsuffering of God waited in the days of Noah, while the ark was a preparing, wherein few, that is, eight souls were saved by water." (See also 1 Peter 4:6; D&C 88:99.)

Prepared from before the foundation of the world. D&C 128:5. "You may think this order of things to be very particular; but let me tell you that it is only to answer the will of God, by conforming to the ordinance and preparation that the Lord ordained and prepared before the foundation of the world, for the salvation of the dead who should die without a knowledge of the gospel."

Work for the dead instituted by the Prophet Joseph Smith in accordance with prophecy and revelation. D&C 128:17–19. "And again, in connection with this quotation I will give you a quotation from one of the prophets, who had his eye fixed on the restoration of the priesthood, the glories to be revealed in the last days, and in an especial manner this most glorious of all subjects belonging to the everlasting gospel, namely, the baptism for the dead; for Malachi says, last chapter, verses 5th and 6th: Behold, I will send you Elijah the prophet before the coming of the great and dreadful day of the Lord: And he shall turn the heart of the fathers to the children, and the heart of the children to their fathers, lest I come and smite the earth with a curse. I might have rendered a plainer translation to this, but it is sufficiently plain to suit my purpose as it stands. It is sufficient to know, in this case, that the earth will be smitten with a curse unless there is a welding link of some kind or other between the fathers and the children, upon some subject or other—and behold what is that subject? It is the baptism for the dead. For we without them cannot be made perfect; neither can they without us be made perfect. Neither can they nor we be made perfect without those who have died in the gospel also; for it is necessary in the ushering in of the dispensation of the fulness of times, which dispensation is now beginning to usher in, that a whole and complete and perfect union, and welding together of dispensations, and keys, and powers, and glories should take place, and be revealed from the days of Adam even to the present time. And not only this, but those things which never have been revealed from the foundation of the world, but have been kept hid from the wise and prudent, shall be revealed unto babes and sucklings in this, the dispensation of the fulness of times. Now, what do we hear in the gospel which we have received? A voice of gladness! A voice of mercy from heaven; and a voice of truth out of the earth; glad tidings for the dead; a voice of gladness for the living and the dead; glad tidings of great joy. How beautiful upon the mountains are the feet of those that bring glad tidings of good things, and that say unto Zion: Behold, thy God reigneth! As the dews of Carmel, so shall the knowledge of God descend upon them!"

Celestial kingdom available to those who would have received the gospel. D&C 137:7. "Thus came the voice of the Lord unto me, saying: All who have died without a knowledge of this gospel, who would have received it if they had been permitted to tarry, shall be heirs of the celestial kingdom of God."

From the vision of President Joseph F. Smith concerning work in the spirit world. D&C 138:11–20. "As I pondered over these things which are written [1 Peter 3:18–20; 1 Peter 4:6], the eyes of my understanding were opened, and the Spirit of the Lord rested upon me, and I saw the hosts of the dead, both small and great. And there were gathered together in one place an innumerable company of the spirits of the just, who had been faithful in the testimony of Jesus while they lived in mortality; And who had offered sacrifice in the similitude of the great sacrifice of the Son of God, and had suffered tribulation in their Redeemer's name. All these had departed the mortal life, firm in the hope of a glorious resurrection, through the grace of God the Father and his Only Begotten Son, Jesus Christ. I beheld that they were filled with joy and gladness, and were rejoicing together because the day of their deliverance was at hand. They were assembled awaiting the advent of the Son of God into the spirit world, to declare their redemption from the bands of death. Their sleeping dust was to be restored unto its perfect frame, bone to his bone, and the sinews and the flesh upon them, the spirit and the body to be united never again to be divided, that they might receive a fulness of joy. While this vast multitude waited and conversed, rejoicing in the hour of their deliverance from the chains of death, the Son of God appeared, declaring liberty to the captives who had been faithful; And there he preached to them the everlasting gospel, the doctrine of the resurrection and the redemption of mankind from the fall, and from individual sins on conditions of repentance. But unto the wicked he did not go, and among the ungodly and the unrepentant who had defiled themselves while in the flesh, his voice was not raised." (See also D&C 138:25–34, 57.)

What is the special role of the Book of Mormon in advancing the cause of the gospel?

To restore the fulness and promises of the gospel. D&C 1:22–23. "That mine everlasting covenant might be established; That the fulness of my gospel might be proclaimed by the weak and the simple unto the ends of the world, and before kings and rulers."(See also 1 Nephi 13:35–37; D&C 3:19–20; 10:45–52; 27:5; 42:12; JS—H 1:34.)

To restore the true points of Christ's doctrine. D&C 10:61–62. "And I will bring to light their marvelous works, which they did in my name; Yea, and I will also bring to light my gospel which was ministered unto them, and, behold, they shall not deny that which you have received, but they shall build it up, and shall bring to light the true points of my doctrine, yea, and the only doctrine which is in me."

To enlighten the Gentiles, and then the Jews. D&C 19:26–27. "And again, I command thee that thou shalt not covet thine own property, but impart it freely to the printing of the Book of Mormon, which contains the truth and the word of God—Which is my word to the Gentile, that soon it may go to the Jew, of whom the Lamanites are a remnant, that they may believe the gospel, and look not for a Messiah to come who has already come."

WORDS OF THE PROPHETS | **Gordon B. Hinckley on the gospel.** "I encourage you to go forward and live the gospel and love the gospel. Make it a part of your lives—this great and glorious thing which has come to us through the providence of the Almighty. Live the gospel. Love the gospel. Read the scriptures. You won't get a testimony of the Book of Mormon unless you read the Book of Mormon. You won't get a testimony of the Doctrine and Covenants unless you read the Doctrine and Covenants. Faith comes of drinking at the fountain of eternal truth. . . . The gospel of Jesus Christ is the only thing that will bless the lands of the world. Many people live in poverty and ignorance. They have a long way to go, and the gospel provides a bridge over which they walk, as it were, from their present situation to a brighter future." —Gordon B. Hinckley, *Teachings of Gordon B. Hinckley* (Salt Lake City: Deseret Book, 1997), 245.

Cross reference to "Gospel": see Preach My Gospel, *1–3, 5–6, 32, 36–37, 60–70.*

GRATITUDE [1]. Gratitude is one of the cardinal virtues of life. Gratitude has the power to bring about monumental change for good. It is typically characterized as a gentle quality—tender, sweet, modest, serene, temperate, humble, kindly, unassuming, and peaceful. But at its heart, gratitude also partakes of power, light, and majesty: power to transform human relationships in enduring ways; light that attracts the admiration of others and the loyalty of willing followership; and majesty that lifts the sons and daughters of God closer in nature to their divine parentage. Truly, the miracle of gratitude is its ability to empower, illuminate, and lift almost instantaneously.

1 Chronicles 29:11–13. "Thine, O Lord, is the greatness, and the power, and the glory, and the victory, and the majesty: for all that is in the heaven and in the earth is thine; thine is the kingdom, O Lord, and thou art exalted as head above all. Both riches and honour come of thee, and thou reignest over all; and in thine hand is power and might; and in thine hand it is to make great, and to give strength unto all. Now therefore, our God, we thank thee, and praise thy glorious name."

2 Nephi 25:26. "And we talk of Christ, we rejoice in Christ, we preach of Christ, we prophesy of Christ, and we write according to our prophecies, that our children may know to what source they may look for a remission of their sins."

Alma 34:37–38. "And now, my beloved brethren, I desire that ye should remember these things, and that ye should work out your salvation with fear before God, and that ye should no more deny the coming of Christ; That ye contend no more against the Holy Ghost, but that ye receive it, and take upon you the name of Christ; that ye humble yourselves even to the dust, and worship God, in whatsoever place ye may be in, in spirit and in truth; and that ye live in thanksgiving daily, for the many mercies and blessings which he doth bestow upon you."

D&C 46:32. "And ye must give thanks unto God in the Spirit for whatsoever blessing ye are blessed with."

D&C 78:19. "He who receiveth all things with thankfulness shall be made glorious."

D&C 98:1. "Verily I say unto you my friends, fear not, let your hearts be comforted; yea, rejoice evermore, and in everything give thanks."

D&C 109:1. "Thanks be to thy name, O Lord God of Israel, who keepest covenant and showest mercy unto thy servants who walk uprightly before thee, with all their hearts."

Words of the Prophets | **Howard W. Hunter on having gratitude.** "We pay our debt of gratitude by living in such a way as to bring credit to our parents and the name we bear, by doing good to others, by being of service, by being willing to share the light and knowledge we have received so that others will also have joy and happiness, by living the principles of the gospel in their fulness. Paul told us we should be filled with the Spirit, 'giving thanks always for all things unto God and the Father in the name of our Lord Jesus Christ' (Ephesians 5:20)." —Howard W. Hunter, *The Teachings of Howard W. Hunter*, edited by Clyde J. Williams (Salt Lake City: Bookcraft, 1997), 93.

GRIEF [34]. Grief is an inevitable dimension of the mortal experience—sometimes from inescapable natural events, such as death or separation; sometimes from suffering due to the wickedness of others; and sometimes from avoidable causes relating to personal unrighteousness. The comfort and grace of the gospel help to overcome the former two causes of grief through the blessings of the Spirit; repentance and godly sorrow help to overcome the last-named cause of grief through the power and healing balm of the Atonement of Jesus Christ. The Lord experiences grief over our disobedience but joy over our obedience and spiritual growth (see D&C 18:11–13).

Genesis 49:22–23, 26. "Joseph is a fruitful bough, even a fruitful bough by a well; whose branches run over the wall: The archers have sorely grieved him, and shot at him, and hated him. . . . The blessings of thy father have prevailed above the blessings of my progenitors unto the utmost bound of the everlasting hills: they shall be on the head of Joseph, and on the crown of the head of him that was separate from his brethren."

1 Samuel 1:8, 15–17. "Then said Elkanah her husband to her, Hannah, why weepest thou? and why eatest thou not? and why is thy heart grieved? am not I better to thee than ten sons? . . . And Hannah answered [Eli] and said, No, my lord, I am a woman of a sorrowful spirit: I have drunk neither wine nor strong drink, but have poured out my soul before the Lord. Count not thine handmaid for a daughter of Belial: for out of the abundance of my complaint and grief have I spoken hitherto. Then Eli answered and said, Go in peace: and the God of Israel grant thee thy petition that thou hast asked of him."

Psalm 119:158. "I beheld the transgressors, and was grieved; because they kept not thy word."

Isaiah 53:3–10. "He is despised and rejected of men; a man of sorrows, and acquainted with grief: and we hid as it were our faces from him; he was despised, and we esteemed him not. Surely he hath borne our griefs, and carried our sorrows: yet we did esteem him stricken, smitten of God, and afflicted. But he was wounded for our transgressions, he was bruised for our iniquities: the chastisement of our peace was upon him; and with his stripes we are healed. All we like sheep have gone astray; we have turned every one to his own way; and the Lord hath laid on him the iniquity of us all. He was oppressed, and he was afflicted, yet he opened not his mouth: he is brought as a lamb to the slaughter, and as a sheep before her shearers is dumb, so he openeth not his mouth. He was taken from prison and from judgment: and who shall declare his generation? for he was cut off out of the land of the living: for the transgression of my people was he stricken. And he made his grave with the wicked, and with the rich in his death; because he had done no violence, neither was any deceit in his mouth. Yet it pleased the Lord to bruise him; he hath put him to grief: when thou shalt make his soul an offering for sin, he shall see his seed, he shall prolong his days, and the pleasure of the Lord shall prosper in his hand." (See also Psalm 69; Mosiah 14:3–10.)

2 Nephi 1:21. "And now that my soul might have joy in you, and that my heart might leave this world with gladness because of you, that I [Lehi] might not be brought down with grief and sorrow to the grave, arise from the dust, my sons, and be men, and be determined in one mind and in one heart, united in all things, that ye may not come down into captivity."

2 Nephi 4:17–18, 28. "Yea, my heart sorroweth because of my flesh; my soul grieveth because of mine iniquities. I am encompassed about, because of the temptations and the sins which do so easily beset me. . . . Awake, my soul! No longer droop in sin. Rejoice, O my heart, and give place no more for the enemy of my soul."

2 Nephi 26:11. "For the Spirit of the Lord will not always strive with man. And when the Spirit ceaseth to strive with man then cometh speedy destruction, and this grieveth my soul."

D&C 121:37. "That they [the rights of the priesthood] may be conferred upon us, it is true; but when we undertake to cover our sins, or to gratify our pride, our vain ambition, or to exercise control or dominion or compulsion upon the souls of the children of men, in any degree of unrighteousness, behold, the heavens withdraw themselves; the Spirit of the Lord is grieved; and when it is withdrawn, Amen to the priesthood or the authority of that man."

HAPPINESS [72]. Everyone seeks happiness—it is the design and quest of our existence. The state of happiness comes from righteousness (see Mosiah 2:41) and having the love of God in our hearts (see 4 Nephi 1:15–16).

Proverbs 29:18. "Where there is no vision, the people perish: but he that keepeth the law, happy is he."

John 13:17. "If ye know these things, happy are ye if ye do them."

2 Nephi 5:27. "And it came to pass that we lived after the manner of happiness."

Mosiah 2:41. "And moreover, I would desire that ye should consider on the blessed and happy state of those that keep the commandments of God. For behold, they are blessed in all things, both temporal and spiritual; and if they hold out faithful to the end they are received into heaven, that thereby they may dwell with God in a state of never-ending happiness. O remember, remember that these things are true; for the Lord God hath spoken it."

Alma 41:10. "Behold, I say unto you, wickedness never was happiness."

4 Nephi 1:15–16. "And it came to pass that there was no contention in the land, because of the love of God which did dwell in the hearts of the people. And there were no envyings, nor strifes, nor tumults, nor whoredoms, nor lyings, nor murders, nor any manner of lasciviousness; and surely there could not be a happier people among all the people who had been created by the hand of God."

What is the cause of happiness?

Being obedient. Proverbs 29:18. "Where there is no vision, the people perish: but he that keepeth the law, happy is he." (See also John 13:17; Mosiah 2:41; Alma 50:22–23.)

Charity. Proverbs 14:21. "He that despiseth his neighbour sinneth: but he that hath mercy on the poor, happy is he."

Chastening of the Lord. Job 5:17–18. "Behold, happy is the man whom God correcteth: therefore despise not thou the chastening of the Almighty: For he maketh sore, and bindeth up: he woundeth, and his hands make whole."

Children. Psalm 127:3–5. "Lo, children are an heritage of the Lord: and the fruit of the womb is his reward. As arrows are in the hand of a mighty man; so are children of the youth. Happy is the man that hath his quiver full of them: they shall not be ashamed, but they shall speak with the enemies in the gate." (See also 3 John 1:4.)

Defending the gospel. Acts 26: 1–2. "Then Agrippa said unto Paul, Thou art permitted to speak for thyself. Then Paul stretched forth the hand, and answered for himself: I think myself happy, king Agrippa, because I shall answer for myself this day before thee touching all the things whereof I am accused of the Jews."

Enduring patiently. James 5:11. "Behold, we count them happy which endure. Ye have heard of the patience of Job, and have seen the end of the Lord; that the Lord is very pitiful, and of tender mercy."

Faith in the Lord. Alma 46:41. "But there were many who died with old age; and those who died in the faith of Christ are happy in him, as we must needs suppose."

Following the word of God. Alma 44:5. "And now, Zerahemnah, I [Moroni] command you, in the name of that all-powerful God, who has strengthened our arms that we have gained power over you, by our faith, by our religion, and by our rites of worship, and by our church, and by the sacred support which we owe to our wives and our children, by that liberty which binds us to our lands and our country; yea, and also by the maintenance of the sacred word of God, to which we owe all our happiness; and by all that is most dear unto us."

Gathering together and living the gospel. 2 Nephi 5:27. "And it came to pass that we lived after the manner of happiness."

Humility and wisdom. 2 Nephi 9:42–43. "And whoso knocketh, to him will he open; and the wise, and the learned, and they that are rich, who are puffed up because of their learning, and their wisdom, and their riches—yea, they are they whom he despiseth; and save they shall cast these things away, and consider themselves fools before God, and come down in the depths of humility, he will not open unto them. But the things of the wise and the prudent shall be hid from them forever—yea, that happiness which is prepared for the saints."

Love of God. 4 Nephi 1:15–16. "And it came to pass that there was no contention in the land, because of the love of God which did dwell in the hearts of the people. And there were no envyings, nor strifes, nor tumults, nor whoredoms, nor lyings, nor murders, nor any manner of lasciviousness; and surely there could not be a happier people among all the people who had been created by the hand of God."

Seeking and tasting of the fruit of the tree (love of God). 1 Nephi 8:10–11. "And it came to pass that I beheld a tree, whose fruit was desirable to make one happy. And it came to pass that I did go forth and partake of the fruit thereof; and I beheld that it was most sweet, above all that I ever before tasted. Yea, and I beheld that the fruit thereof was white, to exceed all the whiteness that I had ever seen." (See also 1 Nephi 11:22.)

Wisdom. 1 Kings 10:8. "Happy are thy men, happy are these thy servants, which stand continually before thee, and that hear thy wisdom." (See also Proverbs 3:13, 17–18.)

Words of the Prophets | Ezra Taft Benson speaks of happiness. "If you really want to receive joy and happiness, then serve others with all your heart. Lift their burdens, and your own burdens will be lighter. Truly in the words of Jesus of Nazareth: 'He that findeth his life shall lose it: and he that loseth his life for my sake shall find it' (Matt. 10:39)." —Ezra Taft Benson, *Come, Listen to a Prophet's Voice* (Salt Lake City: Deseret Book, 1990), 59–60.

HELL [137]. In the scriptures, the word *hell* and variants apply to several different but related meanings, including "the domicile of Satan," "the place of confinement for the wicked," "a current state of wickedness in mortality," and "a state of deep distress and spiritual anxiety to avoid the judgment of God." According to the design of the Almighty, there is a place prepared for the wicked—a permanent place for Satan and his minions from the rebellion in the premortal existence, plus the sons of perdition from mortality; and a temporary place of suffering and remorse for those individuals of a telestial character who must pay the price of repentance until the "uttermost farthing" (Matthew 5:26) or the "uttermost senine" (3 Nephi 12:26) have been rendered and the grace of heaven can encompass them and bring them to their assigned level of glory in the eternities. The gospel of Jesus Christ provides a way forward that allows the obedient and valiant to avoid the pains and oppressions of hell.

1 Nephi 15:34–35. "But behold, I say unto you, the kingdom of God is not filthy, and there cannot any unclean thing enter into the kingdom of God; wherefore there must needs be a place of filthiness prepared for that which is filthy. And there is a place prepared, yea, even that awful hell of which I have spoken, and the devil is the preparator of it; wherefore the final state of the souls of men is to dwell in the kingdom of God, or to be cast out because of that justice of which I have spoken."

D&C 10:69–70. "And now, behold, whosoever is of my church, and endureth of my church to the end, him will I establish upon my rock, and the gates of hell shall not prevail against them. And now, remember the words of him who is the life and light of the world, your Redeemer, your Lord and your God."

D&C 21:4–6. "Wherefore, meaning the church, thou shalt give heed unto all his words [the prophet] and commandments which he shall give unto you as he receiveth them, walking in all holiness before me; For his word ye shall receive, as if from mine own mouth, in all patience and faith. For by doing these things the gates of hell shall not prevail against you; yea, and the Lord God will disperse the powers of darkness from before you, and cause the heavens to shake for your good, and his name's glory."

D&C 122:1, 7–8. "The ends of the earth shall inquire after thy name, and fools shall have thee in derision, and hell shall rage against thee; . . . and above all, if the very jaws of hell shall gape open the mouth wide after thee, know thou, my son, that all these things shall give thee experience, and shall be for thy good. The Son of Man hath descended below them all. Art thou greater than he?"

HEALTH [20]. There is wisdom in giving heed to the Lord's counsel on health by avoiding that which harms the body and promoting the wise use of nature's abundance to improve and preserve our health. The riches of the earth, given through the grace and blessing of God, offer grand opportunities for mankind to choose that which will have the most beneficial impact on health and well-being. There are grave physical and spiritual consequences when we stray from the Lord's counsel on health, just as there are magnificent physical and spiritual advantages awaiting those who heed the word of the Lord in humble gratitude.

1 Corinthians 3:16–17. "Know ye not that ye are the temple of God, and that the Spirit of God dwelleth in you? If any man defile the temple of God, him shall God destroy; for the temple of God is holy, which temple ye are."

1 Corinthians 6:19–20. "What? know ye not that your body is the temple of the Holy Ghost which is in you, which ye have of God, and ye are not your own? For ye are bought with a price: therefore glorify God in your body, and in your spirit, which are God's."

D&C 89:18–21. "And all saints who remember to keep and do these sayings [the Word of Wisdom], walking in obedience to the commandments, shall receive health in their navel and marrow to their bones; And shall find wisdom and great treasures of knowledge, even hidden treasures; And shall run and not be weary, and shall walk and not faint. And I, the Lord, give unto them a promise, that the destroying angel shall pass by them, as the children of Israel, and not slay them." (See the entire section.)

Words of the Prophets | Harold B. Lee on feeding both body and spirit. "Your spiritual body needs nourishment at frequent intervals in order to assure its health and vigor. Earthly food does not satisfy this need. Food to satisfy your spiritual needs must come from spiritual sources. Principles of eternal truth, as contained in the gospel, and the proper exercise by engaging in spiritual activities are essential to the satisfying of your spiritual selves. Vital processes of the spirit are likewise maintained only by intelligent connection with spiritual fountains of truth. Spiritual sickness and death, which mean separation from the fountain of spiritual light, are sure to follow the severance of your connection with the spiritual nerve center, the Church of Jesus Christ." —Harold B. Lee, *Decisions for Successful Living*, (Salt Lake City: Deseret Book, 1973), 145.

HOLY GHOST [261]. The Holy Ghost is the third member of the Godhead. He bears record of the Father and the Son and confirms the verity of the word of the Lord. The Holy Ghost is involved at every stage of the unfolding of the Father's plan of salvation. He is intimately connected with the instruction and enlightenment of the children of God through the ages. As the Spirit of truth and the Holy Spirit of Promise, He comforts, testifies, sanctifies, and acts as the constant companion of those who have received the gift of the Holy Ghost and live worthy of it. The Holy Ghost is the administering Agent for the light of Christ, by which light, even the light of revelation, we can come to know the Father and the Son and learn to comprehend all things. When we enjoy the companionship and blessings of the Holy Ghost, we will have peace, being comforted in all things and inspired to do good.

Numbers 11:29. "And Moses said unto him, Enviest thou for my sake? would God that all the Lord's people were prophets, and that the Lord would put his spirit upon them!"

1 Kings 19:11–12. "But the Lord was not in the wind: and after the wind an earthquake; but the Lord was not in the earthquake: And after the earthquake a fire; but the Lord was not in the fire: and after the fire a still small voice."

Joel 2:28–29. "And it shall come to pass afterward, that I will pour out my spirit upon all flesh; and your sons and your daughters shall prophesy, your old men shall dream dreams, your young men shall see visions: And also upon the servants and upon the handmaids in those days will I pour out my spirit."

John 14:26. "But the Comforter, which is the Holy Ghost, whom the Father will send in my name, he shall teach you all things, and bring all things to your remembrance, whatsoever I have said unto you."

Romans 5:5. "And hope maketh not ashamed; because the love of God is shed abroad in our hearts by the Holy Ghost which is given unto us."

1 Corinthians 12:3. "Wherefore I give you to understand, that no man speaking by the Spirit of God calleth Jesus accursed: and that no man can say that Jesus is the Lord, but by the Holy Ghost."

Galatians 5:22–23. "But the fruit of the Spirit is love, joy, peace, longsuffering, gentleness, goodness, faith, Meekness, temperance: against such there is no law."

Ephesians 1:12–14. "That we should be to the praise of his glory, who first trusted in Christ. In whom ye also trusted, after that ye heard the word of truth, the gospel of your salvation: in whom also after that ye believed, ye were sealed with that holy Spirit of promise, Which is the earnest of our inheritance until the redemption of the purchased possession, unto the praise of his glory."

2 Peter 1:20–21. "Knowing this first, that no prophecy of the scripture is of any private interpretation. For the prophecy came not in old time by the will of man: but holy men of God spake as they were moved by the Holy Ghost."

2 Nephi 32:5. "For behold, again I say unto you that if ye will enter in by the way, and receive the Holy Ghost, it will show unto you all things what ye should do."

Alma 5:46. "Behold, I say unto you they are made known unto me by the Holy Spirit of God. Behold, I have fasted and prayed many days that I might know these things of myself. And now I do know of myself that they are true; for the Lord God hath made them manifest unto me by his Holy Spirit; and this is the spirit of revelation which is in me."

Alma 17:3. "But this is not all; they [sons of Mosiah] had given themselves to much prayer, and fasting; therefore they had the spirit of prophecy, and the spirit of revelation, and when they taught, they taught with power and authority of God."

Moroni 10:4–5. "And when ye shall receive these things, I would exhort you that ye would ask God, the Eternal Father, in the name of Christ, if these things are not true; and if ye shall ask with a sincere heart, with real intent, having faith in Christ, he will manifest the truth of it unto you, by the power of the Holy Ghost. And by the power of the Holy Ghost ye may know the truth of all things."

D&C 11:12–13. "And now, verily, verily, I say unto thee, put your trust in that Spirit which leadeth to do good—yea, to do justly, to walk humbly, to judge righteously; and this is my Spirit. Verily, verily, I say unto you, I will impart unto you of my Spirit, which shall enlighten your mind, which shall fill your soul with joy."

D&C 20:27–28. "The Holy Ghost, which beareth record of the Father and of the Son; Which Father, Son, and Holy Ghost are one God, infinite and eternal, without end."

D&C 42:17. "For, behold, the Comforter knoweth all things, and beareth record of the Father and of the Son."

D&C 42:61. "If thou shalt ask, thou shalt receive revelation upon revelation, knowledge upon knowledge, that thou mayest know the mysteries and peaceable things—that which bringeth joy, that which bringeth life eternal."

D&C 76:7. "And to them will I reveal all mysteries, yea, all the hidden mysteries of my kingdom from days of old, and for ages to come, will I make known unto them the good pleasure of my will concerning all things pertaining to my kingdom."

D&C 130:22. "The Father has a body of flesh and bones as tangible as man's; the Son also; but the Holy Ghost has not a body of flesh and bones, but is a personage of Spirit. Were it not so, the Holy Ghost could not dwell in us."

Words of the Prophets | Lorenzo Snow on living by the Spirit. "Make up your minds to live humbly and in such a way that you will always have the spirit of the Lord to be your friend, to make suggestions to you from time to time as shall be needed under the peculiar circumstances in which you may be placed. . . . I do desire, and it is something that you should desire, to have that humility, and that meekness, and that simplicity, to enjoy the spirit of revelation. It is your privilege, every one of you, to have enough of the spirit of revelation

to know exactly what is proper for you to do. It is your privilege to know when men speak by the spirit of God and whether the counsel they give is proper or not." —Lorenzo Snow, *The Teachings of Lorenzo Snow*, ed. Clyde J. Williams (Salt Lake City: Deseret Book, 1984), 114.
Cross reference to "Holy Ghost": see Preach My Gospel, *18, 90–91.*

HOPE [217]. Hope in the Lord is the anchor of our existence, the compelling force that carries us forward on wings of faith toward the realization of our destiny as sons and daughters of God. A life without hope is empty, but a life filled with hope is a life filled with light and meaning, a life of exuberance in doing the will of the Lord, a life devoted to the preparations required for the fulfillment of our divine promises of glory, exaltation, and eternal life.

Proverbs 10:28. "The hope of the righteous shall be gladness: but the expectation of the wicked shall perish."

Jeremiah 17:7. "Blessed is the man that trusteth in the Lord, and whose hope the Lord is."

1 Corinthians 15:19–22. "If in this life only we have hope in Christ, we are of all men most miserable. But now is Christ risen from the dead, and become the firstfruits of them that slept. For since by man came death, by man came also the resurrection of the dead. For as in Adam all die, even so in Christ shall all be made alive."

Hebrews 11:1. "Now faith is the substance of things hoped for, the evidence of things not seen."

2 Nephi 31:20. "Wherefore, ye must press forward with a steadfastness in Christ, having a perfect brightness of hope, and a love of God and of all men. Wherefore, if ye shall press forward, feasting upon the word of Christ, and endure to the end, behold, thus saith the Father: Ye shall have eternal life."

Alma 32:21. "And now as I said concerning faith—faith is not to have a perfect knowledge of things; therefore if ye have faith ye hope for things which are not seen, which are true."

Ether 12:4. "Wherefore, whoso believeth in God might with surety hope for a better world, yea, even a place at the right hand of God, which hope cometh of faith, maketh an anchor to the souls of men, which would make them sure and steadfast, always abounding in good works, being led to glorify God."

Moroni 8:26. "And the remission of sins bringeth meekness, and lowliness of heart; and because of meekness and lowliness of heart cometh the visitation of the Holy Ghost, which Comforter filleth with hope and perfect love, which love endureth by diligence unto prayer, until the end shall come, when all the saints shall dwell with God."

D&C 4:5. "And faith, hope, charity and love, with an eye single to the glory of God, qualify him for the work."

Thirteenth Article of Faith. "We believe in being honest, true, chaste, benevolent, virtuous, and in doing good to all men; indeed, we may say that we follow the admonition of Paul—We believe all things, we hope all things, we have endured many things, and hope to be able to endure all things. If there is anything virtuous, lovely, or of good report or praiseworthy, we seek after these things."

What is the source of hope?

Jesus Christ. 1 Timothy 1:1. "Paul, an apostle of Jesus Christ by the commandment of God our Saviour, and Lord Jesus Christ, which is our hope."

Grace of the Lord. 2 Thessalonians 2:16–17. "Now our Lord Jesus Christ himself, and God, even our Father, which hath loved us, and hath given us everlasting consolation and good hope through grace, Comfort your hearts, and stablish you in every good word and work."

The Holy Ghost. Romans 15:13. "Now the God of hope fill you with all joy and peace in believing, that ye may abound in hope, through the power of the Holy Ghost." (See also Moroni 8:26.)

Scriptures. Romans 15:4. "For whatsoever things were written aforetime were written for our learning, that we through patience and comfort of the scriptures might have hope." (See also Jacob 4:6.)

Faith and meekness. Moroni 7:40–44. "And again, my beloved brethren, I would speak unto you concerning hope. How is it that you can attain unto faith, save ye shall have hope? And what is it that ye shall hope for? Behold I say unto you that ye shall have hope through the atonement of Christ and the power of his resurrection, to be raised unto life eternal, and this because of your faith in him according to the promise. Wherefore, if a man have faith he must needs have hope; for without faith there cannot be any hope. And again, behold I say unto you that he cannot have faith and hope, save he shall be meek, and lowly of heart. If so, his faith and hope is vain, for none is acceptable before God, save the meek and lowly in heart; and if a man be meek and lowly in heart, and confesses by the power of the Holy Ghost that Jesus is the Christ, he must needs have charity."

The ministering of heavenly beings. D&C 128:21. "And again, the voice of God in the chamber of old Father Whitmer, in Fayette, Seneca county, and at sundry times, and in divers places through all the travels and tribulations of this Church of Jesus Christ of Latter-day Saints! And the voice of Michael, the archangel; the voice of Gabriel, and of Raphael, and of divers angels, from Michael or Adam down to the present time, all declaring their dispensation, their rights, their keys, their honors, their majesty and glory, and the power of their priesthood; giving line upon line, precept upon precept; here a little, and there a little; giving us consolation by holding forth that which is to come, confirming our hope!"

HUMILITY [193]. When we are humble—being submissive, easily entreated, and teachable—we receive blessings of peace, inspiration, hope, and the guidance of the Lord. We have a broken heart and a contrite spirit. By cultivating a pattern of living grounded in humility, we can relate to God in gratitude and love.

Proverbs 16:19. "Better it is to be of an humble spirit with the lowly, than to divide the spoil with the proud."

Micah 6:8. "He hath shewed thee, O man, what is good; and what doth the Lord require of thee, but to do justly, and to love mercy, and to walk humbly with thy God?"

Matthew 18:3–4. "And said, Verily I say unto you, Except ye be converted, and become as little children, ye shall not enter into the kingdom of heaven. Whosoever therefore shall humble himself as this little child, the same is greatest in the kingdom of heaven."

James 4:10. "Humble yourselves in the sight of the Lord, and he shall lift you up."

Mosiah 3:18–19. "For behold he judgeth, and his judgment is just; and the infant perisheth not that dieth in his infancy; but men drink damnation to their own souls except they humble themselves and become as little children, and believe that salvation was, and is, and is to come, in and through the atoning blood of Christ, the Lord Omnipotent. For the natural man is an enemy to God, and has been from the fall of Adam, and will be, forever and ever, unless he yields to the enticings of the Holy Spirit, and putteth off the natural man and becometh a saint through the atonement of Christ the Lord, and becometh as a child, submissive, meek, humble, patient, full of love, willing to submit to all things which the Lord seeth fit to inflict upon him, even as a child doth submit to his father."
Alma 7:23. "And now I would that ye should be humble, and be submissive and gentle; easy to be entreated; full of patience and long-suffering; being temperate in all things; being diligent in keeping the commandments of God at all times; asking for whatsoever things ye stand in need, both spiritual and temporal; always returning thanks unto God for whatsoever things ye do receive."
Alma 32:16. "Therefore, blessed are they who humble themselves without being compelled to be humble; or rather, in other words, blessed is he that believeth in the word of God, and is baptized without stubbornness of heart, yea, without being brought to know the word, or even compelled to know, before they will believe."
Ether 12:27. "And if men come unto me I will show unto them their weakness. I give unto men weakness that they may be humble; and my grace is sufficient for all men that humble themselves before me; for if they humble themselves before me, and have faith in me, then will I make weak things become strong unto them."
D&C 11:12. "And now, verily, verily, I say unto thee, put your trust in that Spirit which leadeth to do good—yea, to do justly, to walk humbly, to judge righteously; and this is my Spirit."
D&C 12:8. "And no one can assist in this work except he shall be humble and full of love, having faith, hope, and charity, being temperate in all things, whatsoever shall be entrusted to his care."
D&C 20:37. "And again, by way of commandment to the church concerning the manner of baptism—All those who humble themselves before God, and desire to be baptized, and come forth with broken hearts and contrite spirits, and witness before the church that they have truly repented of all their sins, and are willing to take upon them the name of Jesus Christ, having a determination to serve him to the end, and truly manifest by their works that they have received of the Spirit of Christ unto the remission of their sins, shall be received by baptism into his church."
D&C 97:8. "Verily I say unto you, all among them who know their hearts are honest, and are broken, and their spirits contrite, and are willing to observe their covenants by sacrifice—yea, every sacrifice which I, the Lord, shall command—they are accepted of me."
D&C 112:10. "Be thou humble; and the Lord thy God shall lead thee by the hand, and give thee answer to thy prayers."

Words of the Prophets | Spencer W. Kimball on how to be humble. "How does one get humble? To me, one must constantly be reminded of his dependence. On whom dependent? On the Lord. How remind one's self? By real, constant, worshipful, grateful prayer. . . . Humility is gracious, quiet, serene, not pompous, spectacular, nor histrionic. It is subdued, kindly, and understanding—not crude, blatant, loud, or ugly. Humility is not just a man or a woman, but a perfect gentleman and a gentlelady. It never struts nor swaggers. Its faithful, quiet works will be the badge of its own accomplishments. It never sets itself in the center of the stage, leaving all others in supporting roles. Humility is never accusing nor contentious. It is not boastful." —Spencer W. Kimball, *The Teachings of Spencer W. Kimball*, edited by Edward L. Kimball (Salt Lake City: Bookcraft, 1982), 233.

IMAGE, GOD'S [8]. The scriptures confirm that man was created "in the image of God" (Genesis 1:27; Genesis 9:6; Mosiah 7:27). Thus the spirit children of God were endowed at birth with a physical framework patterned after that of their Father in Heaven, who blessed them with the divine capacity to grow and develop in spirit and body to become more and more like Him. The Father and Son are not an ethereal essence, without form or substance, but personages of infinite glory and power who have tangible bodies of flesh and bones (see Hebrews 1:3; D&C 130:22). The Holy Ghost does not have such a physical body, "but is a personage of Spirit" (D&C 130:22), enabling Him to dwell within us and accomplish His commission as the source of inspiration and guidance for those receptive of the truths of the gospel of Jesus Christ. One of the most sacred treasures is to come forth in the resurrection as "just men [and women] made perfect through Jesus the mediator of the new covenant . . . whose bodies are celestial, whose glory is that of the sun, even the glory of God, the highest of all" (D&C 76:69-70). With their spirits and bodies forever united and glorified, such children of God cross the threshold of ascendancy to become even as their Father in Heaven and His Only Begotten Son. God's image is thus everlastingly preserved in their beings as sons and daughters of God.

Genesis 1:27. "So God created man in his own image, in the image of God created he him; male and female created he them." (See also Genesis 9:6; Moses 2:26; Abraham 4:26.)

2 Corinthians 4:3–4. "But if our gospel be hid, it is hid to them that are lost: In whom the god of this world hath blinded the minds of them which believe not, lest the light of the glorious gospel of Christ, who is the image of God, should shine unto them."

Hebrews 1:3. "Who being the brightness of his glory, and the express image of his person, and upholding all things by the word of his power, when he had by himself purged our sins, sat down on the right hand of the Majesty on high."

Mosiah 7:26–28. "And a prophet of the Lord have they slain; yea, a chosen man of God, who told them of their wickedness and abominations, and prophesied of many things which are to come, yea, even the coming of Christ. And because he [Abinadi] said unto them that Christ was the God, the Father of all things, and said that he should take upon him the image of man, and it should be the image after which man was created in the beginning; or in other words, he said that man was created after the image of God, and that God should come down among the children of men, and take upon him flesh and blood, and go forth upon the face of the earth— And now, because he said this, they did put him to death."

Alma 5:19. "I say unto you, can ye look up to God at that day with a pure heart and clean hands? I say unto you, can you look up, having the image of God engraven upon your countenances?"
Alma 18:33–34. "And king Lamoni said: I believe all these things which thou hast spoken. Art thou sent from God? Ammon said unto him: I am a man; and man in the beginning was created after the image of God, and I am called by his Holy Spirit to teach these things unto this people, that they may be brought to a knowledge of that which is just and true."
D&C 76:69–70. "These are they who are just men made perfect through Jesus the mediator of the new covenant, who wrought out this perfect atonement through the shedding of his own blood. These are they whose bodies are celestial, whose glory is that of the sun, even the glory of God, the highest of all, whose glory the sun of the firmament is written of as being typical."
D&C 130:22. "The Father has a body of flesh and bones as tangible as man's; the Son also; but the Holy Ghost has not a body of flesh and bones, but is a personage of Spirit. Were it not so, the Holy Ghost could not dwell in us."
Moses 6:8–9. "Now this prophecy Adam spake, as he was moved upon by the Holy Ghost, and a genealogy was kept of the children of God. And this was the book of the generations of Adam, saying: In the day that God created man, in the likeness of God made he him; In the image of his own body, male and female, created he them, and blessed them, and called their name Adam, in the day when they were created and became living souls in the land upon the footstool of God."

How is the physical aspect of the glory of the Father, Son, and Holy Ghost confirmed in events recorded in the scriptures?

Resurrected Lord shows unto His disciples that He has a body of flesh and bones. Luke 24:36–40. "And as they thus spake, Jesus himself stood in the midst of them, and saith unto them, Peace be unto you. But they were terrified and affrighted, and supposed that they had seen a spirit. And he said unto them, Why are ye troubled? and why do thoughts arise in your hearts? Behold my hands and my feet, that it is I myself: handle me, and see; for a spirit hath not flesh and bones, as ye see me have. And when he had thus spoken, he shewed them his hands and his feet."
Nephi shown in vision that the Holy Ghost is a personage of Spirit without a physical body yet "in the form of a man." 1 Nephi 11:8–11. "And it came to pass that the Spirit said unto me [Nephi]: Look! And I looked and beheld a tree; and it was like unto the tree which my father had seen; and the beauty thereof was far beyond, yea, exceeding of all beauty; and the whiteness thereof did exceed the whiteness of the driven snow. And it came to pass after I had seen the tree, I said unto the Spirit: I behold thou hast shown unto me the tree which is precious above all. And he said unto me: What desirest thou? And I said unto him: To know the interpretation thereof—for I spake unto him as a man speaketh; for I beheld that he was in the form of a man; yet nevertheless, I knew that it was the Spirit of the Lord; and he spake unto me as a man speaketh with another."
Resurrected Lord shows unto the Saints in ancient America that He has a body of flesh and bones. 3 Nephi 11:13–15. "And it came to pass that the Lord spake unto them saying:

Arise and come forth unto me, that ye may thrust your hands into my side, and also that ye may feel the prints of the nails in my hands and in my feet, that ye may know that I am the God of Israel, and the God of the whole earth, and have been slain for the sins of the world. And it came to pass that the multitude went forth, and thrust their hands into his side, and did feel the prints of the nails in his hands and in his feet; and this they did do, going forth one by one until they had all gone forth, and did see with their eyes and did feel with their hands, and did know of a surety and did bear record, that it was he, of whom it was written by the prophets, that should come."

Joseph Smith shown in the First Vision that the Father and Son are separate personages. JS—H 1:16–17. "I saw a pillar of light exactly over my head, above the brightness of the sun, which descended gradually until it fell upon me. It no sooner appeared than I found myself delivered from the enemy which held me bound. When the light rested upon me I saw two Personages, whose brightness and glory defy all description, standing above me in the air. One of them spake unto me, calling me by name and said, pointing to the other—*This is My Beloved Son. Hear Him!*"

Joseph Smith and Oliver Cowdery shown in vision in the Kirtland Temple on April 3, 1836, the glorious nature of the Lord Jesus Christ. D&C 110:1–4. "The veil was taken from our minds, and the eyes of our understanding were opened. We saw the Lord standing upon the breastwork of the pulpit, before us; and under his feet was a paved work of pure gold, in color like amber. His eyes were as a flame of fire; the hair of his head was white like the pure snow; his countenance shone above the brightness of the sun; and his voice was as the sound of the rushing of great waters, even the voice of Jehovah, saying: I am the first and the last; I am he who liveth, I am he who was slain; I am your advocate with the Father."

Words of the Prophets | Joseph Smith concerning God's image. "If the veil were rent today, and the great God who holds this world in its orbit, and who upholds all worlds and all things by His power, was to make himself visible,—I say, if you were to see him today, you would see him like a man in form—like yourselves in all the person, image, and very form as a man; for Adam was created in the very fashion, image and likeness of God, and received instruction from, and walked, talked and conversed with Him, as one man talks and communes with another." —Joseph Smith, *HC* 6:305.

INTELLIGENCE [17]. Intelligence is the light of truth that enlivens and edifies the thoughts and actions of a person committed to doing the will of the Father and the Son. Intelligence cleaves unto the divine and rejects evil. The quest for and acquisition of intelligence is a principle that unites the Saints of God in a mutual bond of working toward the state of perfection, according to their divine destiny.

D&C 88:38–41. "And unto every kingdom is given a law; and unto every law there are certain bounds also and conditions. All beings who abide not in those conditions are not justified. For intelligence cleaveth unto intelligence; wisdom receiveth wisdom; truth embraceth truth; virtue loveth virtue; light cleaveth unto light; mercy hath compassion on mercy and claimeth her own; justice continueth its course and claimeth its own; judgment goeth before the face of him who sitteth upon the throne and governeth and executeth all things. He comprehendeth all things, and all things are before him, and all things are round about him; and he is above all things, and in all things, and is through all things, and is round about all things; and all things are by him, and of him, even God, forever and ever."

D&C 93:29–30. "Man was also in the beginning with God. Intelligence, or the light of truth, was not created or made, neither indeed can be. All truth is independent in that sphere in which God has placed it, to act for itself, as all intelligence also; otherwise there is no existence."

D&C 93:36. "The glory of God is intelligence, or, in other words, light and truth."

JS—H 1:54. "Accordingly, as I had been commanded, I went at the end of each year, and at each time I found the same messenger there, and received instruction and intelligence from him [Moroni] at each of our interviews, respecting what the Lord was going to do, and how and in what manner his kingdom was to be conducted in the last days."

JEHOVAH [14]. Jehovah (meaning "the Unchangeable One") is a principal name for Jesus Christ, generally rendered in small caps as LORD or GOD in the KJV of the Bible. The sublime and eternal implication of the name was expressed to Moses by the Lord Himself: "And Moses said unto God, Behold, when I come unto the children of Israel, and shall say unto them, The God of your fathers hath sent me unto you; and they shall say to me, What is his name? what shall I say unto them? And God said unto Moses, I AM THAT I AM: and he said, Thus shalt thou say unto the children of Israel, I AM hath sent me unto you. And God said moreover unto Moses, Thus shalt thou say unto the children of Israel, The LORD [i.e., Jehovah] God of your fathers, the God of Abraham, the God of Isaac, and the God of Jacob, hath sent me unto you: this is my name for ever, and this is my memorial unto all generations" (Exodus 3:13–15). The name Jehovah is not used in the KJV of the New Testament and is used only four times in the KJV of the Old Testament:

Exodus 6:2–3. "And God spake unto Moses, and said unto him, I am the LORD: And I appeared unto Abraham, unto Isaac, and unto Jacob, by *the name of* God Almighty, but by my name JEHOVAH was I not known to them." (Note: the Joseph Smith Translation corrects this last phrase as follows: "And unto Jacob. I am the Lord God Almighty; the Lord JEHOVAH. AND WAS NOT MY NAME KNOWN UNTO THEM?")

Psalm 83:18. "That men may know that thou, whose name alone is JEHOVAH, art the most high over all the earth." (See also Psalm 68:4, where the term JAH is used.)

Isaiah 12:2. "Behold, God is my salvation; I will trust, and not be afraid: for the LORD JEHOVAH is my strength and my song; he also is become my salvation."

Isaiah 26:4. "Trust ye in the Lord for ever: for in the LORD JEHOVAH is everlasting strength." (Note: In addition, the Old Testament mentions the place name Jehovah-jireh—Genesis 22:14.)

JERUSALEM, NEW (20). The New Jerusalem to be built by the Lord and His Saints will be the glorious and holy abode of Deity and His redeemed sons and daughters. There will be a duality of capitals of gathering and sanctuary in the kingdom of God in the millennial era and beyond: the Old Jerusalem restored to its state of sanctity and the New Jerusalem built up in glory to receive and embrace the translated city of Enoch from olden times.

3 Nephi 20:21–22. "And it shall come to pass that I will establish my people, O house of Israel. And behold, this people will I establish in this land, unto the fulfilling of the covenant which I made with your father Jacob; and it shall be a New Jerusalem. And the powers of heaven shall be in the midst of this people; yea, even I will be in the midst of you."

3 Nephi 21:23–24. "And they [those who repent and come unto Christ] shall assist my people, the remnant of Jacob, and also as many of the house of Israel as shall come, that they may build a city, which shall be called the New Jerusalem. And then shall they assist my people that they may be gathered in, who are scattered upon all the face of the land, in unto the New Jerusalem."

Ether 13:5–6, 8. "And he [Ether] spake also concerning the house of Israel, and the Jerusalem from whence Lehi should come—after it should be destroyed it should be built up again, a holy city unto the Lord; wherefore, it could not be a new Jerusalem for it had been in a time of old; but it should be built up again, and become a holy city of the Lord; and it should be built unto the house of Israel—And that a New Jerusalem should be built up upon this land, unto the remnant of the seed of Joseph. . . . Wherefore, the remnant of the house of Joseph shall be built upon this land; and it shall be a land of their inheritance; and they shall build up a holy city unto the Lord, like unto the Jerusalem of old; and they shall no more be confounded, until the end come when the earth shall pass away."

D&C 133:56. "And the graves of the saints shall be opened; and they shall come forth and stand on the right hand of the Lamb, when he shall stand upon Mount Zion, and upon the holy city, the New Jerusalem; and they shall sing the song of the Lamb, day and night forever and ever."

Tenth Article of Faith. "We believe in the literal gathering of Israel and in the restoration of the Ten Tribes; that Zion (the New Jerusalem) will be built upon the American continent; that Christ will reign personally upon the earth; and, that the earth will be renewed and receive its paradisiacal glory."

JESUS CHRIST [Jesus 1,285; Jesus Christ 357; Christ 1,108]. The quintessence and enduring spirit of all the scriptures—the Old Testament, New Testament, Book of Mormon, the Doctrine and Covenants, and Pearl of Great Price—is to communicate to mankind the glory and power of the gospel of Jesus Christ. It is through "the merits, and mercy, and grace of the Holy Messiah" (2 Nephi 2:8), the Mediator of the sacred covenant with the Father, that the immortality, eternal life, and exaltation of the sons and daughters of God are realized. The word of God is indeed the Word of God (John 1:1). Among the numerous offices and titles of the Lord revealed through the scriptural record, the following six might be considered the principal and predominant ones: (1) Jehovah ("Unchangeable One"), (2) Messiah or Christ ("Anointed One"), (3) Creator, (4) Emmanuel ("God Among Us"), (5) Jesus ("God is help" or "Savior") and (6) King. Understanding the interrelated functions of the mission of the Lord serves as a kind of lens through which to view the unfolding panorama of God's dealings with His people during the dispensations of time.

2 Nephi 31:21. "And now, behold, my beloved brethren, this is the way; and there is none other way nor name given under heaven whereby man can be saved in the kingdom of God. And now, behold, this is the doctrine of Christ, and the only and true doctrine of the Father, and of the Son, and of the Holy Ghost, which is one God, without end. Amen." (See also Moses 6:51–52.)

Six Key Dimensions of Jesus Christ's mission of love and mercy in the scriptures.

Jehovah. The name Jehovah signifies everlasting, endless, and eternal God, a reflection of the supernal constancy of Deity, the Word of God. D&C 35:1. "Listen to the voice of the Lord your God, even Alpha and Omega, the beginning and the end, whose course is one eternal round, the same today as yesterday, and forever." (See also Exodus 3:13–15; Hebrews 13:8; 2 Nephi 2:4; 27:23; 29:9; Alma 31:17; Mormon 9:9; Moroni 10:19; D&C 20:12.)

Messiah/Christ. The meaning of the name is "Anointed." The Greek equivalent of Messiah was Christ. Moses 7:53. "And the Lord said: Blessed is he through whose seed Messiah shall come; for he saith—I am Messiah, the King of Zion, the Rock of Heaven, which is broad as eternity; whoso cometh in at the gate and climbeth up by me shall never fall; wherefore, blessed are they of whom I have spoken, for they shall come forth with songs of everlasting joy." (See also Daniel 9:25–26; Moses 6:52, 57; 7:50; 8:24.)

Creator. The Unchangeable and Anointed One served as the principal divine agent in laying the foundation of the world through the Creation itself. When God directed by His word that the Creation should proceed (Genesis 1–2; Deuteronomy 4:32; Moses 2–3), it was through the Word of God (Jehovah, Messiah, Christ) that this divine process was initiated and completed. Isaiah 44:24. "Thus saith the Lord, thy redeemer, and he that formed thee from the womb, I am the Lord that maketh all things; that stretcheth forth the heavens alone; that spreadeth abroad the earth by myself." (See also Psalm 33:6; Isaiah 41:20; John 1:1–5; Colossians 1:16; Revelation 5:13; 10:6; 2 Nephi 2:14; 29:7; Mosiah 4:2, 9; 5:15; Alma 18:28–29; 22:10; Helaman 14:12; 3 Nephi 9:15; Mormon 9:11, 17; D&C 14:9.)

Emmanuel (Immanuel). One of the greatest of all the miracles of the gospel is the condescension of God, that the great Jehovah—the "Unchangeable One," the "Anointed One"—should deem it His essential mission to do the will of the Father and come among mortals to bring to pass for all mankind the effectual conditions of faith, salvation, and redemption. In this capacity, His office and title are known as Emmanuel (also rendered "Immanuel")—that is, "God Among Us." As the Only Begotten of the Father, He accepted His mortal mission to serve as the Messenger of the covenant, and He experienced birth, grew to manhood, completed His ministry as the Good Shepherd, and suffered betrayal and death as the "author of eternal salvation" (Hebrews 5:8–9). Isaiah 53:1–5. "Who hath believed our report? and to whom is the arm of the Lord revealed? For he shall grow up before him as a tender plant, and as a root out of a dry ground: he hath no form nor comeliness; and when we shall see him, there is no beauty that we should desire him. He is despised and rejected of men; a man of sorrows, and acquainted with grief: and we hid as it were our faces from him; he was despised, and we esteemed him not. Surely he hath borne our griefs, and carried our sorrows: yet we did esteem him stricken, smitten of God, and afflicted. But he was wounded for our transgressions, he was bruised for our iniquities: the chastisement of our peace was upon him; and with his stripes we are healed." (See also 1 Samuel 16:1; 17:12; 2 Samuel 7:12–17; Psalm 132:11–18; Isaiah 9:6–7; 11:1–10; Jeremiah 23:5–6; 33:14–16; Zechariah 3:8–9; 6:10–15; 12:7–12.)

Jesus. The name Jesus *is the Greek form of the name* Joshua *or* Jeshua, *meaning "God is help" or "Jehovah is help" (i.e., "Savior"). The name implies the sacred office of Redeemer; Lamb of Life; Bread of Life; the One who brings about the Atonement through the sacrificial crucifixion; the One who ushers in the process of the resurrection; the One who is therefore, in all respects, the Life of the World. In this capacity as Savior, the Son of God—even Jehovah, Messiah, Christ, Creator, Emmanuel—is the means for rescuing all mankind from the effects of the temporal death and enabling the faithful and obedient to escape the clutches of the second (or spiritual) death through compliance with the principles and ordinances of the gospel. The New Testament is a vibrant and compelling witness of the office of Savior and Redeemer as consummated in the crucifixion and resurrection of Jesus. Alma 34:15–16.* "And thus he shall bring salvation to all those who shall believe on his name; this being the intent of this last sacrifice, to bring about the bowels of mercy, which overpowereth justice, and bringeth about means unto men that they may have faith unto repentance. And thus mercy can satisfy the demands of justice, and encircles them in the arms of safety, while he that exercises no faith unto repentance is exposed to the whole law of the demands of justice; therefore only unto him that has faith unto repentance is brought about the great and eternal plan of redemption." (See also Psalm 22:16–19; Isaiah 53; Zechariah 12:10.)

King. In the final chapter of the history of this world, Jesus Christ will return in glory as King, Judge, Law-Giver, Mediator, Advocate, and Prince of Peace to usher in the millennial reign and take His place as the covenant Father of all the righteous and redeemed. With great clarity, the Old Testament account confirms this divine design of consummation and the ultimate royal ascension of the Son to the throne of glory. Joel 3:15–17. "The sun and the moon shall be darkened, and the stars shall withdraw their shining. The Lord also shall roar out of Zion, and utter his voice from Jerusalem; and the heavens and the earth shall shake: but the Lord will be the hope of his people, and the strength of the children of Israel. So shall ye know that I am the Lord your God dwelling in Zion, my holy mountain: then shall Jerusalem be holy, and there shall no strangers pass through her any more." (See also Job 19:25; Psalm 24:7–10; Daniel 7:13; Micah 1:3–4; Haggai 2:6–7; Malachi 3:1–3.)

Words of the Prophets | **Ezra Taft Benson on the pervasive presence of the Savior in the Book of Mormon.** "The honest seeker after truth can gain the testimony that Jesus is the Christ as he prayerfully ponders the inspired words of the Book of Mormon. Over one-half of all the verses in the Book of Mormon refer to our Lord. Some form of Christ's name is mentioned more frequently per verse in the Book of Mormon than even in the New Testament. He is given over one hundred different names in the Book of Mormon. Those

names have a particular significance in describing His divine nature." —Ezra Taft Benson, "Come unto Christ," *Ensign*, November 1987, 83.
Cross reference to "Jesus Christ": see Preach My Gospel, *34, 37, 47–48, 51–52, 60–61.*

JUDGMENT, FINAL [590]. Just as the Creation, Fall, and Atonement are considered to be the three pillars of eternity (see Mormon 9:12), so likewise is the judgment of God a central and inevitable aspect of the plan of salvation. The ultimate Judge of all is Jesus Christ, commissioned of the Father. Grounded in grace, justice, mercy, and truth, the judgment of the Lord is universal in application, since "every knee shall bow, and every tongue confess before him" (Mosiah 27:31), and He will, at that confession and judgment, place us in the station we have earned in this life—whether it be to a station of glory or darkness. All our doings, thoughts, words, and deeds factor into our accountability before the Lord in the process of divine judgment. We can rejoice in the assurance that the power of redemption extends to all who repent in obedience and endure to the end in righteousness, for the promise is given to such that their sins are forgiven (see D&C 58:42). Thus, if we prepare ourselves for the day of judgment in faith and valor, heed the prophets, follow the word of God, and look to Him in the spirit of reverence and love—just as He loves us—the ultimate judgment will be one of joy and glory, with our coming forth in the morning of the first resurrection as "joint-heirs with Christ" (Romans 8:17) and partakers of everlasting life in the mansions of heaven.

Ecclesiastes 12:13–14. "Let us hear the conclusion of the whole matter: Fear God, and keep his commandments: for this is the whole duty of man. For God shall bring every work into judgment, with every secret thing, whether it be good, or whether it be evil."

Isaiah 9:6–7. "For unto us a child is born, unto us a son is given: and the government shall be upon his shoulder: and his name shall be called Wonderful, Counsellor, The mighty God, The everlasting Father, The Prince of Peace. Of the increase of his government and peace there shall be no end, upon the throne of David, and upon his kingdom, to order it, and to establish it with judgment and with justice from henceforth even for ever. The zeal of the Lord of hosts will perform this." (See also 2 Nephi 19:6–7.)

Philippians 2:9–11. "Wherefore God also hath highly exalted him, and given him a name which is above every name: That at the name of Jesus every knee should bow, of things in heaven, and things in earth, and things under the earth; And that every tongue should confess that Jesus Christ is Lord, to the glory of God the Father."

Hebrews 6:1–3. "Therefore leaving the principles of the doctrine of Christ, let us go on unto perfection; not laying again the foundation of repentance from dead works, and of faith toward God, Of the doctrine of baptisms, and of laying on of hands, and of resurrection of the dead, and of eternal judgment. And this will we do, if God permit."

2 Nephi 9:21–22. "And he cometh into the world that he may save all men if they will hearken unto his voice; for behold, he suffereth the pains of all men, yea, the pains of every living creature, both men, women, and children, who belong to the family of Adam. And he suffereth this that the resurrection might pass upon all men, that all might stand before him at the great and judgment day."

Mormon 7:7. "And he hath brought to pass the redemption of the world, whereby he that is found guiltless before him at the judgment day hath it given unto him to dwell in the presence of God in his kingdom, to sing ceaseless praises with the choirs above, unto the Father, and unto the Son, and unto the Holy Ghost, which are one God, in a state of happiness which hath no end."

Mormon 8:20. "Behold what the scripture says—man shall not smite, neither shall he judge; for judgment is mine, saith the Lord, and vengeance is mine also, and I will repay."

D&C 82:23. "Leave judgment alone with me, for it is mine and I will repay. Peace be with you; my blessings continue with you."

D&C 84:87–88. "Behold, I send you out to reprove the world of all their unrighteous deeds, and to teach them of a judgment which is to come. And whoso receiveth you, there I will be also, for I will go before your face. I will be on your right hand and on your left, and my Spirit shall be in your hearts, and mine angels round about you, to bear you up."

D&C 101:78. "That every man may act in doctrine and principle pertaining to futurity, according to the moral agency which I have given unto him, that every man may be accountable for his own sins in the day of judgment."

JUSTICE AND MERCY [34]. Justice connotes the righteous judgment of God as it relates to the thoughts, words, and deeds of all His spirit children and all those who enter mortality. Those who have received and understand the commandments of God are subject to the demands of justice, which extend great blessings for obedience and exact exquisite punishment for disobedience. Since no mortals, left to their own devices, can satisfy with perfection the standards prescribed by the framework of justice (see 2 Nephi 2:5), the Atonement brings about the operation of mercy in the lives of all who follow in the footsteps of the Master and enter His fold through faith, repentance, and the baptism of water and fire—and thereafter endure to the end. For the faithful and obedient, mercy satisfies the demands of justice through the power and grace of the redemption.

Psalm 89:14. "Justice and judgment are the habitation of thy throne: mercy and truth shall go before thy face."

2 Nephi 9:25–26. "Wherefore, he has given a law; and where there is no law given there is no punishment; and where there is no punishment there is no condemnation; and where there is no condemnation the mercies of the Holy One of Israel have claim upon them, because of the atonement; for they are delivered by the power of him. For the atonement satisfieth the demands of his justice upon all those who have not the law given to them, that they are delivered from that awful monster, death and hell, and the devil, and the lake of fire and brimstone, which is endless torment; and they are restored to that God who gave them breath, which is the Holy One of Israel."

Jacob 4:10. "Wherefore, brethren, seek not to counsel the Lord, but to take counsel from his hand. For behold, ye yourselves know that he counseleth in wisdom, and in justice, and in great mercy, over all his works."

Mosiah 15:8–9. "And thus God breaketh the bands of death, having gained the victory over death; giving the Son power to make intercession for the children of men—Having ascended into heaven, having the bowels of mercy; being filled with compassion towards the children of men; standing betwixt them and justice; having broken the bands of death, taken upon himself their iniquity and their transgressions, having redeemed them, and satisfied the demands of justice."

Alma 34:15–17. "And thus he shall bring salvation to all those who shall believe on his name; this being the intent of this last sacrifice, to bring about the bowels of mercy, which overpowereth justice, and bringeth about means unto men that they may have faith unto repentance. And thus mercy can satisfy the demands of justice, and encircles them in the arms of safety, while he that exercises no faith unto repentance is exposed to the whole law of the demands of justice; therefore only unto him that has faith unto repentance is brought about the great and eternal plan of redemption. Therefore may God grant unto you, my brethren, that ye may begin to exercise your faith unto repentance, that ye begin to call upon his holy name, that he would have mercy upon you."

Alma 42:13–15. "Therefore, according to justice, the plan of redemption could not be brought about, only on conditions of repentance of men in this probationary state, yea, this preparatory state; for except it were for these conditions, mercy could not take effect except it should destroy the work of justice. Now the work of justice could not be destroyed; if so, God would cease to be God. And thus we see that all mankind were fallen, and they were in the grasp of justice; yea, the justice of God, which consigned them forever to be cut off from his presence. And now, the plan of mercy could not be brought about except an atonement should be made; therefore God himself atoneth for the sins of the world, to bring about the plan of mercy, to appease the demands of justice, that God might be a perfect, just God, and a merciful God also. (See also verses 21–25.)

3 Nephi 26:4–5. "And even unto the great and last day, when all people, and all kindreds, and all nations and tongues shall stand before God, to be judged of their works, whether they be good or whether they be evil—If they be good, to the resurrection of everlasting life; and if they be evil, to the resurrection of damnation; being on a parallel, the one on the one hand and the other on the other hand, according to the mercy, and the justice, and the holiness which is in Christ, who was before the world began."

KINGDOM OF GOD [126]. The kingdom of God is an expression for the divinely regulated society of the sons and daughters of God as they are gathered under the power of the priesthood to prepare for and obtain the blessings of eternal glory and everlasting life. In a sense, the kingdom of God is a state of worthiness achieved by those who are accepted of the Father and Son (as in the Lord's words in Luke 17:20–21); but in a more express sense, the kingdom of God is indeed the Church of Jesus Christ—organized and empowered to bring about the perfection of the Saints through their obedience and through the grace and guidance of heaven in providing prophets, seers, and revelators to convey the will of the Lord and administer all the essential ordinances of the gospel.

Matthew 6:33. "But seek ye first the kingdom of God, and his righteousness; and all these things shall be added unto you." (See also Luke 12:31; Jacob 2:18; 3 Nephi 13:33; D&C 11:23.)

Luke 17:20–21. "And when he was demanded of the Pharisees, when the kingdom of God should come, he answered them and said, The kingdom of God cometh not with observation: Neither shall they say, Lo here! or, lo there! for, behold, the kingdom of God is within you."

Luke 21:29–31. "And he spake to them a parable; Behold the fig tree, and all the trees; When they now shoot forth, ye see and know of your own selves that summer is now nigh at hand. So likewise ye, when ye see these things come to pass, know ye that the kingdom of God is nigh at hand."

John 3:3–5. "Jesus answered and said unto him, Verily, verily, I say unto thee, Except a man be born again, he cannot see the kingdom of God. Nicodemus saith unto him, How can a man be born when he is old? can he enter the second time into his mother's womb, and be born? Jesus answered, Verily, verily, I say unto thee, Except a man be born of water and of the Spirit, he cannot enter into the kingdom of God."

Romans 14:17. "For the kingdom of God is not meat and drink; but righteousness, and peace, and joy in the Holy Ghost."

2 Nephi 10:25. "Wherefore, may God raise you from death by the power of the resurrection, and also from everlasting death by the power of the atonement, that ye may be received into the eternal kingdom of God, that ye may praise him through grace divine."

D&C 6:13. "If thou wilt do good, yea, and hold out faithful to the end, thou shalt be saved in the kingdom of God, which is the greatest of all the gifts of God; for there is no gift greater than the gift of salvation."

D&C 20:29. "And we know that all men must repent and believe on the name of Jesus Christ, and worship the Father in his name, and endure in faith on his name to the end, or they cannot be saved in the kingdom of God."

D&C 65:2, 5–6. "The keys of the kingdom of God are committed unto man on the earth, and from thence shall the gospel roll forth unto the ends of the earth, as the stone which is cut out of the mountain without hands shall roll forth, until it has filled the whole earth . . . Call upon the Lord, that his kingdom may go forth upon the earth, that the inhabitants thereof may receive it, and be prepared for the days to come, in the which the Son of Man shall come down in heaven, clothed in the brightness of his glory, to meet the kingdom of God which is set up on the earth. Wherefore, may the kingdom of God go forth, that the kingdom of heaven may come, that thou, O God, mayest be glorified in heaven so on earth, that thine enemies may be subdued; for thine is the honor, power and glory, forever and ever." (See also D&C 138:44.)

Ninth Article of Faith. "We believe all that God has revealed, all that He does now reveal, and we believe that He will yet reveal many great and important things pertaining to the Kingdom of God."

Words of the Prophets | Joseph Smith on the kingdom of God. "Now I will give my testimony. I care not for man. I speak boldly and faithfully and with authority. How is it with the kingdom of God? Where did the kingdom of God begin? Where there is no kingdom of God there is no salvation. What constitutes the kingdom of God? Where there is a prophet, a priest, or a righteous man unto whom God gives His oracles, there is the kingdom of God; and where the oracles of God are not, there the kingdom of God is not." —Joseph Smith, *Teachings of the Prophet Joseph Smith* (Salt Lake City: Deseret Book, 1938), 271–272.

KNOWLEDGE [362]. God, in His mercy and lovingkindness, grants unto His sons and daughters the knowledge essential for their salvation and exaltation—including knowledge about the nature of God and about the doctrines, principles, ordinances, and covenants of the gospel of Jesus Christ. Such knowledge is supplied through the scriptures, the voice of the living prophets, the truths dispensed in the temples, and the continual whisperings of the Spirit. Knowledge is willingly received by hearts that are humble and then applied with faith and trust in the Almighty. The essence of all saving knowledge is conveyed in the celebrated words from the Savior's intercessory prayer: "And this is life eternal, that they might know thee the only true God, and Jesus Christ, whom thou hast sent" (John 17:3). That being the case, there is plainness and clarity in the words of Joseph Smith: "It is impossible for a man to be saved in ignorance" (D&C 131:6).

Genesis 2:17. "But of the tree of the knowledge of good and evil, thou shalt not eat of it: for in the day that thou eatest thereof thou shalt surely die." (See also Moses 3:17; Abraham 5:13.)

Proverbs 9:10. "The fear of the Lord is the beginning of wisdom: and the knowledge of the holy is understanding."

2 Corinthians 4:6. "For God, who commanded the light to shine out of darkness, hath shined in our hearts, to give the light of the knowledge of the glory of God in the face of Jesus Christ."

1 Nephi 15:14. "And at that day shall the remnant of our seed know that they are of the house of Israel, and that they are the covenant people of the Lord; and then shall they know and come to the knowledge of their forefathers, and also to the knowledge of the gospel of their Redeemer, which was ministered unto their fathers by him; wherefore, they shall come to the knowledge of their Redeemer and the very points of his doctrine, that they may know how to come unto him and be saved."

Alma 37:8. "And now, it has hitherto been wisdom in God that these things should be preserved; for behold, they have enlarged the memory of this people, yea, and convinced many of the error of their ways, and brought them to the knowledge of their God unto the salvation of their souls."

D&C 42:61. "If thou shalt ask, thou shalt receive revelation upon revelation, knowledge upon knowledge, that thou mayest know the mysteries and peaceable things—that which bringeth joy, that which bringeth life eternal."

D&C 84:19–21. "And this greater priesthood administereth the gospel and holdeth the key of the mysteries of the kingdom, even the key of the knowledge of God. Therefore, in the ordinances thereof, the power of godliness is manifest. And without the ordinances thereof, and the authority of the priesthood, the power of godliness is not manifest unto men in the flesh."

D&C 93:24. "And truth is knowledge of things as they are, and as they were, and as they are to come."

D&C 130:18–19. "Whatever principle of intelligence we attain unto in this life, it will rise with us in the resurrection. And if a person gains more knowledge and intelligence in this life through his diligence and obedience than another, he will have so much the advantage in the world to come."

LOVE [628]. Love is the motivating essence of the divine mission, the substance of everlasting life, the key to eternal hope and peace, and the binding power of the relationship between God and His children. God loves us with a perfect love (charity), and we are to love Him with all our heart, might, mind, and strength. The gospel of Jesus Christ is founded upon the principle of enduring love. It constitutes obtaining the divine nature of Christ through faith, virtue, knowledge, temperance, patience, brotherly kindness, and godliness with all humility and diligence (see D&C 4:6). This pure love of Christ is total, complete, enduring, and characteristic of the divine being. When we are possessed of this love, our desires are like unto our Savior's—to bless and serve mankind. Charity never fails. Christ did not fail His Father, nor did He fail us; His pure love motivated His great sacrifice—the eternal, infinite, vicarious Atonement. When we embody that love, we act in our lives according to the principles of the Atonement. When we possess this charity—this pure love of Christ, this love for all men, this desire to bless and serve—we then possess the qualities of charity, and we never fail. For in the strength of the Lord we can do all things, just as Ammon did (see Alma 26:12). Empowered by charity, through the Atonement of Christ, we begin to acquire this unconditional godly love, this divine nature of Christ. Love marks the pathway to salvation and exaltation.

Deuteronomy 10:12. "And now, Israel, what doth the Lord thy God require of thee, but to fear the Lord thy God, to walk in all his ways, and to love him, and to serve the Lord thy God with all thy heart and with all thy soul."

Matthew 22:37–39. "Jesus said unto him, Thou shalt love the Lord thy God with all thy heart, and with all thy soul, and with all thy mind. This is the first and great commandment. And the second is like unto it, Thou shalt love thy neighbour as thyself."

John 3:16. "For God so loved the world, that he gave his only begotten Son, that whosoever believeth in him should not perish, but have everlasting life."

John 13:34–35. "A new commandment I give unto you, That ye love one another; as I have loved you, that ye also love one another. By this shall all men know that ye are my disciples, if ye have love one to another."

John 14:15. "If ye love me, keep my commandments."

John 15:13. "Greater love hath no man than this, that a man lay down his life for his friends."

1 Corinthians 2:9–10. "But as it is written, Eye hath not seen, nor ear heard, neither have entered into the heart of man, the things which God hath prepared for them that love him. But God hath revealed them unto us by his Spirit: for the Spirit searcheth all things, yea, the deep things of God."

1 Timothy 6:10–11. "For the love of money is the root of all evil: which while some coveted after, they have erred from the faith, and pierced themselves through with many sorrows. But thou, O man of God, flee these things; and follow after righteousness, godliness, faith, love, patience, meekness."

2 Timothy 1:7. "For God hath not given us the spirit of fear; but of power, and of love, and of a sound mind."

1 John 4:7–8. "Beloved, let us love one another: for love is of God; and every one that loveth is born of God, and knoweth God. He that loveth not knoweth not God; for God is love."

2 Nephi 31:20. "Wherefore, ye must press forward with a steadfastness in Christ, having a perfect brightness of hope, and a love of God and of all men. Wherefore, if ye shall press forward, feasting upon the word of Christ, and endure to the end, behold, thus saith the Father: Ye shall have eternal life."

Mosiah 3:19. "For the natural man is an enemy to God, and has been from the fall of Adam, and will be, forever and ever, unless he yields to the enticings of the Holy Spirit, and putteth off the natural man and becometh a saint through the atonement of Christ the Lord, and becometh as a child, submissive, meek, humble, patient, full of love, willing to submit to all things which the Lord seeth fit to inflict upon him, even as a child doth submit to his father."

Moroni 7:47–48. "But charity is the pure love of Christ, and it endureth forever; and whoso is found possessed of it at the last day, it shall be well with him. Wherefore, my beloved brethren, pray unto the Father with all the energy of heart, that ye may be filled with this love, which he hath bestowed upon all who are true followers of his Son, Jesus Christ; that ye may become the sons of God; that when he shall appear we shall be like him, for we shall see him as he is; that we may have this hope; that we may be purified even as he is pure."

What are the key sources of love?

God. Moroni 7:13. "But behold, that which is of God inviteth and enticeth to do good continually; wherefore, every thing which inviteth and enticeth to do good, and to love God, and to serve him, is inspired of God." (See also Moroni 7:47–48.)

Obedience to the commandments. D&C 6:20. "Behold, thou art Oliver, and I have spoken unto thee because of thy desires; therefore treasure up these words in thy heart. Be faithful and diligent in keeping the commandments of God, and I will encircle thee in the arms of my love."

The Atonement of Jesus Christ. Alma 5:9. "And again I ask, were the bands of death broken, and the chains of hell which encircled them about, were they loosed? I say unto you, Yea, they were loosed, and their souls did expand, and they did sing redeeming love. And I say unto you that they are saved." (See also Mosiah 3:19; 4:11–12; Alma 5:26.)

The bridling of passions. Alma 38:12. "Use boldness, but not overbearance; and also see that ye bridle all your passions, that ye may be filled with love; see that ye refrain from idleness."

The Holy Ghost. Romans 5:5. "And hope maketh not ashamed; because the love of God is shed abroad in our hearts by the Holy Ghost which is given unto us." (See also Galatians 5:22–23; Alma 13:27–29; Moroni 8:26.)

The teachings of God's worthy servants. Mosiah 2:4. "And also that they might give thanks to the Lord their God, who had brought them out of the land of Jerusalem, and who had delivered them out of the hands of their enemies, and had appointed just men to be their teachers, and also a just man to be their king, who had established peace in the land of Zarahemla, and who had taught them to keep the commandments of God, that they might rejoice and be filled with love towards God and all men." (See also Mosiah 4:14–15.)

The word of the Lord. Alma 26:13–15. "Behold, how many thousands of our brethren has he loosed from the pains of hell; and they are brought to sing redeeming love, and this because of the power of his word which is in us, therefore have we not great reason to rejoice? Yea, we have reason to praise him forever, for he is the Most High God, and has loosed our brethren from the chains of hell. Yea, they were encircled about with everlasting darkness and destruction; but behold, he has brought them into his everlasting light, yea, into everlasting salvation; and they are encircled about with the matchless bounty of his love; yea, and we have been instruments in his hands of doing this great and marvelous work."

WORDS OF THE PROPHETS | **Joseph Smith speaks about love.** "Love is one of the chief characteristics of Deity, and ought to be manifested by those who aspire to be the sons of God. A man filled with the love of God, is not content with blessing his family alone, but ranges through the whole world, anxious to bless the whole human race." —Joseph Smith, *HC* 4:227.

MAGNIFYING YOUR CALLING [51]. To "magnify," as used in the scriptures, means to make greater, to make more splendid. There are at least four kinds of magnifying evidenced in the gospel. First, there is the process of magnifying an office by accepting it with humility, gratitude, soberness, and devotion. By doing so, we next magnify the Lord and enlarge His holy name before the world. This process results in our being magnified ourselves through His blessings unto us, thus allowing us to magnify the gospel message for others so that the pathway to salvation and exaltation is illuminated with the light of Christ. This four-fold process of enlargement—the eternal circle of service in which we magnify an office, magnify the Lord, magnify ourselves, and magnify the gospel—is a buoyant force, a lifting force. When the four stages are completed, the cycle starts again at a higher level. Thus we see emerging a magnificent spiral that carries us ever upward as we contribute to and are nurtured by the process of magnification. What a grand and magnanimous blessing it is to have part in such a program of enlargement as the kingdom of God expands and grows like the stone that was cut from the mountain without hands and rolls forth to fill the whole world (Daniel 2:34–35; D&C 65:2).

Magnifying an office. Jacob 1:19. "And we did magnify our office unto the Lord, taking upon us the responsibility, answering the sins of the people upon our own heads if we did not teach them the word of God with all diligence; wherefore, by laboring with our might their blood might not come upon our garments; otherwise their blood would come upon our garments, and we would not be found spotless at the last day."

Magnifying the Lord. 2 Nephi 25:13. "Wherefore, my soul delighteth to prophesy concerning him, for I have seen his day, and my heart doth magnify his holy name."

Magnify the person serving. Joshua 3:7. "And the Lord said unto Joshua, This day will I begin to magnify thee in the sight of all Israel, that they may know that, as I was with Moses, so I will be with thee."

Magnify the gospel plan. Isaiah 42:21. "The Lord is well pleased for his righteousness' sake; he will magnify the law, and make it honourable."

WORDS OF THE PROPHETS | **Howard W. Hunter on the Lord providing ways to magnify callings.** "The Lord never calls a man to any office in his Church but what he will by revelation help that man to magnify his calling." —Howard W. Hunter, *The Teachings of Howard W. Hunter*, ed. Clyde J. Williams (Salt Lake City: Bookcraft, 1997), 215.

MARRIAGE [33]. In "The Family: A Proclamation to the World" (1995), the fundamental role of the family in the divine plan of happiness is confirmed: "We, the First Presidency and the Council of the Twelve Apostles of The Church of Jesus Christ of Latter-day Saints, solemnly proclaim that marriage between a man and a woman is ordained of God and that the family is central to the Creator's plan for the eternal destiny of His children." Through obedience to the will of God and by virtue of the power and efficacy of the priesthood, families can endure as celestial units through all eternity.

Genesis 1:27–28. "So God created man in his own image, in the image of God created he him; male and female created he them. And God blessed them, and God said unto them, Be fruitful, and multiply, and replenish the earth, and subdue it: and have dominion over the fish of the sea, and over the fowl of the air, and over every living thing that moveth upon the earth." (See also Moses 2:27–28.)

Genesis 2:18, 21–24. "And the Lord God said, It is not good that the man should be alone; I will make him an help meet for him. . . . And the Lord God caused a deep sleep to fall upon Adam, and he slept: and he took one of his ribs, and closed up the flesh instead thereof; And the rib, which the Lord God had taken from man, made he a woman, and brought her unto the man. And Adam said, This is now bone of my bones, and flesh of my flesh: she shall be called Woman, because she was taken out of Man. Therefore shall a man leave his father and his mother, and shall cleave unto his wife: and they shall be one flesh." (See also Moses 3:18, 21–24.)

1 Corinthians 11:11–12. "Nevertheless neither is the man without the woman, neither the woman without the man, in the Lord. For as the woman is of the man, even so is the man also by the woman; but all things of God."

Hebrews 13:4. "Marriage is honourable in all."

What are the conditions placed by the Lord on the marriage relationship?

Cooperation. Ephesians 5:22–23. "Wives, submit yourselves unto your own husbands, as unto the Lord. For the husband is the head of the wife, even as Christ is the head of the church: and he is the saviour of the body."

Fidelity. D&C 42:22. "Thou shalt love thy wife with all thy heart, and shalt cleave unto her and none else."

Living in keeping with the promises of the Lord. 4 Nephi 1:10–11. "And now, behold, it came to pass that the people of Nephi did wax strong, and did multiply exceedingly fast, and became an exceedingly fair and delightsome people. And they were married, and given in marriage, and were blessed according to the multitude of the promises which the Lord had made unto them."

Purity. D&C 42:23–26. "And he that looketh upon a woman to lust after her shall deny the faith, and shall not have the Spirit; and if he repents not he shall be cast out. Thou shalt not commit adultery; and he that committeth adultery, and repenteth not, shall be cast out. But he that has committed adultery and repents with all his heart, and forsaketh it, and doeth it no more, thou shalt forgive; But if he doeth it again, he shall not be forgiven, but shall be cast out."

What do the scriptures teach about the principle of celestial marriage?

Essential for obtaining the highest degree of glory. D&C 131:1–4. "In the celestial glory there are three heavens or degrees; And in order to obtain the highest, a man must enter into this order of the priesthood [meaning the new and everlasting covenant of marriage]; And if he does not, he cannot obtain it. He may enter into the other, but that is the end of his kingdom; he cannot have an increase."

The pathway to eternal increase. D&C 132:19. "And again, verily I say unto you, if a man marry a wife by my word, which is my law, and by the new and everlasting covenant, and it is sealed unto them by the Holy Spirit of promise, by him who is anointed, unto whom I have appointed this power and the keys of this priesthood; and it shall be said unto them—Ye shall come forth in the first resurrection; and if it be after the first resurrection, in the next resurrection; and shall inherit thrones, kingdoms, principalities, and powers, dominions, all heights and depths—then shall it be written in the Lamb's Book of Life, that he shall commit no murder whereby to shed innocent blood, and if ye abide in my covenant, and commit no murder whereby to shed innocent blood, it shall be done unto them in all things whatsoever my servant hath put upon them, in time, and through all eternity; and shall be of full force when they are out of the world; and they shall pass by the angels, and the gods, which are set there, to their exaltation and glory in all things, as hath been sealed upon their heads, which glory shall be a fulness and a continuation of the seeds forever and ever."

Consummated through the sealing powers of the priesthood. Matthew 16:19. "And I will give unto thee the keys of the kingdom of heaven: and whatsoever thou shalt bind on earth shall be bound in heaven: and whatsoever thou shalt loose on earth shall be loosed in heaven."

MERCY [550]. The Lord is the God of mercy. Mercy is the divine quality that loves, creates, enlivens, guides, gathers, forgives, redeems, comforts, heals, and exalts the sons and daughters of the covenant through the power of the Atonement. Mercy brings all mankind, as immortals, before the bar of justice for an accounting of all thoughts, desires, and deeds prior to consignment to the eternal abode (whether to glory or darkness) that accords with the level obedience and faithfulness demonstrated. Without mercy, we would all be consigned to darkness without the beneficent intercession of the Lord, but because of mercy, we, through Christ, do have a final judgment and can, through worthiness, attain glory.

1 Chronicles 16:34. "O give thanks unto the Lord; for he is good; for his mercy endureth for ever.

Isaiah 49:13. "Sing, O heavens; and be joyful, O earth; and break forth into singing, mountains: for the Lord hath comforted his people, and will have mercy upon his afflicted."

Micah 6:8. "He hath shewed thee, O man, what is good; and what doth the Lord require of thee, but to do justly, and to love mercy, and to walk humbly with thy God?"

Matthew 5:7. "Blessed are the merciful: for they shall obtain mercy." (See also 3 Nephi 12:7.)

Luke 6:36. "Be ye therefore merciful, as your Father also is merciful."

James 3:17–18. "But the wisdom that is from above is first pure, then peaceable, gentle, and easy to be intreated, full of mercy and good fruits, without partiality, and without hypocrisy. And the fruit of righteousness is sown in peace of them that make peace."

1 Nephi 1:20. "And when the Jews heard these things they were angry with him [Lehi]; yea, even as with the prophets of old, whom they had cast out, and stoned, and slain; and they also sought his life, that they might take it away. But behold, I, Nephi, will show unto you that the tender mercies of the Lord are over all those whom he hath chosen, because of their faith, to make them mighty even unto the power of deliverance."

Jacob 4:10. "Wherefore, brethren, seek not to counsel the Lord, but to take counsel from his hand. For behold, ye yourselves know that he counseleth in wisdom, and in justice, and in great mercy, over all his works."

Mosiah 29:20. "But behold, he did deliver them because they did humble themselves before him; and because they cried mightily unto him he did deliver them out of bondage; and thus doth the Lord work with his power in all cases among the children of men, extending the arm of mercy towards them that put their trust in him."

Alma 26:37. "Now my brethren, we see that God is mindful of every people, whatsoever land they may be in; yea, he numbereth his people, and his bowels of mercy are over all the earth. Now this is my joy, and my great thanksgiving; yea, and I will give thanks unto my God forever."

Alma 34:15–18. "And thus he shall bring salvation to all those who shall believe on his name; this being the intent of this last sacrifice, to bring about the bowels of mercy, which overpowereth justice, and bringeth about means unto men that they may have faith unto repentance. And thus mercy can satisfy the demands of justice, and encircles them in the arms of safety, while he that exercises no faith unto repentance is exposed to the whole law of the demands of justice; therefore only unto him that has faith unto repentance is brought about the great and eternal plan of redemption. Therefore may God grant unto you, my brethren, that ye may begin to exercise your faith unto repentance, that ye begin to call upon his holy name, that he would have mercy upon you; Yea, cry unto him for mercy; for he is mighty to save."

Alma 34:37–38. "And now, my beloved brethren, I desire that ye should remember these things, and that ye should work out your salvation with fear before God, and that ye should no more deny the coming of Christ; That ye contend no more against the Holy Ghost, but that ye receive it, and take upon you the name of Christ; that ye humble yourselves even to the dust, and worship God, in whatsoever place ye may be in, in spirit and in truth; and that ye live in thanksgiving daily, for the many mercies and blessings which he doth bestow upon you."

Alma 42:15. "And now, the plan of mercy could not be brought about except an atonement should be made; therefore God himself atoneth for the sins of the world, to bring about the plan of mercy, to appease the demands of justice, that God might be a perfect, just God, and a merciful God also."

3 Nephi 9:14. "Yea, verily I say unto you, if ye will come unto me ye shall have eternal life. Behold, mine arm of mercy is extended towards you, and whosoever will come, him will I receive; and blessed are those who come unto me."

Moroni 10:3. "Behold, I would exhort you that when ye shall read these things, if it be wisdom in God that ye should read them, that ye would remember how merciful the Lord hath been unto the children of men, from the creation of Adam even down until the time that ye shall receive these things, and ponder it in your hearts."

MILLENNIUM [2]. The Millennium, comprising the final thousand years of the earth's history prior to its celestialization, will be ushered in with the dawning glory of the Second Coming of our Lord and Savior Jesus Christ. During the Millennium, "Christ will reign personally upon the earth" (Tenth Article of Faith). Because telestial culture will have been eradicated through the cleansing of the earth, peace will finally be established and righteousness will prevail. Enmity among all the Lord's creatures will cease. Satan will be bound and have no power over the people. There will be grand opportunities during the Millennium for the Saints, being of a celestial order, to preach the gospel among those of a terrestrial order and spread the good news about the Atonement and the saving and exalting ordinances of the gospel. Revelation will be poured out and temple work will abound. After the thousand years have ended, Satan will be loosed for a season until Michael and his hosts defeat the forces of evil and consign them to their eternal isolation in darkness. Then the earth will be celestialized, and the obedient and faithful will attain to an everlasting heritage of glory and eternal lives, having been perfected in Christ and made joint heirs with Him forever.

Isaiah 2:4–5. "And he shall judge among the nations, and shall rebuke many people: and they shall beat their swords into plowshares, and their spears into pruninghooks: nation shall not lift up sword against nation, neither shall they learn war any more. O house of Jacob, come ye, and let us walk in the light of the Lord."

Isaiah 11:6–9. "The wolf also shall dwell with the lamb, and the leopard shall lie down with the kid; and the calf and the young lion and the fatling together; and a little child shall lead them. And the cow and the bear shall feed; their young ones shall lie down together: and the lion shall eat straw like the ox. And the sucking child shall play on the hole of the asp, and the weaned child shall put his hand on the cockatrice' den. They shall not hurt nor destroy in all my holy mountain: for the earth shall be full of the knowledge of the Lord, as the waters cover the sea."

Isaiah 54:13–14. "And all thy children shall be taught of the Lord; and great shall be the peace of thy children. In righteousness shalt thou be established: thou shalt be far from oppression; for thou shalt not fear: and from terror; for it shall not come near thee." (See also 3 Nephi 22:13-14.)

Matthew 6:10. "Thy kingdom come. Thy will be done in earth, as it is in heaven." (See also Luke 11:2; 3 Nephi 13:9–13.)

D&C 29:11. "For I will reveal myself from heaven with power and great glory, with all the hosts thereof, and dwell in righteousness with men on earth a thousand years, and the wicked shall not stand."

D&C 43:29–33. "For in mine own due time will I come upon the earth in judgment, and my people shall be redeemed and shall reign with me on earth. For the great Millennium, of which I have spoken by the mouth of my servants, shall come. For Satan shall be bound, and when he is loosed again he shall only reign for a little season, and then cometh the end of the earth. And he that liveth in righteousness shall be changed in the twinkling of an eye, and the earth shall pass away so as by fire. And the wicked shall go away into unquenchable fire, and their end no man knoweth on earth, nor ever shall know, until they come before me in judgment."

D&C 77:12. "Q. What are we to understand by the sounding of the trumpets, mentioned in the 8th chapter of Revelation? A. We are to understand that as God made the world in six days, and on the seventh day he finished his work, and sanctified it, and also formed man out of the dust of the earth, even so, in the beginning of the seventh thousand years will the Lord God sanctify the earth, and complete the salvation of man, and judge all things, and shall redeem all things, except that which he hath not put into his power, when he shall have sealed all things, unto the end of all things; and the sounding of the trumpets of the seven angels are the preparing and finishing of his work, in the beginning of the seventh thousand years—the preparing of the way before the time of his coming."

D&C 130:1–2. "When the Savior shall appear we shall see him as he is. We shall see that he is a man like ourselves. And that same sociality which exists among us here will exist among us there, only it will be coupled with eternal glory, which glory we do not now enjoy."

Moses 7:63–65. "And the Lord said unto Enoch: Then shalt thou and all thy city meet them there, and we will receive them into our bosom, and they shall see us; and we will fall upon their necks, and they shall fall upon our necks, and we will kiss each other; And there shall be mine abode, and it shall be Zion, which shall come forth out of all the creations which I have made; and for the space of a thousand years the earth shall rest. And it came to pass that Enoch saw the day of the coming of the Son of Man, in the last days, to dwell on the earth in righteousness for the space of a thousand years."

Words of the Prophets | John Taylor on the ruling power of the priesthood. "When the will of God is done on earth as it is in heaven, that Priesthood will be the only legitimate ruling power under the whole heavens; for every other power and influence will be subject to it. When the millennium . . . is introduced, all potentates, powers, and authorities—every man, woman, and child will be in subjection to the kingdom of God; they will be under the power and dominion of the Priesthood of God: then the will of God will be done on the earth as it is done in heaven." —John Taylor, "The Kingdom of God or Nothing," *Journal of Discourses*, 6:25, November 1, 1857.

MISSIONARY WORK [0]. We can all contribute to the growth of the kingdom of God by embarking with faith, devotion, and courage upon the pathway of missionary service. Nephi declared: "For we labor diligently to write, to persuade our children, and also our brethren, to believe in Christ, and to be reconciled to God; for we know that it is by grace that we are saved, after all we can do" (2 Nephi 25:23). It is within the framework of "all we can do" that the vision and opportunity of missionary work arises in its refulgent glory. The degree of our commitment to this covenant principle will in large measure determine our worthiness before the Lord of grace and mercy when the hour of accountability arrives. By following the example of superlative missionaries, such as Peter and Paul, Alma and Amulek, the sons of

Mosiah, and many others in the Lord's vineyard, we can do our part in helping to build the kingdom of God with compassion and devotion.

Matthew 4:18–20. "And Jesus, walking by the sea of Galilee, saw two brethren, Simon called Peter, and Andrew his brother, casting a net into the sea: for they were fishers. And he saith unto them, Follow me, and I will make you fishers of men. And they straightway left their nets, and followed him." (See also Mark 1:16–18.)

Matthew 28:19–20. "Go ye therefore, and teach all nations, baptizing them in the name of the Father, and of the Son, and of the Holy Ghost: Teaching them to observe all things whatsoever I have commanded you: and, lo, I am with you alway, even unto the end of the world."

Mark 16:15–16. "And he said unto them, Go ye into all the world, and preach the gospel to every creature. He that believeth and is baptized shall be saved; but he that believeth not shall be damned."

1 Peter 3:15. "But sanctify the Lord God in your hearts: and be ready always to give an answer to every man that asketh you a reason of the hope that is in you with meekness and fear."

Mosiah 28:3. "Now they [sons of Mosiah] were desirous that salvation should be declared to every creature, for they could not bear that any human soul should perish; yea, even the very thoughts that any soul should endure endless torment did cause them to quake and tremble."

3 Nephi 12:16. "Therefore let your light so shine before this people, that they may see your good works and glorify your Father who is in heaven." (See also Matthew 5:16.)

D&C 18:15–16. "And if it so be that you should labor all your days in crying repentance unto this people, and bring, save it be one soul unto me, how great shall be your joy with him in the kingdom of my Father! And now, if your joy will be great with one soul that you have brought unto me into the kingdom of my Father, how great will be your joy if you should bring many souls unto me!"

D&C 88:81. "Behold, I sent you out to testify and warn the people, and it becometh every man who hath been warned to warn his neighbor."

Abraham 2:9–11. "And I will make of thee a great nation, and I will bless thee above measure, and make thy name great among all nations, and thou shalt be a blessing unto thy seed after thee, that in their hands they shall bear this ministry and Priesthood unto all nations; And I will bless them through thy name; for as many as receive this Gospel shall be called after thy name, and shall be accounted thy seed, and shall rise up and bless thee, as their father; And I will bless them that bless thee, and curse them that curse thee; and in thee (that is, in thy Priesthood) and in thy seed (that is, thy Priesthood), for I give unto thee a promise that this right shall continue in thee, and in thy seed after thee (that is to say, the literal seed, or the seed of the body) shall all the families of the earth be blessed, even with the blessings of the Gospel, which are the blessings of salvation, even of life eternal." (See also D&C 132:31–32.)

What are the essential ingredients of successful missionary work?

Be a righteous example. 3 Nephi 18:24. "Therefore, hold up your light that it may shine unto the world. Behold I am the light which ye shall hold up—that which ye have seen me do. Behold ye see that I have prayed unto the Father, and ye all have witnessed." (See also Matthew 5:16; 3 Nephi 12:16; D&C 115:5–6.)

Be bold yet temperate. Alma 38:12. "Use boldness, but not overbearance; and also see that ye bridle all your passions, that ye may be filled with love; see that ye refrain from idleness."

Be patient. Alma 26:27. "Now when our hearts were depressed, and we were about to turn back, behold, the Lord comforted us, and said: Go amongst thy brethren, the Lamanites, and bear with patience thine afflictions, and I will give unto you success."

Cultivate desire and commitment. Alma 29:9–10. "I [Alma] do not glory of myself, but I glory in that which the Lord hath commanded me; yea, and this is my glory, that perhaps I may be an instrument in the hands of God to bring some soul to repentance; and this is my joy." (See also Mosiah 28:3.)

Cultivate love and compassion. Luke 22:32. "I have prayed for thee, that thy faith fail not: and when thou art converted, strengthen thy brethren." (See also Romans 5:5; Galatians 5:22; 1 Thessalonians 1:3; Enos 1:9–11; Mosiah 18:8–9; Moroni 7:48; D&C 12:8; 108:7.)

Cultivate the divine nature. D&C 4:5–6. "And faith, hope, charity and love, with an eye single to the glory of God, qualify him for the work. Remember faith, virtue, knowledge, temperance, patience, brotherly kindness, godliness, charity, humility, diligence." (See also 2 Peter 1:4–8.)

Depend upon the strength and support of the Lord. Proverbs 3:5–6. "Trust in the Lord with all thine heart; and lean not unto thine own understanding. In all thy ways acknowledge him, and he shall direct thy paths." (See also 1 Peter 3:15; Alma 26:11–13; D&C 84:87–88.)

Find those seeking the truth. D&C 123:12. "For there are many yet on the earth among all sects, parties, and denominations, who are blinded by the subtle craftiness of men, whereby they lie in wait to deceive, and who are only kept from the truth because they know not where to find it."

Follow the Spirit. Mark 13:11. "But when they shall lead you, and deliver you up, take no thought beforehand what ye shall speak, neither do ye premeditate: but whatsoever shall be given you in that hour, that speak ye: for it is not ye that speak, but the Holy Ghost." (See also Luke 12:11–12; 21:14–15; John 15:26–27; 1 Corinthians 12:3; 2 Nephi 31:18; 32:5; Alma 21:16–17; 3 Nephi 11:32–33; Moroni 10:3–5; D&C 42:6; 42:13–14; 68:2–6; D&C 84:85; D&C 100:5–8; D&C 124:97; Moses 1:24.)

Give it your all. D&C 4:1–4. "Now behold, a marvelous work is about to come forth among the children of men. Therefore, O ye that embark in the service of God, see that ye serve him with all your heart, might, mind and strength, that ye may stand blameless before God at the last day. Therefore, if ye have desires to serve God ye are called to the work; For behold the field is white already to harvest; and lo, he that thrusteth in his sickle with his might, the same layeth up in store that he perisheth not, but bringeth salvation to his soul." (See also Jacob 5:71; D&C 6:3–5; 11:3–5; 24:7; 82:3.)

Have the courage to speak out. D&C 28:16. "And thou must open thy mouth at all times, declaring my gospel with the sound of rejoicing." (See also D&C 33:8–11; 60:2–3.)

Keep the commandments of the Lord. D&C 11:9. "Say nothing but repentance unto this generation. Keep my commandments, and assist to bring forth my work, according to my commandments, and you shall be blessed."

Keep the Lord foremost in mind while serving others. Matthew 25:40. "And the King shall answer and say unto them, Verily I say unto you, Inasmuch as ye have done it unto one of the least of these my brethren, ye have done it unto me." (See also Mosiah 2:17.)

Labor with the promised joy in mind. Jacob 5:71. "And the Lord of the vineyard said unto them: Go to, and labor in the vineyard, with your might. For behold, this is the last time that I shall nourish my vineyard; for the end is nigh at hand, and the season speedily cometh; and if ye labor with your might with me ye shall have joy in the fruit which I shall lay up unto myself against the time which will soon come." (See also Alma 29:9–10; D&C 18:15–16.)

Purify yourself. D&C 112:28. "But purify your hearts before me; and then go ye into all the world, and preach my gospel unto every creature who has not received it."

Study and pray. Alma 6:6. "Nevertheless the children of God were commanded that they should gather themselves together oft, and join in fasting and mighty prayer in behalf of the welfare of the souls of those who knew not God." (See also Alma 17:2–4; 26:21–22; D&C 4:7; 11:21; 88:78–80; 90:24.)

Teach from the Book of Mormon (subtitle: "Another Testament of Jesus Christ"). D&C 20:8–12. "And gave him power from on high, by the means which were before prepared, to translate the Book of Mormon; Which contains a record of a fallen people, and the fulness of the gospel of Jesus Christ to the Gentiles and to the Jews also; Which was given by inspiration, and is confirmed to others by the ministering of angels, and is declared unto the world by them— Proving to the world that the holy scriptures are true, and that God does inspire men and call them to his holy work in this age and generation, as well as in generations of old; Thereby showing that he is the same God yesterday, today, and forever." (See also D&C 84:57.)

Teach rather than be taught. D&C 43:15. "Again I say, hearken ye elders of my church, whom I have appointed: Ye are not sent forth to be taught, but to teach the children of men the things which I have put into your hands by the power of my Spirit."

WORDS OF THE PROPHETS | **Joseph Smith on the progression of missionary work.** "Our missionaries are going forth to different nations, and in Germany, Palestine, New Holland, Australia, the East Indies, and other places, the Standard of Truth has been erected; no unhallowed hand can stop the work from progressing; persecutions may rage, mobs may combine, armies may assemble, calumny may defame, but the truth of God will go forth boldly, nobly, and independent, till it has penetrated every continent, visited every clime, swept every country, and sounded in every ear, till the purposes of God shall be accomplished, and the Great Jehovah shall say the work is done." —Joseph Smith, *HC* 4:540.

Harold B. Lee on developing a testimony and sharing it. "The most important responsibility that you . . . have is to see that you are converted. That is number one. In this sense, all of us should be converts to the Church. We should all be converted to the truthfulness of the gospel. Then we can share this truth with others." —Harold B. Lee, "When Your Heart Tells You Things Your Mind Does Not Know," *New Era*, February 1971, 2–4.

Ezra Taft Benson on missionary work. "One of the greatest secrets of missionary work is work. If a missionary works, he will get the Spirit; if he gets the Spirit, he will teach by the Spirit; if he teaches by the Spirit, he will touch the hearts of the people, and he will be happy. Then there will be no homesickness nor worrying about families, for all time and talents and interests are centered on the work of the ministry. Work, work, work—there is no satisfactory substitute, especially in missionary work." —Ezra Taft Benson, *Come unto Christ* (Salt Lake City: Deseret Book, 1983), 95; "I have a conviction: The more we teach and preach from the Book of Mormon, the more we shall please the Lord and the greater will be our power of speaking. By so doing, we shall greatly increase our converts, both within the Church and among those we proselyte. The Lord expects us to use this book, and we remain under His condemnation if we do not (see D&C 84:57)" —Ezra Taft Benson, *The Teachings of Ezra Taft Benson* (Salt Lake City: Bookcraft, 1988), 58.
Cross reference to "Missionary Work": see Preach My Gospel, *the most comprehensive manual on missionary work available.*

MIRACLES [96]. From the perspective of man, the Father's divine plan of immortality and eternal life—in all its glory and magnificence—is a transcendent miracle: the Creation is a miracle; the Atonement of Jesus Christ is a miracle; the operation of the Holy Spirit for the blessing of God's children is a miracle; rebirth with a mighty change of heart for the obedient and faithful is a miracle; the inexorable unfolding of the kingdom of God on the earth is a miracle; the ever-expanding canon of scripture is a miracle; the coming heritage of glory and eternal lives for the righteous is a miracle—all of these magnificent blessings from heaven being the key to eternal happiness and joy. In addition, those who follow in the footsteps of the Master and seek to do good have a touch of a miracle empowered in their service that enables them to do things of a miraculous nature for the blessing of mankind, for that is the promise of the Father and Son.

2 Nephi 27:23. "For behold, I am God; and I am a God of miracles; and I will show unto the world that I am the same yesterday, today, and forever; and I work not among the children of men save it be according to their faith."

Mormon 9:10–11. "And now, if ye have imagined up unto yourselves a god who doth vary, and in whom there is shadow of changing, then have ye imagined up unto yourselves a god who is not a God of miracles. But behold, I will show unto you a God of miracles, even the God of Abraham, and the God of Isaac, and the God of Jacob; and it is that same God who created the heavens and the earth, and all things that in them are." (See also verses 9–20.)

Ether 12:11–12, 18. "Wherefore, by faith was the law of Moses given. But in the gift of his Son hath God prepared a more excellent way; and it is by faith that it hath been fulfilled. For if there be no faith among the children of men God can do no miracle among them; wherefore, he showed not himself until after their faith. . . . And neither at any time hath any wrought miracles until after their faith; wherefore they first believed in the Son of God."

Moroni 7:27–29, 33–37. "Wherefore, my beloved brethren, have miracles ceased because Christ hath ascended into heaven, and hath sat down on the right hand of God, to claim of the Father his rights of mercy which he hath upon the children of men? For he hath answered the ends of the law, and he claimeth all those who have faith in him; and they who have faith in him will cleave unto every good thing; wherefore he advocateth the cause of the children of men; and he dwelleth eternally in the heavens. And because he hath done this, my beloved brethren, have miracles ceased? Behold I say unto you, Nay; neither have angels ceased to minister unto the children of men. . . . And Christ hath said: If ye will have faith in me ye shall have power to do whatsoever thing is expedient in me. And he hath said: Repent all ye ends of the earth, and come unto me, and be baptized in my name, and have faith in me, that ye may be saved. And now, my beloved brethren, if this be the case that these things are true which I have spoken unto you, and God will show unto you, with power and great glory at the last day, that they are true, and if they are true has the day of miracles ceased? Or have angels ceased to appear unto the children of men? Or has he withheld the power of the Holy Ghost from them? Or will he, so long as time shall last, or the earth shall stand, or there shall be one man upon the face thereof to be saved? Behold I say unto you, Nay; for it is by faith that miracles are wrought; and it is by faith that angels appear and minister unto men; wherefore, if these things have ceased wo be unto the children of men, for it is because of unbelief, and all is vain."

D&C 45:8. "I came unto mine own, and mine own received me not; but unto as many as received me gave I power to do many miracles, and to become the sons of God; and even unto them that believed on my name gave I power to obtain eternal life."

Seventh Article of Faith. "We believe in the gift of tongues, prophecy, revelation, visions, healing, interpretation of tongues, and so forth."

MORTALITY [32]. Mortality is the short intermediate act in the magnificent three-act drama comprising our eternal journey of life. It is the brief temporal sojourn on earth following our premortal spiritual state in the presence of the Father and Son and preceding the ultimate and final state of immortality. Mortality is a probationary time in which each individual receives a mortal body and has the opportunity to use his or her God-given agency to obey the word of God, follow the Spirit, keep the commandments, and prepare to return to the heavenly home with honor and valor, being lifted through the Atonement and eternal grace to a state of glory and eternal life. In the strength of the Lord, we can endure the trials and tribulations of mortal life and endure to the end in joy and peace. The scriptures provide a blueprint for understanding the purpose and nature of life in mortality and how we can honor our covenants in preparation for the coming state of immortality and eternal life.

1 Corinthians 15:22. "For as in Adam all die, even so in Christ shall all be made alive."

2 Nephi 2:25. "Adam fell that men might be; and men are, that they might have joy."

2 Nephi 2:27. "Wherefore, men are free according to the flesh; and all things are given them which are expedient unto man. And they are free to choose liberty and eternal life, through the great Mediator of all men, or to choose captivity and death, according to the captivity and power of the devil; for he seeketh that all men might be miserable like unto himself."

Mosiah 3:19. "For the natural man is an enemy to God, and has been from the fall of Adam, and will be, forever and ever, unless he yields to the enticings of the Holy Spirit, and putteth off the natural man and becometh a saint through the atonement of Christ the Lord, and becometh as a child, submissive, meek, humble, patient, full of love, willing to submit to all things which the Lord seeth fit to inflict upon him, even as a child doth submit to his father."

Alma 11:45. "Now, behold, I have spoken unto you concerning the death of the mortal body, and also concerning the resurrection of the mortal body. I say unto you that this mortal body is raised to an immortal body, that is from death, even from the first death unto life, that they can die no more; their spirits uniting with their bodies, never to be divided; thus the whole becoming spiritual and immortal, that they can no more see corruption."

3 Nephi 12:48. "Therefore I would that ye should be perfect even as I, or your Father who is in heaven is perfect."

Ether 12:27. "And if men come unto me I will show unto them their weakness. I give unto men weakness that they may be humble; and my grace is sufficient for all men that humble themselves before me; for if they humble themselves before me, and have faith in me, then will I make weak things become strong unto them."

Moses 3:7. "And I, the Lord God, formed man from the dust of the ground, and breathed into his nostrils the breath of life; and man became a living soul, the first flesh upon the earth, the first man also; nevertheless, all things were before created; but spiritually were they created and made according to my word." (See also Abraham 5:7.)

Moses 5:10–11. "And in that day Adam blessed God and was filled, and began to prophesy concerning all the families of the earth, saying: Blessed be the name of God, for because of my transgression my eyes are opened, and in this life I shall have joy, and again in the flesh I shall see God. And Eve, his wife, heard all these things and was glad, saying: Were it not for our transgression we never should have had seed, and never should have known good and evil, and the joy of our redemption, and the eternal life which God giveth unto all the obedient."

Abraham 3:24–26. "And there stood one among them [in the premortal existence] that was like unto God, and he said unto those who were with him: We will go down, for there is space there, and we will take of these materials, and we will make an earth whereon these may dwell; And we will prove them herewith, to see if they will do all things whatsoever the Lord their God shall command them; And they who keep their first estate shall be added upon; and they who keep not their first estate shall not have glory in the same kingdom with those who keep their first estate; and they who keep their second estate shall have glory added upon their heads for ever and ever."

Words of the Prophets | **Gordon B. Hinckley on the mission of this life.** "Life is a mission, not just the sputtering of a candle between a chance lighting and a gust of wind that blows it out forever. . . . While here, we have learning to gain, work to do, service to give. We are here with a marvelous inheritance, a divine endowment. How different this world would be if every person realized that all of his actions have eternal consequences. How much more satisfying our years may be if in our accumulation of knowledge, in our relationships with others, in our business affairs, in our courtship and marriage, and in our family rearing, we recognize that we form each day the stuff of which eternity is made. . . . Life is forever. Live each day as if you were going to live eternally, for you surely shall." —Gordon B. Hinckley, "Pillars of Truth," *Ensign*, January 1994, 2–4.

OBEDIENCE [231]. Obedience is a commandment from God. Obedience is an act in which one is fully committed to keeping the Lord's commandments with honor and devotion. Obedience is the pathway to salvation and eternal life because it is a complete demonstration of one's willingness to do the Lord's will.

1 Samuel 15:22. "And Samuel said, Hath the Lord as great delight in burnt offerings and sacrifices, as in obeying the voice of the Lord? Behold, to obey is better than sacrifice, and to hearken than the fat of rams."

Acts 5:29. "Then Peter and the other apostles answered and said, We ought to obey God rather than men."

Mosiah 5:8. "And under this head [Jesus Christ] ye are made free, and there is no other head whereby ye can be made free. There is no other name given whereby salvation cometh; therefore, I would that ye should take upon you the name of Christ, all you that have entered into the covenant with God that ye should be obedient unto the end of your lives."

D&C 59:20–21. "And it pleaseth God that he hath given all these things unto man; for unto this end were they made to be used, with judgment, not to excess, neither by extortion. And in nothing doth man offend God, or against none is his wrath kindled, save those who confess not his hand in all things, and obey not his commandments."

D&C 63:5. "Behold, I, the Lord, utter my voice, and it shall be obeyed."

D&C 64:33–35. "Wherefore, be not weary in well-doing, for ye are laying the foundation of a great work. And out of small things proceedeth that which is great. Behold, the Lord requireth the heart and a willing mind; and the willing and obedient shall eat the good of the land of Zion in these last days. And the rebellious shall be cut off out of the land of Zion, and shall be sent away, and shall not inherit the land."

D&C 93:1. "Verily, thus saith the Lord: It shall come to pass that every soul who forsaketh his sins and cometh unto me, and calleth on my name, and obeyeth my voice, and keepeth my commandments, shall see my face and know that I am."

D&C 130:19–21. "And if a person gains more knowledge and intelligence in this life through his diligence and obedience than another, he will have so much the advantage in the world to come. There is a law, irrevocably decreed in heaven before the foundations of this world, upon which all blessings are predicated—And when we obtain any blessing from God, it is by obedience to that law upon which it is predicated."

Third Articles of Faith. "We believe that through the Atonement of Christ, all mankind may be saved, by obedience to the laws and ordinances of the Gospel."

Words of the Prophets | **Brigham Young on obeying with a willing heart.** "Every son and daughter of God is expected to obey with a willing heart every word which the Lord has spoken, and which He will in the future speak to us. It is expected that we hearken

to the revelations of His will, and adhere to them, cleave to them with all our might; for this is salvation, and any thing short of this clips the salvation and the glory of the Saints."
—Brigham Young, *Journal of Discourses,* 2:2, October 23, 1853.
Cross reference to "Obedience": see Preach My Gospel, *122.*

OPPOSITION IN ALL THINGS [7]. Man's agency operates in an environment of opposites, where choices between a duality of good and evil, righteousness and wickedness, valor and apostasy can be made—the former in each case leading to eternal life and the latter leading to damnation. It is the design of heaven that our choices accord fully with the divine plan of salvation and exaltation. Opposition helps us see the magnitude of God's grace and love in contrast to Satan's destruction and hatred.

2 Nephi 2:10–11, 15–16, 27. "And because of the intercession for all, all men come unto God; wherefore, they stand in the presence of him, to be judged of him according to the truth and holiness which is in him. Wherefore, the ends of the law which the Holy One hath given, unto the inflicting of the punishment which is affixed, which punishment that is affixed is in opposition to that of the happiness which is affixed, to answer the ends of the atonement—For it must needs be, that there is an opposition in all things. If not so, my first-born in the wilderness, righteousness could not be brought to pass, neither wickedness, neither holiness nor misery, neither good nor bad. Wherefore, all things must needs be a compound in one; wherefore, if it should be one body it must needs remain as dead, having no life neither death, nor corruption nor incorruption, happiness nor misery, neither sense nor insensibility. . . . And to bring about his eternal purposes in the end of man, after he had created our first parents, and the beasts of the field and the fowls of the air, and in fine, all things which are created, it must needs be that there was an opposition; even the forbidden fruit in opposition to the tree of life; the one being sweet and the other bitter. Wherefore, the Lord God gave unto man that he should act for himself. Wherefore, man could not act for himself save it should be that he was enticed by the one or the other. . . . Wherefore, men are free according to the flesh; and all things are given them which are expedient unto man. And they are free to choose liberty and eternal life, through the great Mediator of all men, or to choose captivity and death, according to the captivity and power of the devil; for he seeketh that all men might be miserable like unto himself."

PATIENCE [93]. To become like the Savior requires the enduring application of the virtue of patience. Patience is part of the divine nature—and it is our opportunity and commandment to become patient like unto the Father and the Son. The blessings of eternal life and exaltation depend upon our patience, as well as all the other related qualities we are counseled to inculcate into our lives, including faith, virtue, knowledge, temperance, brotherly kindness, godliness, charity, humility, and diligence. Patience is a manifestation of nobility of character and a governing virtue of success in all dimensions of life.

Luke 21:19. "In your patience possess ye your souls."

James 5:7–11. "Be patient therefore, brethren, unto the coming of the Lord. Behold, the husbandman waiteth for the precious fruit of the earth, and hath long patience for it, until he receive the early and latter rain. Be ye also patient; stablish your hearts: for the coming of the Lord draweth nigh. Grudge not one against another, brethren, lest ye be condemned: behold, the judge standeth before the door. Take, my brethren, the prophets, who have spoken in the name of the Lord, for an example of suffering affliction, and of patience. Behold, we count them happy which endure. Ye have heard of the patience of Job, and have seen the end of the Lord; that the Lord is very pitiful, and of tender mercy."

Alma 7:23. "And now I would that ye should be humble, and be submissive and gentle; easy to be entreated; full of patience and long-suffering; being temperate in all things; being diligent in keeping the commandments of God at all times; asking for whatsoever things ye stand in need, both spiritual and temporal; always returning thanks unto God for whatsoever things ye do receive."

D&C 4:6–7. "Remember faith, virtue, knowledge, temperance, patience, brotherly kindness, godliness, charity, humility, diligence. Ask, and ye shall receive; knock, and it shall be opened unto you."

D&C 101:37–38. "Therefore, care not for the body, neither the life of the body; but care for the soul, and for the life of the soul. And seek the face of the Lord always, that in patience ye may possess your souls, and ye shall have eternal life."

Words of the Prophets | **Ezra Taft Benson on having self-control.** "Patience is another form of self-control. It is the ability to postpone gratification and to bridle one's passions. In his relationships with loved ones, a patient man does not engage in impetuous behavior that he will later regret. Patience is composure under stress. A patient man is understanding of others' faults. A patient man also waits on the Lord. We sometimes read or hear of people who seek a blessing from the Lord, then grow impatient when it does not come swiftly. Part of the divine nature is to trust in the Lord enough to 'be still and know that [he is] God' (D&C 101:16). A priesthood holder who is patient will be tolerant of the mistakes and failings of his loved ones. Because he loves them, he will not find fault nor criticize nor blame." —Ezra Taft Benson, "Godly Characteristics of the Master," *Ensign*, November 1986, 47.

PATRIARCHAL BLESSINGS [1]. A patriarchal blessing, given to a worthy member of the Church by an authorized and ordained patriarch, is a unique and wonderful gift of personal revelation declaring one's assigned lineage in the family of God and presenting counsel and guidance for one's life, as well as promised blessings if one is true and faithful to his or her covenants with the Lord. A patriarchal blessing in our day (see D&C 124:92) is in accordance with the pattern of the priesthood blessings granted under inspiration by the ancient patriarchs to family members whose task it was to carry on the work of the Lord for the immortality and eternal life of His children.

Genesis 49:22–26. "Joseph is a fruitful bough, even a fruitful bough by a well; whose branches run over the wall: The archers have sorely grieved him, and shot at him, and hated him: But his bow abode in strength, and the arms of his hands were made strong by the hands of the mighty God of Jacob; (from thence is the shepherd, the stone of Israel:) Even by the God of thy father, who shall help thee; and by the Almighty, who shall bless thee with blessings of heaven above, blessings of the deep that lieth under, blessings of the breasts, and of the womb: The blessings of thy father have prevailed above the blessings of my progenitors unto the utmost bound of the everlasting hills: they shall be on the head of Joseph, and on the crown of the head of him that was separate from his brethren."

2 Nephi 3:1–3. "And now I speak unto you, Joseph, my last-born. Thou wast born in the wilderness of mine afflictions; yea, in the days of my greatest sorrow did thy mother bear thee. And may the Lord consecrate also unto thee this land, which is a most precious land, for thine inheritance and the inheritance of thy seed with thy brethren, for thy security forever, if it so be that ye shall keep the commandments of the Holy One of Israel. And now, Joseph, my last-born, whom I have brought out of the wilderness of mine afflictions, may the Lord bless thee forever, for thy seed shall not utterly be destroyed."

Words of the Prophets | **Ezra Taft Benson on studying patriarchal blessings.** "I would encourage you . . . to receive a patriarchal blessing. Study it carefully and regard it as personal scripture to you—for that is what it is. A patriarchal blessing is the inspired and prophetic statement of your life's mission together with blessings, cautions, and admonitions as the patriarch may be prompted to give. . . . [R]eceive your patriarchal blessing under the influence of fasting and prayer, and then read it regularly that you may know God's will for you." —Ezra Taft Benson, "To the Youth of the Noble Birthright," *Ensign*, May 1986, 43–44.

PEACE [615]. Peace, being one of the most desired and cherished of conditions, is a divine endowment of love and mercy from the Almighty and is reserved for those who follow the gospel path in righteousness and with enduring commitment and faith.

Psalm 29:11. "The Lord will give strength unto his people; the Lord will bless his people with peace."

Isaiah 9:6–7. "For unto us a child is born, unto us a son is given: and the government shall be upon his shoulder: and his name shall be called Wonderful, Counsellor, The mighty God, The everlasting Father, The Prince of Peace. Of the increase of his government and peace there shall be no end, upon the throne of David, and upon his kingdom, to order it, and to establish it with judgment and with justice from henceforth even for ever. The zeal of the Lord of hosts will perform this." (See also 2 Nephi 19:6–7.)

Isaiah 48:22. "There is no peace, saith the Lord, unto the wicked." (See also 1 Nephi 20:22.)

Ezekiel 37:25–26. "And they shall dwell in the land that I have given unto Jacob my servant, wherein your fathers have dwelt; and they shall dwell therein, even they, and their children, and their children's children for ever: and my servant David shall be their prince for ever. Moreover I will make a covenant of peace with them; it shall be an everlasting covenant with them: and I will place them, and multiply them, and will set my sanctuary in the midst of them for evermore."

Matthew 5:9. "Blessed are the peacemakers: for they shall be called the children of God." (See also 3 Nephi 12:9.)

Mark 4:39. "And he arose, and rebuked the wind, and said unto the sea, Peace, be still. And the wind ceased, and there was a great calm."

Luke 2:13–14. "And suddenly there was with the angel a multitude of the heavenly host praising God, and saying, Glory to God in the highest, and on earth peace, good will toward men."
John 14:27. "Peace I leave with you, my peace I give unto you: not as the world giveth, give I unto you. Let not your heart be troubled, neither let it be afraid."
John 16:32–33. "Behold, the hour cometh, yea, is now come, that ye shall be scattered, every man to his own, and shall leave me alone: and yet I am not alone, because the Father is with me. These things I have spoken unto you, that in me ye might have peace. In the world ye shall have tribulation: but be of good cheer; I have overcome the world."
Romans 5:1–2. "Therefore being justified by faith, we have peace with God through our Lord Jesus Christ: By whom also we have access by faith into this grace wherein we stand, and rejoice in hope of the glory of God."
Romans 8:6. "For to be carnally minded is death; but to be spiritually minded is life and peace."
1 Corinthians 14:33. "For God is not the author of confusion, but of peace, as in all churches of the saints."
2 Corinthians 13:11. "Finally, brethren, farewell. Be perfect, be of good comfort, be of one mind, live in peace; and the God of love and peace shall be with you."
James 3:17–18. "But the wisdom that is from above is first pure, then peaceable, gentle, and easy to be intreated, full of mercy and good fruits, without partiality, and without hypocrisy. And the fruit of righteousness is sown in peace of them that make peace."
Alma 40:11–12. "Now, concerning the state of the soul between death and the resurrection—Behold, it has been made known unto me by an angel, that the spirits of all men, as soon as they are departed from this mortal body, yea, the spirits of all men, whether they be good or evil, are taken home to that God who gave them life. And then shall it come to pass, that the spirits of those who are righteous are received into a state of happiness, which is called paradise, a state of rest, a state of peace, where they shall rest from all their troubles and from all care, and sorrow."
D&C 19:23–24. "Learn of me, and listen to my words; walk in the meekness of my Spirit, and you shall have peace in me. I am Jesus Christ; I came by the will of the Father, and I do his will."
D&C 39:5-6. "And verily, verily, I say unto you, he that receiveth my gospel receiveth me; and he that receiveth not my gospel receiveth not me. And this is my gospel—repentance and baptism by water, and then cometh the baptism of fire and the Holy Ghost, even the Comforter, which showeth all things, and teacheth the peaceable things of the kingdom."
D&C 42:61. "If thou shalt ask, thou shalt receive revelation upon revelation, knowledge upon knowledge, that thou mayest know the mysteries and peaceable things—that which bringeth joy, that which bringeth life eternal."
D&C 59:23. "But learn that he who doeth the works of righteousness shall receive his reward, even peace in this world, and eternal life in the world to come."
D&C 88:125. "And above all things, clothe yourselves with the bond of charity, as with a mantle, which is the bond of perfectness and peace."

PERFECTION [199]. It is a commandment of the Lord to be perfect (see Matthew 5:48; 3 Nephi 12:48). Our model for perfection is our Father in Heaven and His Son Jesus Christ. Those who achieve perfection will inherit an eternal heavenly abode in the presence of the Father and Son and an "innumerable company of angels" (Hebrews 12:22; D&C 76:67). Perfection is a process that unfolds through the application of a myriad of qualities, such as obedience, patience, humility, love, charity, service, and receiving and applying the word of God. Through the power and grace of the Lord as evidenced through the Atonement, the gateway to perfection is opened to all who are willing to receive light in greater and greater measure "until the perfect day" (D&C 50:24; Proverbs 4:18).

Psalm 37:37. "Mark the perfect man, and behold the upright: for the end of that man is peace."

Isaiah 26:3. "Thou wilt keep him in perfect peace, whose mind is stayed on thee: because he trusteth in thee."

Matthew 5:48. "Be ye therefore perfect, even as your Father which is in heaven is perfect." See also 3 Nephi 12:48—"Therefore I would that ye should be perfect even as I, or your Father who is in heaven is perfect."

2 Corinthians 13:11. "Be perfect, be of good comfort, be of one mind, live in peace; and the God of love and peace shall be with you."

Ephesians 4:11–13. "And he gave some, apostles; and some, prophets; and some, evangelists; and some, pastors and teachers; For the perfecting of the saints, for the work of the ministry, for the edifying of the body of Christ: Till we all come in the unity of the faith, and of the knowledge of the Son of God, unto a perfect man, unto the measure of the stature of the fulness of Christ."

Colossians 3:14. "And above all these things put on charity, which is the bond of perfectness." (See also D&C 88:125.)

2 Timothy 3:16–17. "All scripture is given by inspiration of God, and is profitable for doctrine, for reproof, for correction, for instruction in righteousness: That the man of God may be perfect, throughly furnished unto all good works."

Hebrews 5:9. "And being made perfect, he became the author of eternal salvation unto all them that obey him."

2 Nephi 9:23. "And he commandeth all men that they must repent, and be baptized in his name, having perfect faith in the Holy One of Israel, or they cannot be saved in the kingdom of God."

2 Nephi 31:20. "Wherefore, ye must press forward with a steadfastness in Christ, having a perfect brightness of hope, and a love of God and of all men. Wherefore, if ye shall press forward, feasting upon the word of Christ, and endure to the end, behold, thus saith the Father: Ye shall have eternal life."

Moroni 10:32–33. "Yea, come unto Christ, and be perfected in him, and deny yourselves of all ungodliness; and if ye shall deny yourselves of all ungodliness, and love God with all your might, mind and strength, then is his grace sufficient for you, that by his grace ye may be perfect in Christ; and if by the grace of God ye are perfect in Christ, ye can in nowise deny the power of God. And again, if ye by the grace of God are perfect in Christ, and deny not his power, then are ye sanctified in Christ by the grace of God, through the shedding of the blood of Christ, which is in the covenant of the Father unto the remission of your sins, that ye become holy, without spot."

D&C 50:24. "That which is of God is light; and he that receiveth light, and continueth in God, receiveth more light; and that light groweth brighter and brighter until the perfect day."

D&C 76:69. "These are they [of the Celestial kingdom] who are just men made perfect through Jesus the mediator of the new covenant, who wrought out this perfect atonement through the shedding of his own blood."

D&C 128:15, 18. "And now, my dearly beloved brethren and sisters, let me assure you that these are principles in relation to the dead and the living that cannot be lightly passed over, as pertaining to our salvation. For their salvation is necessary and essential to our salvation, as Paul says concerning the fathers—that they without us cannot be made perfect—neither can we without our dead be made perfect. . . . For we without them cannot be made perfect; neither can they without us be made perfect. Neither can they nor we be made perfect without those who have died in the gospel also; for it is necessary in the ushering in of the dispensation of the fulness of times, which dispensation is now beginning to usher in, that a whole and complete and perfect union, and welding together of dispensations, and keys, and powers, and glories should take place, and be revealed from the days of Adam even to the present time."

PLAN OF HAPPINESS [2; plus 29 similar alternatives]. The plan of happiness is the gospel of Jesus Christ. It is the plan of deliverance, mercy, redemption, and salvation. It is the "great plan of the Eternal God" (Alma 34:9)—empowered through the Atonement of the Only Begotten—through which the obedient and faithful can inherit eternal life and exaltation.

Alma 29:1–2. "O That I were an angel, and could have the wish of mine heart, that I might go forth and speak with the trump of God, with a voice to shake the earth, and cry repentance unto every people! Yea, I would declare unto every soul, as with the voice of thunder, repentance and the plan of redemption, that they should repent and come unto our God, that there might not be more sorrow upon all the face of the earth."

Alma 34:9–10. "For it is expedient that an atonement should be made; for according to the great plan of the Eternal God there must be an atonement made, or else all mankind must unavoidably perish; yea, all are hardened; yea, all are fallen and are lost, and must perish except it be through the atonement which it is expedient should be made. For it is expedient that there should be a great and last sacrifice; yea, not a sacrifice of man, neither of beast, neither of any manner of fowl; for it shall not be a human sacrifice; but it must be an infinite and eternal sacrifice."

How is the word* plan *(meaning God's plan of happiness or plan of salvation) used in the scriptures?

Alma to his son Corianton. Alma 42:7–8. "And now, ye see by this that our first parents were cut off both temporally and spiritually from the presence of the Lord; and thus we see they became subjects to follow after their own will. Now behold, it was not expedient that man should be reclaimed from this temporal death, for that would destroy the great plan of happiness. Therefore, as the soul could never die, and the fall had brought upon all mankind a spiritual death as well as a temporal, that is, they were cut off from the presence of the Lord, it was expedient that mankind should be reclaimed from this spiritual death." (See also Alma 42:16.)

Witness of Nephi. 2 Nephi 11:5–6. "And also my soul delighteth in the covenants of the Lord which he hath made to our fathers; yea, my soul delighteth in his grace, and in his justice, and power, and mercy in the great and eternal plan of deliverance from death. And my soul delighteth in proving unto my people that save Christ should come all men must perish."

Alma to his son Corianton. Alma 42:15, 31. "And now, the plan of mercy could not be brought about except an atonement should be made; therefore God himself atoneth for the sins of the world, to bring about the plan of mercy, to appease the demands of justice, that God might be a perfect, just God, and a merciful God also. . . . And now, O my son, ye are called of God to preach the word unto this people. And now, my son, go thy way, declare the word with truth and soberness, that thou mayest bring souls unto repentance, that the great plan of mercy may have claim upon them. And may God grant unto you even according to my words."

Jacob to the Saints of his day. Jacob 6:8. "Behold, will ye reject these words? Will ye reject the words of the prophets; and will ye reject all the words which have been spoken concerning Christ, after so many have spoken concerning him; and deny the good word of Christ, and the power of God, and the gift of the Holy Ghost, and quench the Holy Spirit, and make a mock of the great plan of redemption, which hath been laid for you?"

The Lord to Adam concerning the plan of salvation. Moses 6:57, 60–62. "Wherefore teach it unto your children, that all men, everywhere, must repent, or they can in nowise inherit the kingdom of God. . . . For by the water ye keep the commandment; by the Spirit ye are justified, and by the blood ye are sanctified; Therefore it is given to abide in you; the record of heaven; the Comforter; the peaceable things of immortal glory; the truth of all things; that which quickeneth all things, which maketh alive all things; that which knoweth all things, and hath all power according to wisdom, mercy, truth, justice, and judgment. And now, behold, I say unto you: This is the plan of salvation unto all men, through the blood of mine Only Begotten, who shall come in the meridian of time."

Amulek to the wayward Zoramites in the city of Antionum. Alma 34:9–10. "For it is expedient that an atonement should be made; for according to the great plan of the Eternal God there must be an atonement made, or else all mankind must unavoidably perish; yea, all are hardened; yea, all are fallen and are lost, and must perish except it be through the atonement which it is expedient should be made. For it is expedient that there should be a great and last sacrifice; yea, not a sacrifice of man, neither of beast, neither of any manner of fowl; for it shall not be a human sacrifice; but it must be an infinite and eternal sacrifice."

Alma to his son Corianton. Alma 41:1–2. "And now, my son, I have somewhat to say concerning the restoration of which has been spoken; for behold, some have wrested the scriptures, and have gone far astray because of this thing. And I perceive that thy mind has been worried also concerning this thing. But behold, I will explain it unto thee. I say unto thee, my son, that the plan of restoration is requisite with the justice of God; for it is requisite that all things should be restored to their proper order. Behold, it is requisite and just, according to the power and resurrection of Christ, that the soul of man should be restored to its body, and that every part of the body should be restored to itself."

Cross reference to "Plan of Happiness": see Preach My Gospel, *47–54.*

POSTMORTAL WORLD [0]. The great plan of happiness encompasses all stages of life: premortal, mortal, and postmortal. It is all part of the Lord's universal design for His children (see 1 Nephi 10:18–19). We learn in the scriptures that "Adam fell that men might be; and men are, that they might have joy" (2 Nephi 2:25). We also learn the indispensable nature and role of the Atonement for empowering the plan for achieving that joy (see Alma 42:15). Through modern-day revelation, we have marvelous confirmation of these truths in ways that inspire the mind and strengthen our resolve to prepare for our introduction into the spirit world—very much as "prisoners," temporarily separated from our bodies and awaiting the resurrection and the day of coming glory and eternal life, according to the divine plan of salvation and redemption.

Isaiah 61:1–2. "The Spirit of the Lord God is upon me; because the Lord hath anointed me to preach good tidings unto the meek; he hath sent me to bind up the brokenhearted, to proclaim liberty to the captives, and the opening of the prison to them that are bound; To proclaim the acceptable year of the Lord, and the day of vengeance of our God; to comfort all that mourn."

Alma 40:11–14. "Now, concerning the state of the soul between death and the resurrection—Behold, it has been made known unto me by an angel, that the spirits of all men, as soon as they are departed from this mortal body, yea, the spirits of all men, whether they be good or evil, are taken home to that God who gave them life. And then shall it come to pass, that the spirits of those who are righteous are received into a state of happiness, which is called paradise, a state of rest, a state of peace, where they shall rest from all their troubles and from all care, and sorrow. And then shall it come to pass, that the spirits of the wicked, yea, who are evil—for behold, they have no part nor portion of the Spirit of the Lord; for behold, they chose evil works rather than good; therefore the spirit of the devil did enter into them, and take possession of their house—and these shall be cast out into outer darkness; there shall be weeping, and wailing, and gnashing of teeth, and this because of their own iniquity, being led captive by the will of the devil. Now this is the state of the souls of the wicked, yea, in darkness, and a state of awful, fearful looking for the fiery indignation of the wrath of God upon them; thus they remain in this state, as well as the righteous in paradise, until the time of their resurrection."

D&C 128:22. "Brethren, shall we not go on in so great a cause? Go forward and not backward. Courage, brethren; and on, on to the victory! Let your hearts rejoice, and be exceedingly glad. Let the earth break forth into singing. Let the dead speak forth anthems of eternal praise to the King Immanuel, who hath ordained, before the world was, that which would enable us to redeem them out of their prison; for the prisoners shall go free."

D&C 138:18–19. "While this vast multitude [in the spirit world] waited and conversed, rejoicing in the hour of their deliverance from the chains of death, the Son of God appeared, declaring liberty to the captives who had been faithful; And there he preached to them the everlasting gospel, the doctrine of the resurrection and the redemption of mankind from the fall, and from individual sins on conditions of repentance."

WORDS OF THE PROPHETS | **Brigham Young on life in the postmortal world.** "When the breath leaves the body, your life has not become extinct; your life is still in existence. And when you are in the spirit world, everything there will appear as natural as things now do. Spirits will be familiar with spirits in the spirit world—will converse, behold, and exercise every variety of communication with one another as familiarly and naturally as while here in tabernacles. There, as here, all things will be natural, and you will understand them as you now understand natural things." —Brigham Young, *Journal of Discourses*, 7:239.

PRAYER [830]. We receive light and truth from the Spirit through the power of prayer. Prayer has many dimensions: it is the intimate communication with God, the channel for inspiration, the most direct means for expressing gratitude, the posture and essence of humility, the witness of a broken heart, the voice of a contrite spirit, and the start and the finish of the quest for forgiveness. All of these dimensions and many more characterize the nobility and the sacredness of praying to our Heavenly Father, for prayer is the very soul of gospel living.

Psalm 4:1. "Hear me when I call, O God of my righteousness: thou hast enlarged me when I was in distress; have mercy upon me, and hear my prayer."

Psalm 55:16–17. "As for me, I will call upon God; and the Lord shall save me. Evening, and morning, and at noon, will I pray, and cry aloud: and he shall hear my voice."

Isaiah 55:6. "Seek ye the Lord while he may be found, call ye upon him while he is near."

Matthew 7: 7–8. "Ask, and it shall be given you; seek, and ye shall find; knock, and it shall be opened unto you: For every one that asketh receiveth; and he that seeketh findeth; and to him that knocketh it shall be opened." (See also 3 Nephi 14:7–8.)

1 Thessalonians 5:16–21. "Rejoice evermore. Pray without ceasing. In every thing give thanks: for this is the will of God in Christ Jesus concerning you. Quench not the Spirit. Despise not prophesyings. Prove all things; hold fast that which is good."

James 1:5–6. "If any of you lack wisdom, let him ask of God, that giveth to all men liberally, and upbraideth not; and it shall be given him. But let him ask in faith, nothing wavering. For he that wavereth is like a wave of the sea driven with the wind and tossed." (See also JS—H 1:11–14, 26.)

James 5:16. "The effectual fervent prayer of a righteous man availeth much."

2 Nephi 32:8–9. "And now, my beloved brethren, I perceive that ye ponder still in your hearts; and it grieveth me that I must speak concerning this thing. For if ye would hearken unto the Spirit which teacheth a man to pray ye would know that ye must pray; for the evil spirit teacheth not a man to pray, but teacheth him that he must not pray. But behold, I say unto you that ye must pray always, and not faint; that ye must not perform any thing unto the Lord save in the first place ye shall pray unto the Father in the name of Christ, that he will consecrate thy performance unto thee, that thy performance may be for the welfare of thy soul."

Alma 5:45–46. "And this is not all. Do ye not suppose that I know of these things myself? Behold, I testify unto you that I do know that these things whereof I have spoken are true. And how do ye suppose that I know of their surety? Behold, I say unto you they are made known unto me by the Holy Spirit of God. Behold, I have fasted and prayed many days that I might know these things of myself. And now I do know of myself that they are true; for the Lord God hath made them manifest unto me by his Holy Spirit; and this is the spirit of revelation which is in me."

Alma 34:18–27. "Yea, cry unto him for mercy; for he is mighty to save. Yea, humble yourselves, and continue in prayer unto him. Cry unto him when ye are in your fields, yea, over all your flocks. Cry unto him in your houses, yea, over all your household, both morning, mid-day, and evening. Yea, cry unto him against the power of your enemies. Yea, cry unto him against the devil, who is an enemy to all righteousness. Cry unto him over the crops of your fields, that ye may prosper in them. Cry over the flocks of your fields, that they may increase. But this is not all; ye must pour out your souls in your closets, and your secret places, and in your wilderness. Yea, and when you do not cry unto the Lord, let your hearts be full, drawn out in prayer unto him continually for your welfare, and also for the welfare of those who are around you."

Alma 37:36–37. "Yea, and cry unto God for all thy support; yea, let all thy doings be unto the Lord, and whithersoever thou goest let it be in the Lord; yea, let all thy thoughts be directed unto the Lord; yea, let the affections of thy heart be placed upon the Lord forever. Counsel with the Lord in all thy doings, and he will direct thee for good; yea, when thou liest down at night lie down unto the Lord, that he may watch over you in your sleep; and when thou risest in the morning let thy heart be full of thanks unto God; and if ye do these things, ye shall be lifted up at the last day."

Helaman 3:35. "Nevertheless they [the more humble people] did fast and pray oft, and did wax stronger and stronger in their humility, and firmer and firmer in the faith of Christ, unto the filling their souls with joy and consolation, yea, even to the purifying and the sanctification of their hearts, which sanctification cometh because of their yielding their hearts unto God."

Moroni 10:4–5. "And when ye shall receive these things, I would exhort you that ye would ask God, the Eternal Father, in the name of Christ, if these things are not true; and if ye shall ask with a sincere heart, with real intent, having faith in Christ, he will manifest the truth of it unto you, by the power of the Holy Ghost. And by the power of the Holy Ghost ye may know the truth of all things."

D&C 46:7. "But ye are commanded in all things to ask of God, who giveth liberally; and that which the Spirit testifies unto you even so I would that ye should do in all holiness of heart, walking uprightly before me, considering the end of your salvation, doing all things with prayer and thanksgiving, that ye may not be seduced by evil spirits, or doctrines of devils, or the commandments of men; for some are of men, and others of devils."

D&C 46:30. "He that asketh in the Spirit asketh according to the will of God; wherefore it is done even as he asketh."

D&C 90:24. "Search diligently, pray always, and be believing, and all things shall work together for your good, if ye walk uprightly and remember the covenant wherewith ye have covenanted one with another."

D&C 112:10. "Be thou humble; and the Lord thy God shall lead thee by the hand, and give thee answer to thy prayers."
Moses 5:8. "Wherefore, thou shalt do all that thou doest in the name of the Son, and thou shalt repent and call upon God in the name of the Son forevermore."

Words of the Prophets | Joseph Smith on gaining wisdom through prayer. "The best way to obtain truth and wisdom is not to ask it from books, but to go to God in prayer, and obtain divine teaching." —Joseph Smith, *HC* 4:425.
Harold B. Lee on the importance of talking to God. "The most important thing you can do is to learn to talk to God. Talk to Him as you would talk to your father, for He is your Father, and He wants you to talk to Him. He wants you to cultivate ears to listen, when He gives you the impressions of the Spirit to tell you what to do. If you learn to give heed to the sudden ideas which come to your minds, you will find those things coming through in the very hour of your need. If you will cultivate an ear to hear these promptings, you will have learned to walk by the spirit of revelation." —Harold B. Lee, *The Teachings of Harold B. Lee*, edited by Clyde J. Williams (Salt Lake City: Bookcraft, 1996), 130.
Cross reference to "Prayer": see Preach My Gospel, *93–95.*

PREMORTAL EXISTENCE [0]. The gospel of Jesus Christ teaches us of the eternal relationship we have with our Heavenly Father, thus filling our lives with the grateful knowledge that we are the offspring of Deity and that our home was in His premortal mansions. He created our spirits, and we walked and talked with Him before we came to this earth. We sat in His presence as He taught us all things we needed to know to prepare to come to earth—including the great plan of salvation in the premortal council. He taught us of our potential to become like Him. With insight into such roots, we are more readily persuaded to abide by God's precepts and commandments in order to return to His presence one day. God is our Father in Heaven. We are His children, and He knows us personally. As the children of our Heavenly Father (Romans 8:16), each of us is truly a divine being who, in the premortal existence, chose to come to earth to live up to the obligation of proving ourselves worthy in this life of returning to our Heavenly Father's presence (Abraham 3:25).

Job 38:5–7. "Who hath laid the measures thereof, if thou knowest? or who hath stretched the line upon it? Whereupon are the foundations thereof fastened? or who laid the corner stone thereof; When the morning stars sang together, and all the sons of God shouted for joy [i.e., in the premortal council]?"
Acts 17:28–29. "For in him we live, and move, and have our being; as certain also of your own poets have said, For we are also his offspring. Forasmuch then as we are the offspring of God, we ought not to think that the Godhead is like unto gold, or silver, or stone, graven by art and man's device."
Romans 8:16. "The Spirit itself beareth witness with our spirit, that we are the children of God."
D&C 76:22–24. "And now, after the many testimonies which have been given of him, this is the testimony, last of all, which we [Joseph Smith and Sidney Rigdon] give of

him: That he lives! For we saw him, even on the right hand of God; and we heard the voice bearing record that he is the Only Begotten of the Father—That by him, and through him, and of him, the worlds are and were created, and the inhabitants thereof are begotten sons and daughters unto God."

D&C 93:21–23. "And now, verily I say unto you, I was in the beginning with the Father, and am the Firstborn; And all those who are begotten through me are partakers of the glory of the same, and are the church of the Firstborn. Ye were also in the beginning with the Father; that which is Spirit, even the Spirit of truth."

D&C 93:29. "Man was also in the beginning with God. Intelligence, or the light of truth, was not created or made, neither indeed can be."

D&C 138:55–56. "I observed that they were also among the noble and great ones who were chosen in the beginning to be rulers in the Church of God. Even before they were born, they, with many others, received their first lessons in the world of spirits and were prepared to come forth in the due time of the Lord to labor in his vineyard for the salvation of the souls of men."

Abraham 3:22–26. "Now the Lord had shown unto me, Abraham, the intelligences that were organized before the world was; and among all these there were many of the noble and great ones; And God saw these souls that they were good, and he stood in the midst of them, and he said: These I will make my rulers; for he stood among those that were spirits, and he saw that they were good; and he said unto me: Abraham, thou art one of them; thou wast chosen before thou wast born. And there stood one among them that was like unto God, and he said unto those who were with him: We will go down, for there is space there, and we will take of these materials, and we will make an earth whereon these may dwell; And we will prove them herewith, to see if they will do all things whatsoever the Lord their God shall command them; And they who keep their first estate shall be added upon; and they who keep not their first estate shall not have glory in the same kingdom with those who keep their first estate; and they who keep their second estate shall have glory added upon their heads for ever and ever."

WORDS OF THE PROPHETS | **Spencer W. Kimball on foreordination.** "Remember, in the world before we came here, faithful women were given certain assignments while faithful men were foreordained to certain priesthood tasks. While we do not now remember the particulars, this does not alter the glorious reality of what we once agreed to. We are accountable for those things which long ago were expected of us just as are those whom we sustain as prophets and apostles." —Spencer W. Kimball, *My Beloved Sisters* (Salt Lake City: Deseret Book, 1979), 37.

PRIDE [198]. Pride masks and disables our remembrance of the goodness and power of God as the source of all growth and advancement. Pride is the gateway to temptation and the catalyst for all greater sin. Pride is the haughty air that inflates our ego to a position of assumed superiority over those errantly perceived as somehow inferior to ourselves—even though God Himself, our Exemplar, is "no respecter of persons" (Acts 10:34; D&C 1:35; 38:16). Pride is the founding force behind false churches and evil empires. Pride fuels an obsession with worldly wealth when the only authentic wealth consists of the treasures of eternal life and everlasting glory. Unrepentant pride in all its manifestations is the condition that invites the inevitable judgment of the Almighty. The only thing certain about pride is its inexorable fall—its collapse before the enveloping light of the gospel of Jesus Christ. Pride is the universal sin that can be overcome only by following the word of the Lord in righteousness and coming unto Him with broken hearts and contrite spirits (Psalm 51:17).

Proverbs 16:18. "Pride goeth before destruction, and an haughty spirit before a fall."

Malachi 4:1. "For, behold, the day cometh, that shall burn as an oven; and all the proud, yea, and all that do wickedly, shall be stubble: and the day that cometh shall burn them up, saith the Lord of hosts, that it shall leave them neither root nor branch."

Mark 7:18–19, 21–23. "And he saith unto them, Are ye so without understanding also? Do ye not perceive, that whatsoever thing from without entereth into the man, it cannot defile him; Because it entereth not into his heart. . . . For from within, out of the heart of men, proceed evil thoughts, adulteries, fornications, murders, Thefts, covetousness, wickedness, deceit, lasciviousness, an evil eye, blasphemy, pride, foolishness: All these evil things come from within, and defile the man."

James 4:6. "But he giveth more grace. Wherefore he saith, God resisteth the proud, but giveth grace unto the humble."

1 John 2:15–16. "Love not the world, neither the things that are in the world. If any man love the world, the love of the Father is not in him. For all that is in the world, the lust of the flesh, and the lust of the eyes, and the pride of life, is not of the Father, but is of the world."

1 Nephi 11:36. "And it came to pass that I saw and bear record, that the great and spacious building was the pride of the world; and it fell, and the fall thereof was exceedingly great. And the angel of the Lord spake unto me again, saying: Thus shall be the destruction of all nations, kindreds, tongues, and people, that shall fight against the twelve apostles of the Lamb."

1 Nephi 12:18–19. "And the large and spacious building, which thy father saw, is vain imaginations and the pride of the children of men. And a great and a terrible gulf divideth them; yea, even the word of the justice of the Eternal God, and the Messiah who is the Lamb of God, of whom the Holy Ghost beareth record, from the beginning of the world until this time, and from this time henceforth and forever. And while the angel spake these words, I beheld and saw that the seed of my brethren did contend against my seed, according to the word of the angel; and because of the pride of my seed, and the temptations of the devil, I beheld that the seed of my brethren did overpower the people of my seed."

Alma 4:19. "And this he did [relinquishing the judgment seat to another] that he [Alma] himself might go forth among his people, or among the people of Nephi, that he might preach the word of God unto them, to stir them up in remembrance of their duty, and that he might pull down, by the word of God, all the pride and craftiness and all the contentions which were among his people, seeing no way that he might reclaim them save it were in bearing down in pure testimony against them."

Alma 5:28. "Behold, are ye stripped of pride? I say unto you, if ye are not ye are not prepared to meet God. Behold ye must prepare quickly; for the kingdom of heaven is soon at hand, and such an one hath not eternal life."

Helaman 7:26. "Yea, wo shall come unto you because of that pride which ye have suffered to enter your hearts, which has lifted you up beyond that which is good because of your exceedingly great riches!"
3 Nephi 6:10–12, 15. "But it came to pass in the twenty and ninth year there began to be some disputings among the people; and some were lifted up unto pride and boastings because of their exceedingly great riches, yea, even unto great persecutions; For there were many merchants in the land, and also many lawyers, and many officers. And the people began to be distinguished by ranks, according to their riches and their chances for learning. . . . Now the cause of this iniquity of the people was this—Satan had great power, unto the stirring up of the people to do all manner of iniquity, and to the puffing them up with pride, tempting them to seek for power, and authority, and riches, and the vain things of the world."
D&C 23:1. "Behold, I speak unto you, Oliver, a few words. Behold, thou art blessed, and art under no condemnation. But beware of pride, lest thou shouldst enter into temptation."
D&C 38:39. "And if ye seek the riches which it is the will of the Father to give unto you, ye shall be the richest of all people, for ye shall have the riches of eternity; and it must needs be that the riches of the earth are mine to give; but beware of pride, lest ye become as the Nephites of old."
D&C 121:34–40. "Behold, there are many called, but few are chosen. And why are they not chosen? Because their hearts are set so much upon the things of this world, and aspire to the honors of men, that they do not learn this one lesson—That the rights of the priesthood are inseparably connected with the powers of heaven, and that the powers of heaven cannot be controlled nor handled only upon the principles of righteousness. That they may be conferred upon us, it is true; but when we undertake to cover our sins, or to gratify our pride, our vain ambition, or to exercise control or dominion or compulsion upon the souls of the children of men, in any degree of unrighteousness, behold, the heavens withdraw themselves; the Spirit of the Lord is grieved; and when it is withdrawn, Amen to the priesthood or the authority of that man. Behold, ere he is aware, he is left unto himself, to kick against the pricks, to persecute the saints, and to fight against God. We have learned by sad experience that it is the nature and disposition of almost all men, as soon as they get a little authority, as they suppose, they will immediately begin to exercise unrighteous dominion. Hence many are called, but few are chosen."

WORDS OF THE PROPHETS | **Ezra Taft Benson on pride.** "Pride is the universal sin, the great vice. . . . It manifests itself in competition, selfishness, contention, power-seeking, backbiting, living beyond our means, coveting, climbing the ladder of worldly success at the expense of others, and in a multitude of ways that 'pit our will against God's' and limit our progression. Pride affects all of us at various times and in various degrees. . . . Pride is the stumbling block to Zion. The antidote for pride is humility—meekness, submissiveness." —Ezra Taft Benson, " Beware of Pride," *Ensign*, May 1989, 4.

PRIESTHOOD [182]. The priesthood is the authority and power of God given to man upon the earth to bless and bring about the salvation of God's children. It is the power by which all things are done in the grand and eternal design of God. It is the divine agency and vital administering principle by means of which the Creation was accomplished and the plan of salvation made operational for achieving the "immortality and eternal life of man" (Moses 1:39). There is one priesthood, with different offices and functions, encompassing the two grand divisions—Aaronic and Melchizedek. The priesthood operates as the government of God and gives direction to the Church and kingdom of God here upon the earth under the leadership of the Lord Jesus Christ through His holy prophets. The lineage and descent of priesthood authority are confirmed by the scriptures (see D&C 84:6–28; D&C 86:8–11; D&C 107:40–57). The Holy Ghost inspires those who hold the priesthood to use it in righteousness. The power of the priesthood is faith. The Doctrine and Covenants is the principal scriptural medium in the latter days for codifying, understanding, and applying the principles and policies embodied in the priesthood as it has been restored to the earth once again by divine intervention and blessing (see D&C 13, 20, 84, 107, 121). Few things could be deemed of greater worth to mankind, and few things should inspire more awe, humble devotion, and enduring commitment, than the singular honor of holding and administering the priesthood of God for and in behalf of His sons and daughters.

1 Peter 2:9. "But ye are a chosen generation, a royal priesthood, an holy nation, a peculiar people [i.e. belonging to the Lord]; that ye should shew forth the praises of him who hath called you out of darkness into his marvellous light."

D&C 13:1. "Upon you my fellow servants, in the name of Messiah I confer the Priesthood of Aaron, which holds the keys of the ministering of angels, and of the gospel of repentance, and of baptism by immersion for the remission of sins; and this shall never be taken again from the earth, until the sons of Levi do offer again an offering unto the Lord in righteousness."

D&C 84:19–21. "And this greater priesthood administereth the gospel and holdeth the key of the mysteries of the kingdom, even the key of the knowledge of God. Therefore, in the ordinances thereof, the power of godliness is manifest. And without the ordinances thereof, and the authority of the priesthood, the power of godliness is not manifest unto men in the flesh; For without this no man can see the face of God, even the Father, and live."

D&C 84:26–28. "And the lesser priesthood continued, which priesthood holdeth the key of the ministering of angels and the preparatory gospel; Which gospel is the gospel of repentance and of baptism, and the remission of sins, and the law of carnal commandments, which the Lord in his wrath caused to continue with the house of Aaron among the children of Israel until John, whom God raised up, being filled with the Holy Ghost from his mother's womb."

D&C 84:33–34. "For whoso is faithful unto the obtaining these two priesthoods of which I have spoken, and the magnifying their calling, are sanctified by the Spirit unto the renewing of their bodies. They become the sons of Moses and of Aaron and the seed of Abraham, and the church and kingdom, and the elect of God."

D&C 107:1–6, 13–14. "There are, in the church, two priesthoods, namely, the Melchizedek and Aaronic, including the Levitical Priesthood. Why the first is called the Melchizedek Priesthood is because Melchizedek was such a great high priest. Before his day it was called the Holy Priesthood, after the Order of the Son of God. But out of respect or reverence to the name of the Supreme Being, to avoid the too frequent repetition of his name, they, the church, in ancient days, called that priesthood after Melchizedek, or the Melchizedek Priesthood. All other authorities or offices in the church are appendages to this priesthood. But there are two divisions or grand heads—one is the Melchizedek Priesthood, and the other is the Aaronic or Levitical Priesthood. . . . The second priesthood is called the Priesthood of Aaron, because it was conferred upon Aaron and his seed, throughout all their generations. Why it is called the lesser priesthood is because it is an appendage to the greater, or the Melchizedek Priesthood, and has power in administering outward ordinances."

D&C 107:8–9, 18–19. "The Melchizedek Priesthood holds the right of presidency, and has power and authority over all the offices in the church in all ages of the world, to administer in spiritual things. The Presidency of the High Priesthood, after the order of Melchizedek, have a right to officiate in all the offices in the church. . . . The power and authority of the higher, or Melchizedek Priesthood, is to hold the keys of all the spiritual blessings of the church—To have the privilege of receiving the mysteries of the kingdom of heaven, to have the heavens opened unto them, to commune with the general assembly and church of the Firstborn, and to enjoy the communion and presence of God the Father, and Jesus the mediator of the new covenant."

D&C 107:20. "The power and authority of the lesser, or Aaronic Priesthood, is to hold the keys of the ministering of angels, and to administer in outward ordinances, the letter of the gospel, the baptism of repentance for the remission of sins, agreeable to the covenants and commandments."

D&C 121:34–36. "Behold, there are many called, but few are chosen. And why are they not chosen? Because their hearts are set so much upon the things of this world, and aspire to the honors of men, that they do not learn this one lesson—That the rights of the priesthood are inseparably connected with the powers of heaven, and that the powers of heaven cannot be controlled nor handled only upon the principles of righteousness."

Fifth Article of Faith. "We believe that a man must be called of God, by prophecy, and by the laying on of hands by those who are in authority, to preach the Gospel and administer in the ordinances thereof."

How is the priesthood conveyed to men?

By being called of the Lord as was Aaron. Hebrews 5:1–4. "For every high priest taken from among men is ordained for men in things pertaining to God, that he may offer both gifts and sacrifices for sins: Who can have compassion on the ignorant, and on them that are out of the way; for that he himself also is compassed with infirmity. And by reason hereof he ought, as for the people, so also for himself, to offer for sins. And no man taketh this honour unto himself, but he that is called of God, as was Aaron."

By being called of the Lord through His prophet. Exodus 28:1–3. "And take thou unto thee Aaron thy brother, and his sons with him, from among the children of Israel, that he may minister unto me in the priest's office, even Aaron, Nadab and Abihu, Eleazar and

Ithamar, Aaron's sons. And thou shalt make holy garments for Aaron thy brother for glory and for beauty. And thou shalt speak unto all that are wise hearted, whom I have filled with the spirit of wisdom, that they may make Aaron's garments to consecrate him, that he may minister unto me in the priest's office."

By being anointed unto an everlasting priesthood. Exodus 40:13–15. "And thou shalt put upon Aaron the holy garments, and anoint him, and sanctify him; that he may minister unto me in the priest's office. And thou shalt bring his sons, and clothe them with coats: And thou shalt anoint them, as thou didst anoint their father, that they may minister unto me in the priest's office: for their anointing shall surely be an everlasting priesthood throughout their generations."

By covenant. Numbers 25:10–13. "And the Lord spake unto Moses, saying, Phinehas, the son of Eleazar, the son of Aaron the priest, hath turned my wrath away from the children of Israel, while he was zealous for my sake among them, that I consumed not the children of Israel in my jealousy. Wherefore say, Behold, I give unto him my covenant of peace: And he shall have it, and his seed after him, even the covenant of an everlasting priesthood; because he was zealous for his God, and made an atonement for the children of Israel."

Based on faith, repentance, and righteousness. Alma 13:10. "Now, as I said concerning the holy order, or this high priesthood, there were many who were ordained and became high priests of God; and it was on account of their exceeding faith and repentance, and their righteousness before God, they choosing to repent and work righteousness rather than to perish."

Bestowed under the direction of the priesthood leadership. D&C 20:67. "Every president of the high priesthood (or presiding elder), bishop, high councilor, and high priest, is to be ordained by the direction of a high council or general conference."

Given through the power restored in the latter days. D&C 27:8. "Which John I have sent unto you, my servants, Joseph Smith, Jun., and Oliver Cowdery, to ordain you unto the first priesthood which you have received, that you might be called and ordained even as Aaron."

Called by prophecy and by the laying on of hands by those having authority. Fifth Article of Faith. "We believe that a man must be called of God, by prophecy, and by the laying on of hands by those who are in authority, to preach the Gospel and administer in the ordinances thereof."

Based on worthiness, independent of race. Official Declaration—2 [1978]. "He has heard our prayers, and by revelation has confirmed that the long-promised day has come when every faithful, worthy man in the Church may receive the holy priesthood, with power to exercise its divine authority, and enjoy with his loved ones every blessing that flows therefrom, including the blessings of the temple. Accordingly, all worthy male members of the Church may be ordained to the priesthood without regard for race or color."

What are some ways priesthood holders use the power of God by the laying on of hands?

Gift of the Holy Ghost. D&C 49:13–14. "Repent and be baptized in the name of Jesus Christ, according to the holy commandment, for the remission of sins; And whoso doeth this shall receive the gift of the Holy Ghost, by the laying on of the hands of the elders of the church."

Blessing the sick. Mark 16:17–18. "And these signs shall follow them that believe; In my name shall they cast out devils; they shall speak with new tongues; They shall take up serpents; and if they drink any deadly thing, it shall not hurt them: they shall lay hands on the sick, and they shall recover."

Priesthood commissions. Acts 13:2–3. "As they [Church leaders at Antioch] ministered to the Lord, and fasted, the Holy Ghost said, Separate me Barnabas and Saul for the work whereunto I have called them. And when they had fasted and prayed, and laid their hands on them, they sent them away."

Priesthood ordinations. JS—H 1:68–69. "While we [Joseph Smith and Oliver Cowdery] were thus employed, praying and calling upon the Lord, a messenger from heaven [John the Baptist] descended in a cloud of light, and having laid his hands upon us, he ordained us, saying: Upon you my fellow servants, in the name of Messiah, I confer the Priesthood of Aaron, which holds the keys of the ministering of angels, and of the gospel of repentance, and of baptism by immersion for the remission of sins; and this shall never be taken again from the earth until the sons of Levi do offer again an offering unto the Lord in righteousness" (italics taken out).

Blessing children. Matthew 19:14–15. "But Jesus said, Suffer little children, and forbid them not, to come unto me: for of such is the kingdom of heaven. And he laid his hands on them, and departed thence."

Words of the Prophets | **Harold B. Lee on the power of the Church.** "The strength of the Church is not in a large membership, but the real strength lies in the power and authority of the holy priesthood which our Heavenly Father has given to us in this day. If we exercise properly that power and magnify our callings in the priesthood, we will see to it that the missionary work shall go forward, that the tithing shall be paid, that the welfare plan shall prosper, that our homes shall be safe, and that morality among the youth of Israel shall be safeguarded." —Harold B. Lee, *The Teachings of Harold B. Lee*, edited by Clyde J. Williams (Salt Lake City: Bookcraft, 1996), 487.

Bruce R. McConkie on the doctrine of the priesthood. "What, then, is the doctrine of the priesthood? And how shall we live as the servants of the Lord? This doctrine is that God our Father is a glorified, a perfected, and an exalted being who has all might, all power, and all dominion, who knows all things and is infinite in all his attributes, and who lives in the family unit. It is that our Eternal Father enjoys this high status of glory and perfection and power because his faith is perfect and his priesthood is unlimited. It is that priesthood that is the very name of the power of God, and that if we are to become like him, we must receive and exercise his priesthood or power as he exercises it. It is that he has given us an endowment of heavenly power here on earth, which is after the order of his Son and which, because it is the power of God, is of necessity without beginning of days or end of years. It is that we can enter an order of the priesthood named the new and everlasting covenant of marriage (see D&C 131:2), named also the patriarchal order, because of which order we can create for ourselves eternal family units of our own, patterned after the family of God our Heavenly Father. It is that we have power, by faith, to govern and control all things, both temporal and spiritual; to work miracles and perfect lives; to stand in the presence of God

and be like him because we have gained his faith, his perfections, and his power, or in other words the fulness of his priesthood. This, then, is the doctrine of the priesthood, than which there neither is nor can be anything greater. This is the power we can gain through faith and righteousness. Truly, there is power in the priesthood—power to do all things!" —Bruce R. McConkie, *Ye Are the Light of the World*, (Salt Lake City: Deseret Book, 1974), 56–57.
Cross reference to "Priesthood": see Preach My Gospel, *83–84, 218.*

PROCRASTINATION (4). The word *procrastination* derives from Latin words meaning "forward" and "of tomorrow"—thus putting things off till tomorrow. The implication is that one ignores important things out of laziness or neglect—a most risky and hurtful habit, especially in regard to responsibilities of a spiritual nature. We are counseled by the Lord and His prophets to take decisive action today—right now—in cultivating thoughts and actions that will propel us forward in valor toward our heavenly destination.

Alma 13: 27–29. "And now, my brethren, I wish from the inmost part of my heart, yea, with great anxiety even unto pain, that ye would hearken unto my words, and cast off your sins, and not procrastinate the day of your repentance; But that ye would humble yourselves before the Lord, and call on his holy name, and watch and pray continually, that ye may not be tempted above that which ye can bear, and thus be led by the Holy Spirit, becoming humble, meek, submissive, patient, full of love and all long-suffering; Having faith on the Lord; having a hope that ye shall receive eternal life; having the love of God always in your hearts, that ye may be lifted up at the last day and enter into his rest."

Alma 34:32–36. "For behold, this life is the time for men to prepare to meet God; yea, behold the day of this life is the day for men to perform their labors. And now, as I said unto you before, as ye have had so many witnesses, therefore, I beseech of you that ye do not procrastinate the day of your repentance until the end; for after this day of life, which is given us to prepare for eternity, behold, if we do not improve our time while in this life, then cometh the night of darkness wherein there can be no labor performed. Ye cannot say, when ye are brought to that awful crisis, that I will repent, that I will return to my God. Nay, ye cannot say this; for that same spirit which doth possess your bodies at the time that ye go out of this life, that same spirit will have power to possess your body in that eternal world. For behold, if ye have procrastinated the day of your repentance even until death, behold, ye have become subjected to the spirit of the devil, and he doth seal you his; therefore, the Spirit of the Lord hath withdrawn from you, and hath no place in you, and the devil hath all power over you; and this is the final state of the wicked. And this I know, because the Lord hath said he dwelleth not in unholy temples, but in the hearts of the righteous doth he dwell; yea, and he has also said that the righteous shall sit down in his kingdom, to go no more out; but their garments should be made white through the blood of the Lamb."

Helaman 13:38–39. "But behold, your days of probation are past; ye have procrastinated the day of your salvation until it is everlastingly too late, and your destruction is made sure; yea, for ye have sought all the days of your lives for that which ye could not obtain; and ye have sought for happiness in doing iniquity, which thing is contrary to the nature of that righteousness which is in our great and Eternal Head. O ye people of the land, that ye would hear my words! And I pray that the anger of the Lord be turned away from you, and that ye would repent and be saved."

How do the scriptures convey warnings against procrastination?

Make important decisions today. Joshua 24:15. "Choose you this day whom ye will serve . . . but as for me and my house, we will serve the Lord."

Listen to the Lord today. Psalm 95:6–8. "O come, let us worship and bow down: let us kneel before the Lord our maker. For he is our God; and we are the people of his pasture, and the sheep of his hand. To day if ye will hear his voice, Harden not your heart, as in the provocation, and as in the day of temptation in the wilderness."

Watch continually every day. Matthew 24:42–43. "Watch therefore: for ye know not what hour your Lord doth come. But know this, that if the goodman of the house had known in what watch the thief would come, he would have watched, and would not have suffered his house to be broken up."

Prepare today. Luke 12:47. "And that servant, which knew his lord's will, and prepared not himself, neither did according to his will, shall be beaten with many stripes."

Do not delay repentance until it is too late. 3 Nephi 8:24. "And in one place they were heard to cry, saying: O that we had repented before this great and terrible day, and then would our brethren have been spared, and they would not have been burned in that great city Zarahemla."

PROPHETS [754]. The English word *prophet* derives from Latin and Greek terms meaning "speaker." Thus a prophet is one who speaks the word of God and serves as His messenger. The Hebrew source word is *navi*, also meaning "spokesperson." The words of the prophets, preserved and conveyed in the holy scriptures and provided in the present day by the living prophets of God, open the gateway for His sons and daughters to enter the fold of the Savior and participate in the plan of salvation and exaltation. The most potent force for instilling faith and turning hearts to righteousness is the word of God as presented by His inspired prophets.

Amos 3:7. "Surely the Lord God will do nothing, but he revealeth his secret unto his servants the prophets."

Acts 3:19–21. "Repent ye therefore, and be converted, that your sins may be blotted out, when the times of refreshing shall come from the presence of the Lord; And he shall send Jesus Christ, which before was preached unto you: Whom the heaven must receive until the times of restitution of all things, which God hath spoken by the mouth of all his holy prophets since the world began."

Ephesians 2:19–22. "Now therefore ye are no more strangers and foreigners, but fellowcitizens with the saints, and of the household of God; And are built upon the foundation of the apostles and prophets, Jesus Christ himself being the chief corner stone; In whom all the building fitly framed together groweth unto an holy temple in the Lord: In whom ye also are builded together for an habitation of God through the Spirit."

Ephesians 4:11–13. "And he gave some, apostles; and some, prophets; and some, evangelists; and some, pastors and teachers; For the perfecting of the saints, for the work of the ministry, for the edifying of the body of Christ: Till we all come in the unity of the faith, and of the knowledge of the Son of God, unto a perfect man, unto the measure of the stature of the fulness of Christ."

2 Nephi 25:17–18. "And the Lord will set his hand again the second time to restore his people from their lost and fallen state. Wherefore, he will proceed to do a marvelous work and a wonder among the children of men. Wherefore, he shall bring forth his words unto them, which words shall judge them at the last day, for they shall be given them for the purpose of convincing them of the true Messiah, who was rejected by them; and unto the convincing of them that they need not look forward any more for a Messiah to come, for there should not any come, save it should be a false Messiah which should deceive the people; for there is save one Messiah spoken of by the prophets, and that Messiah is he who should be rejected of the Jews."

3 Nephi 20:23–26. "Behold, I am he of whom Moses spake, saying: A prophet shall the Lord your God raise up unto you of your brethren, like unto me; him shall ye hear in all things whatsoever he shall say unto you. And it shall come to pass that every soul who will not hear that prophet shall be cut off from among the people. Verily I say unto you, yea, and all the prophets from Samuel and those that follow after, as many as have spoken, have testified of me. And behold, ye are the children of the prophets; and ye are of the house of Israel; and ye are of the covenant which the Father made with your fathers, saying unto Abraham: And in thy seed shall all the kindreds of the earth be blessed. The Father having raised me up unto you first, and sent me to bless you in turning away every one of you from his iniquities; and this because ye are the children of the covenant."

3 Nephi 23:5. "And whosoever will hearken unto my words and repenteth and is baptized, the same shall be saved. Search the prophets, for many there be that testify of these things."

D&C 1:38. "What I the Lord have spoken, I have spoken, and I excuse not myself; and though the heavens and the earth pass away, my word shall not pass away, but shall all be fulfilled, whether by mine own voice or by the voice of my servants, it is the same."

D&C 21:4–6. "Wherefore, meaning the church, thou shalt give heed unto all his words and commandments which he [Joseph Smith] shall give unto you as he receiveth them, walking in all holiness before me; For his word ye shall receive, as if from mine own mouth, in all patience and faith. For by doing these things the gates of hell shall not prevail against you; yea, and the Lord God will disperse the powers of darkness from before you, and cause the heavens to shake for your good, and his name's glory."

Sixth Article of Faith. "We believe in the same organization that existed in the Primitive Church, namely, apostles, prophets, pastors, teachers, evangelists, and so forth."

Words of the Prophets | Ezra Taft Benson on prophets providing direction. "We declare that God has not left man to grope in darkness as to His mind and will. By succession and ordination, there stands on earth today a prophet of God, whom we sustain and revere as president of the Church—prophet, seer, and revelator—the same as Moses of ancient days. This is our message. It is intended for all mankind. The Church proclaims that God spoke in times past through His prophets, has spoken again in this dispensation, and speaks now through His appointed servants." —Ezra Taft Benson, *Come unto Christ* (Salt Lake City: Deseret Book, 1983), 78.

Cross reference to "Prophets": see Preach My Gospel, *32–34.*

PURITY AND VIRTUE [236; 31]. A key part of the gospel code for righteous living is the cultivation of a pure and virtuous character. The Lord will have a pure house and pure servants, for He Himself is pure and holy. Purity and cleanliness of mind and body are unconditionally essential to qualify for the blessings of the Spirit. Purity and virtue—sacred qualities of the divine nature—are indispensable attributes of those who labor in the vineyard of the Lord. As Alma counseled his righteous son, Shiblon: "See that ye bridle all your passions, that ye may be filled with love" (Alma 38:12). The Spirit can abide only in temples of holiness and purity. When one chooses to abide by the highest standards of virtue and decency, great blessings flow to sanctify and lift up lives, both now and in the eternities. In a world of fading values and dissipating principles, we can stand forth in courage to practice and manifest virtue and valor. We can be in the world but not of the world.

Psalm 24:3–5. "Who shall ascend into the hill of the Lord? or who shall stand in his holy place? He that hath clean hands, and a pure heart; who hath not lifted up his soul unto vanity, nor sworn deceitfully. He shall receive the blessing from the Lord, and righteousness from the God of his salvation."

Matthew 5:8. "Blessed are the pure in heart: for they shall see God."

James 1:27. "Pure religion and undefiled before God and the Father is this, To visit the fatherless and widows in their affliction, and to keep himself unspotted from the world."

1 John 3:1–3. "Behold, what manner of love the Father hath bestowed upon us, that we should be called the sons of God: therefore the world knoweth us not, because it knew him not. Beloved, now are we the sons of God, and it doth not yet appear what we shall be: but we know that, when he shall appear, we shall be like him; for we shall see him as he is. And every man that hath this hope in him purifieth himself, even as he is pure."

Jacob 3:1–3. "But behold, I, Jacob, would speak unto you that are pure in heart. Look unto God with firmness of mind, and pray unto him with exceeding faith, and he will console you in your afflictions. . . . O all ye that are pure in heart, lift up your heads and receive the pleasing word of God, and feast upon his love; for ye may, if your minds are firm, forever. But, wo, wo, unto you that are not pure in heart, that are filthy this day before God; for except ye repent the land is cursed for your sakes."

3 Nephi 19:28–29. "Father, I thank thee that thou hast purified those whom I have chosen, because of their faith, and I pray for them, and also for them who shall believe on their words, that they may be purified in me, through faith on their words, even as they are purified in me. Father, I pray not for the world, but for those whom thou hast given me out of the world, because of their faith, that they may be purified in me, that I may be in them as thou, Father, art in me, that we may be one, that I may be glorified in them."

D&C 97:21. "Therefore, verily, thus saith the Lord, let Zion rejoice, for this is Zion—THE PURE IN HEART; therefore, let Zion rejoice, while all the wicked shall mourn."

D&C 100:15–17. "Therefore, let your hearts be comforted; for all things shall work together for good to them that walk uprightly, and to the sanctification of the church. For I will raise up unto myself a pure people, that will serve me in righteousness; And all that call upon the name of the Lord, and keep his commandments, shall be saved."

Thirteenth Article of Faith. "We believe in being honest, true, chaste, benevolent, virtuous, and in doing good to all men; indeed, we may say that we follow the admonition of

Paul—We believe all things, we hope all things, we have endured many things, and hope to be able to endure all things. If there is anything virtuous, lovely, or of good report or praiseworthy, we seek after these things."

Words of the Prophets | **Brigham Young on resisting evil.** "The sooner an individual resists temptation to do, say, or think wrong, while he has light to correct his judgment, the quicker he will gain strength and power to overcome every temptation to evil." —Brigham Young, *Journal of Discourses*, 6:94.

REPENTANCE [628]. Repentance is the second principle of the gospel of Jesus Christ, after faith. It calls for godly sorrow, humility in accepting the loving chastening of the Lord, cultivating a forgiving spirit, and honoring the baptismal covenant in righteousness. The blessings are magnificent: joy, peace, comfort, an enhanced love for our Heavenly Father and His Son, greater capacity to receive light and truth, and the ability to bless the lives of others and show them the way of happiness. Repentance is essential for receiving the blessings of salvation and exaltation. From the foundation of the world, it was decreed that our mortal life would be a testing time (see Abraham 3:25). A Savior was provided from the beginning to empower the plan of redemption by means of which the children of God could overcome their weaknesses and transgressions and rise to their divine potential. The Atonement of Jesus Christ makes possible the miracle of repentance and forgiveness. Repentance is the process of becoming clean from sin. All need to repent, for all have sinned (see 1 John 1:8; 2 Nephi 2:5). Through faith on Jesus Christ and sincere repentance and obedience to the commandments, we can be forgiven and our guilt can be swept away.

Acts 2:37–39. "Now when they heard this, they were pricked in their heart, and said unto Peter and to the rest of the apostles, Men and brethren, what shall we do? Then Peter said unto them, Repent, and be baptized every one of you in the name of Jesus Christ for the remission of sins, and ye shall receive the gift of the Holy Ghost. For the promise is unto you, and to your children, and to all that are afar off, even as many as the Lord our God shall call."

Acts 3:19–21. "Repent ye therefore, and be converted, that your sins may be blotted out, when the times of refreshing shall come from the presence of the Lord; And he shall send Jesus Christ, which before was preached unto you: Whom the heaven must receive until the times of restitution of all things, which God hath spoken by the mouth of all his holy prophets since the world began."

2 Corinthians 7:9–10. "Now I rejoice, not that ye were made sorry, but that ye sorrowed to repentance: for ye were made sorry after a godly manner, that ye might receive damage by us in nothing. For godly sorrow worketh repentance to salvation not to be repented of: but the sorrow of the world worketh death."

Revelation 3:19. "As many as I love, I rebuke and chasten: be zealous therefore, and repent."

1 Nephi 10:18. "For he is the same yesterday, to-day, and forever; and the way is prepared for all men from the foundation of the world, if it so be that they repent and come unto him."

Mosiah 4:10. "And again, believe that ye must repent of your sins and forsake them, and humble yourselves before God; and ask in sincerity of heart that he would forgive you; and now, if you believe all these things see that ye do them."

Mosiah 18:20. "Yea, even he commanded them that they should preach nothing save it were repentance and faith on the Lord, who had redeemed his people."

D&C 1:31–33. "For I the Lord cannot look upon sin with the least degree of allowance; Nevertheless, he that repents and does the commandments of the Lord shall be forgiven; And he that repents not, from him shall be taken even the light which he has received; for my Spirit shall not always strive with man, saith the Lord of Hosts."

D&C 13:1. "Upon you my fellow servants, in the name of Messiah I confer the Priesthood of Aaron, which holds the keys of the ministering of angels, and of the gospel of repentance, and of baptism by immersion for the remission of sins; and this shall never be taken again from the earth, until the sons of Levi do offer again an offering unto the Lord in righteousness."

D&C 18:11–17. "For, behold, the Lord your Redeemer suffered death in the flesh; wherefore he suffered the pain of all men, that all men might repent and come unto him. And he hath risen again from the dead, that he might bring all men unto him, on conditions of repentance. And how great is his joy in the soul that repenteth! Wherefore, you are called to cry repentance unto this people. And if it so be that you should labor all your days in crying repentance unto this people, and bring, save it be one soul unto me, how great shall be your joy with him in the kingdom of my Father! And now, if your joy will be great with one soul that you have brought unto me into the kingdom of my Father, how great will be your joy if you should bring many souls unto me! Behold, you have my gospel before you, and my rock, and my salvation."

D&C 19:13–20. "Wherefore, I command you to repent, and keep the commandments which you have received by the hand of my servant Joseph Smith, Jun., in my name; And it is by my almighty power that you have received them; Therefore I command you to repent—repent, lest I smite you by the rod of my mouth, and by my wrath, and by my anger, and your sufferings be sore—how sore you know not, how exquisite you know not, yea, how hard to bear you know not. For behold, I, God, have suffered these things for all, that they might not suffer if they would repent; But if they would not repent they must suffer even as I; Which suffering caused myself, even God, the greatest of all, to tremble because of pain, and to bleed at every pore, and to suffer both body and spirit—and would that I might not drink the bitter cup, and shrink—Nevertheless, glory be to the Father, and I partook and finished my preparations unto the children of men. Wherefore, I command you again to repent, lest I humble you with my almighty power; and that you confess your sins, lest you suffer these punishments of which I have spoken, of which in the smallest, yea, even in the least degree you have tasted at the time I withdrew my Spirit."

D&C 58:42–43. "Behold, he who has repented of his sins, the same is forgiven, and I, the Lord, remember them no more. By this ye may know if a man repenteth of his sins—behold, he will confess them and forsake them."

D&C 68:25. "And again, inasmuch as parents have children in Zion, or in any of her stakes which are organized, that teach them not to understand the doctrine of repentance, faith in Christ the Son of the living God, and of baptism and the gift of the Holy Ghost by the laying on of the hands, when eight years old, the sin be upon the heads of the parents."

D&C 133:62. "And unto him that repenteth and sanctifieth himself before the Lord shall be given eternal life."

Fourth Article of Faith. "We believe that the first principles and ordinances of the Gospel are: first, Faith in the Lord Jesus Christ; second, Repentance; third, Baptism by immersion for the remission of sins; fourth, Laying on of hands for the gift of the Holy Ghost."

Words of the Prophets | Joseph F. Smith on the necessity of repentance. "When we commit sin, it is necessary that we repent of it and make restitution as far as lies in our power. When we cannot make restitution for the wrong we have done, then we must apply for the grace and mercy of God to cleanse us from that iniquity." —Joseph F. Smith, *CR*, October 1899, 42.

Cross reference to "Repentance": see Preach My Gospel, *62–63, 187–190.*

RESTORATION [160]. On April 6, 1830, the Lord's Church was formally organized in this dispensation (see D&C 20:1). The Church is indeed the organized and authorized structure through which the Saints are to be perfected, the gospel preached unto all the world, and salvation administered and secured for all the hosts of Creation—both living and dead—who become heirs of immortality and eternal life. The Restoration is for Latter-day Saints the supreme application of the verb restore because the Restoration represents all that the Lord has brought back for the last time into the lives of His Saints: truth, priesthood keys and powers, continual revelation, guidance from living prophets, ever-unfolding pages of divine scripture, gathering together in secure and holy places, and the hope and confidence that families can be forever in the eternities that lie ahead. At the same time, the word *restore* has other related applications in the scriptures, including the restoration of individual spiritual wellness through the power of the Atonement, the restoration of the union of spirit and body through the Resurrection, the restoration of the continuity of one's character beyond the veil of mortality (good for good, but evil for evil), the restoration of gifts given from the Lord, and restoration of health and life through the miracle of physical healing.

Acts 3:19–21. "Repent ye therefore, and be converted, that your sins may be blotted out, when the times of refreshing shall come from the presence of the Lord; And he shall send Jesus Christ, which before was preached unto you: Whom the heaven must receive until the times of restitution of all things, which God hath spoken by the mouth of all his holy prophets since the world began."

James 1:5–7. "If any of you lack wisdom, let him ask of God, that giveth to all men liberally, and upbraideth not; and it shall be given him. But let him ask in faith, nothing wavering. For he that wavereth is like a wave of the sea driven with the wind and tossed. For let not that man think that he shall receive any thing of the Lord."

Revelation 14:6. "And I saw another angel fly in the midst of heaven, having the everlasting gospel to preach unto them that dwell on the earth, and to every nation, and kindred, and tongue, and people."

2 Nephi 28:29–30. "Wo be unto him that shall say: We have received the word of God, and we need no more of the word of God, for we have enough! For behold, thus saith the Lord God: I will give unto the children of men line upon line, precept upon precept, here a little and there a little; and blessed are those who hearken unto my precepts, and lend an ear unto my counsel, for they shall learn wisdom; for unto him that receiveth I will give more; and from them that shall say, We have enough, from them shall be taken away even that which they have."

D&C 4:1–2. "Now behold, a marvelous work is about to come forth among the children of men. Therefore, O ye that embark in the service of God, see that ye serve him with all your heart, might, mind and strength, that ye may stand blameless before God at the last day."

D&C 20:8–12. "And gave him power from on high, by the means which were before prepared, to translate the Book of Mormon; Which contains a record of a fallen people, and the fulness of the gospel of Jesus Christ to the Gentiles and to the Jews also; Which was given by inspiration, and is confirmed to others by the ministering of angels, and is declared unto the world by them—Proving to the world that the holy scriptures are true, and that God does inspire men and call them to his holy work in this age and generation, as well as in generations of old; Thereby showing that he is the same God yesterday, today, and forever."

JS—H 1:17. "It no sooner appeared than I found myself delivered from the enemy which held me bound. When the light rested upon me I saw two Personages, whose brightness and glory defy all description, standing above me in the air. One of them spake unto me, calling me by name and said, pointing to the other—*This is My Beloved Son. Hear Him!*"

How do the scriptures prophecy, in general, of the restoration of all things in the last days?

Marvelous work and a wonder coming forth. Isaiah 29:13–14. "Wherefore the Lord said, Forasmuch as this people draw near me with their mouth, and with their lips do honour me, but have removed their heart far from me, and their fear toward me is taught by the precept of men: Therefore, behold, I will proceed to do a marvellous work among this people, even a marvellous work and a wonder: for the wisdom of their wise men shall perish, and the understanding of their prudent men shall be hid." (See also D&C 4:1–2.)

New covenant in the latter days. Jeremiah 31:31–34. "Behold, the days come, saith the Lord, that I will make a new covenant with the house of Israel, and with the house of Judah: Not according to the covenant that I made with their fathers in the day that I took them by the hand to bring them out of the land of Egypt; which my covenant they brake, although I was an husband unto them, saith the Lord: But this shall be the covenant that I will make with the house of Israel; After those days, saith the Lord, I will put my law in their inward parts, and write it in their hearts; and will be their God, and they shall be my people. And they shall teach no more every man his neighbour, and every man his brother, saying, Know the Lord: for they shall all know me, from the least of them unto the greatest of them, saith the Lord: for I will forgive their iniquity, and I will remember their sin no more."

Stone cut out of the mountain without hands. Daniel 2: 34–35, 44–45. "Thou sawest till that a stone was cut out without hands . . . and filled the whole earth. . . . And in the days of these kings shall the God of heaven set up a kingdom, which shall never be destroyed: and the kingdom shall not be left to other people, but it shall break in pieces and consume all these kingdoms, and it shall stand for ever. Forasmuch as thou sawest that the stone was cut out of the mountain without hands, and that it brake in pieces the iron, the brass, the clay, the silver, and the gold; the great God hath made known to the king what shall come to pass hereafter: and the dream is certain, and the interpretation thereof sure." (See also D&C 65:2.)

Revelation to the prophets to restore truth. Amos 3:7. "Surely the Lord God will do nothing, but he revealeth his secret unto his servants the prophets."

Dispensation of the fulness of times for gathering together all things. Ephesians 1:9–10. "Having made known unto us the mystery of his will, according to his good pleasure which he hath purposed in himself: That in the dispensation of the fulness of times he might gather together in one all things in Christ, both which are in heaven, and which are on earth; even in him."

Times of refreshing for the restitution of all things. Acts 3:19–21. "Repent ye therefore, and be converted, that your sins may be blotted out, when the times of refreshing shall come from the presence of the Lord; And he shall send Jesus Christ, which before was preached unto you: Whom the heaven must receive until the times of restitution of all things, which God hath spoken by the mouth of all his holy prophets since the world began."

Coming forth of the only true and living church. D&C 1:30. "And also those to whom these commandments were given, might have power to lay the foundation of this church, and to bring it forth out of obscurity and out of darkness, the only true and living church upon the face of the whole earth, with which I, the Lord, am well pleased, speaking unto the church collectively and not individually."

Restoration of all things spoken by the prophets. D&C 86:9–11. "For ye are lawful heirs, according to the flesh, and have been hid from the world with Christ in God—Therefore your life and the priesthood have remained, and must needs remain through you and your lineage until the restoration of all things spoken by the mouths of all the holy prophets since the world began. Therefore, blessed are ye if ye continue in my goodness, a light unto the Gentiles, and through this priesthood, a savior unto my people Israel. The Lord hath said it. Amen." (See also D&C 27:6.)

Fulness of the gospel sent forth, along with the everlasting covenant. D&C 133:57–62. "And for this cause, that men might be made partakers of the glories which were to be revealed, the Lord sent forth the fulness of his gospel, his everlasting covenant, reasoning in plainness and simplicity—To prepare the weak for those things which are coming on the earth, and for the Lord's errand in the day when the weak shall confound the wise, and the little one become a strong nation, and two shall put their tens of thousands to flight. And by the weak things of the earth the Lord shall thrash the nations by the power of his Spirit. And for this cause these commandments were given; they were commanded to be kept from the world in the day that they were given, but now are to go forth unto all flesh—And this according to the mind and will of the Lord, who ruleth over all flesh. And unto him that repenteth and sanctifieth himself before the Lord shall be given eternal life."

Cross reference to "Restoration": see Preach My Gospel, *6–8, 36–38.*

RESURRECTION [155]. No doctrine in the sacred canon of eternal principles captures the imagination with more compelling urgency than the Resurrection. This word derives from the Latin term *resurgere,* meaning "to rise again." Resurrection is the permanent reuniting of the body and the spirit following death in mortality. Through the miracle of the Resurrection, we become immortal. We are restored to a state of existence (level of glory) consonant with our works of righteousness. Resurrection was made possible through the merits, mercy, and grace of the Messiah—by virtue of His infinite and eternal Atonement. We will be resurrected whole, restored to our perfect frame. We take with us all the knowledge and intelligence that we have learned through our experiences here upon the earth. In addition to the blessing of the Resurrection (immortality), there is the magnificent blessing of eternal life and celestial exaltation that we can look forward to through our obedience. If we hold out faithful to the end and endure well—following strictly in the pathway of the Savior—we will eventually receive "all that my Father hath" (D&C 84:38).

John 11:25. "I am the resurrection, and the life: he that believeth in me, though he were dead, yet shall he live."

1 Corinthians 15:22–23. "For as in Adam all die, even so in Christ shall all be made alive. But every man in his own order: Christ the firstfruits; afterward they that are Christ's at his coming."

2 Nephi 2:8–9. "Wherefore, how great the importance to make these things known unto the inhabitants of the earth, that they may know that there is no flesh that can dwell in the presence of God, save it be through the merits, and mercy, and grace of the Holy Messiah, who layeth down his life according to the flesh, and taketh it again by the power of the Spirit, that he may bring to pass the resurrection of the dead, being the first that should rise. Wherefore, he is the firstfruits unto God, inasmuch as he shall make intercession for all the children of men; and they that believe in him shall be saved."

Jacob 4:11–12. "Wherefore, beloved brethren, be reconciled unto him through the atonement of Christ, his Only Begotten Son, and ye may obtain a resurrection, according to the power of the resurrection which is in Christ, and be presented as the first-fruits of Christ unto God, having faith, and obtained a good hope of glory in him before he manifesteth himself in the flesh. And now, beloved, marvel not that I tell you these things; for why not speak of the atonement of Christ, and attain to a perfect knowledge of him, as to attain to the knowledge of a resurrection and the world to come?"

D&C 88:14–16. "Now, verily I say unto you, that through the redemption which is made for you is brought to pass the resurrection from the dead. And the spirit and the body are the soul of man. And the resurrection from the dead is the redemption of the soul."

D&C 130:18–19. "Whatever principle of intelligence we attain unto in this life, it will rise with us in the resurrection. And if a person gains more knowledge and intelligence in this life through his diligence and obedience than another, he will have so much the advantage in the world to come."

D&C 130:22. "The Father has a body of flesh and bones as tangible as man's; the Son also; but the Holy Ghost has not a body of flesh and bones, but is a personage of Spirit. Were it not so, the Holy Ghost could not dwell in us."
Moses 7:62. "And righteousness will I send down out of heaven; and truth will I send forth out of the earth, to bear testimony of mine Only Begotten; his resurrection from the dead; yea, and also the resurrection of all men; and righteousness and truth will I cause to sweep the earth as with a flood, to gather out mine elect from the four quarters of the earth, unto a place which I shall prepare, an Holy City, that my people may gird up their loins, and be looking forth for the time of my coming; for there shall be my tabernacle, and it shall be called Zion, a New Jerusalem."

Words of the Prophets | Ezra Taft Benson on the nonexistence of true death. "There is the ever expectancy of death, but in reality there is no death—no permanent parting. The resurrection is a reality. The scriptures are replete with evidence. Almost immediately after the glorious resurrection of the Lord, Matthew records: 'And the graves were opened; and many bodies of the saints which slept arose, And came out of the graves after his resurrection, and went into the holy city, and appeared unto many' (Matthew 27:52–53). The Apostle John on the Isle of Patmos 'saw the dead, small and great, stand before God' (Revelation 20:12)." —Ezra Taft Benson, "Life is Eternal," *Ensign*, June 1971, 33.

ADDITIONAL INFORMATION—**A concise summary of the sequence of the resurrection.** Four trumpet signals will announce the unfolding of the resurrection, according to the order established from before the foundation of the world, to grant immortality to all souls and is timed according to each soul's level of obedience and righteousness, the first two trumps corresponding to the resurrection of the just at the time of the Second Coming and the second two trumps corresponding to the resurrection of the unjust after the thousand year period has ended (see Acts 24:15; Alma 12:8; D&C 76:17, 50, 65).

Trump 1. D&C 88:96–98. "And the saints that are upon the earth, who are alive, shall be quickened and be caught up to meet him. And they who have slept in their graves shall come forth, for their graves shall be opened; and they also shall be caught up to meet him in the midst of the pillar of heaven—They are Christ's, the first fruits, they who shall descend with him first, and they who are on the earth and in their graves, who are first caught up to meet him; and all this by the voice of the sounding of the trump of the angel of God."
Trump 2. D&C 88:99. "And after this another angel shall sound, which is the second trump; and then cometh the redemption of those who are Christ's at his coming; who have received their part in that prison which is prepared for them, that they might receive the gospel, and be judged according to men in the flesh" (also those who were without the law, and those who were honorable in mortality but not valiant in the testimony of Jesus).
Trump 3. D&C 88:100–101. "And again, another trump shall sound, which is the third trump; and then come the spirits of men who are to be judged, and are found under condemnation; And these are the rest of the dead; and they live not again until the thousand years are ended, neither again, until the end of the earth."

Trump 4. D&C 88:102. "And another trump shall sound, which is the fourth trump, saying: There are found among those who are to remain until that great and last day, even the end, who [the sons of perdition] shall remain filthy still."

REVELATION/REVEAL [125; 138]. Revelation is the word of God communicated to His children—whether directly from the Father or the Son, through the ministration of angels or prophets, or through the inspiration of the Holy Ghost. The Church and kingdom of God is governed by continual revelation. The scriptures canonize the revelations of God down through the dispensations. We as children of our Heavenly Father have the privilege of receiving inspiration and direction in our lives, based on our faith, prayers, and humble capacity to listen and learn the will of God.

Deuteronomy 29:29. "The secret things belong unto the Lord our God: but those things which are revealed belong unto us and to our children for ever, that we may do all the words of this law."

Proverbs 29:18. "Where there is no vision, the people perish: but he that keepeth the law, happy is he."

Amos 3:7. "Surely the Lord God will do nothing, but he revealeth his secret unto his servants the prophets."

Matthew 7:7–8. "Ask, and it shall be given you; seek, and ye shall find; knock, and it shall be opened unto you: For every one that asketh receiveth; and he that seeketh findeth; and to him that knocketh it shall be opened." (See also Luke 11:9–10; 3 Nephi 14:7–8.)

Matthew 16:16–18. "And Simon Peter answered and said, Thou art the Christ, the Son of the living God. And Jesus answered and said unto him, Blessed art thou, Simon Bar-jona: for flesh and blood hath not revealed it unto thee, but my Father which is in heaven. And I say also unto thee, That thou art Peter, and upon this rock [i.e., the rock of revelation empowered by the Redeemer] I will build my church; and the gates of hell shall not prevail against it."

1 Corinthians 2:9–10. "But as it is written, Eye hath not seen, nor ear heard, neither have entered into the heart of man, the things which God hath prepared for them that love him. But God hath revealed them unto us by his Spirit: for the Spirit searcheth all things, yea, the deep things of God." (See also Isaiah 64:4; D&C 76:10; 133:45.)

1 Corinthians 12:3. "Wherefore I give you to understand, that no man speaking by the Spirit of God calleth Jesus accursed: and that no man can say that Jesus is the Lord, but by the Holy Ghost."

James 1:5–6. "If any of you lack wisdom, let him ask of God, that giveth to all men liberally, and upbraideth not; and it shall be given him. But let him ask in faith, nothing wavering. For he that wavereth is like a wave of the sea driven with the wind and tossed."

2 Peter 1:20–21. "Knowing this first, that no prophecy of the scripture is of any private interpretation. For the prophecy came not in old time by the will of man: but holy men of God spake as they were moved by the Holy Ghost."

Revelation 19:10. "And I fell at his feet to worship him. And he said unto me, See thou do it not: I am thy fellowservant, and of thy brethren that have the testimony of Jesus: worship God: for the testimony of Jesus is the spirit of prophecy."

Jacob 4:6–8. "Wherefore, we search the prophets, and we have many revelations and the spirit of prophecy; and having all these witnesses we obtain a hope, and our faith becometh unshaken, insomuch that we truly can command in the name of Jesus and the very trees obey us, or the mountains, or the waves of the sea. Nevertheless, the Lord God showeth us our weakness that we may know that it is by his grace, and his great condescensions unto the children of men, that we have power to do these things. Behold, great and marvelous are the works of the Lord. How unsearchable are the depths of the mysteries of him; and it is impossible that man should find out all his ways. And no man knoweth of his ways save it be revealed unto him; wherefore, brethren, despise not the revelations of God."

Alma 17:2–3. "Now these sons of Mosiah were with Alma at the time the angel first appeared unto him; therefore Alma did rejoice exceedingly to see his brethren; and what added more to his joy, they were still his brethren in the Lord; yea, and they had waxed strong in the knowledge of the truth; for they were men of a sound understanding and they had searched the scriptures diligently, that they might know the word of God. But this is not all; they had given themselves to much prayer, and fasting; therefore they had the spirit of prophecy, and the spirit of revelation, and when they taught, they taught with power and authority of God."

Alma 26:21–22. "And now behold, my brethren, what natural man is there that knoweth these things? I say unto you, there is none that knoweth these things, save it be the penitent. Yea, he that repenteth and exerciseth faith, and bringeth forth good works, and prayeth continually without ceasing—unto such it is given to know the mysteries of God; yea, unto such it shall be given to reveal things which never have been revealed; yea, and it shall be given unto such to bring thousands of souls to repentance, even as it has been given unto us to bring these our brethren to repentance."

D&C 6:22–23. "Verily, verily, I say unto you [Oliver Cowdery], if you desire a further witness, cast your mind upon the night that you cried unto me in your heart, that you might know concerning the truth of these things. Did I not speak peace to your mind concerning the matter? What greater witness can you have than from God?"

D&C 8:1–3. "Oliver Cowdery, verily, verily, I say unto you, that assuredly as the Lord liveth, who is your God and your Redeemer, even so surely shall you receive a knowledge of whatsoever things you shall ask in faith, with an honest heart, believing that you shall receive a knowledge concerning the engravings of old records, which are ancient, which contain those parts of my scripture of which has been spoken by the manifestation of my Spirit. Yea, behold, I will tell you in your mind and in your heart, by the Holy Ghost, which shall come upon you and which shall dwell in your heart. Now, behold, this is the spirit of revelation; behold, this is the spirit by which Moses brought the children of Israel through the Red Sea on dry ground."

D&C 9:7–9. "Behold, you have not understood; you have supposed that I would give it unto you, when you took no thought save it was to ask me. But, behold, I say unto you, that you must study it out in your mind; then you must ask me if it be right, and if it is right I will cause that your bosom shall burn within you; therefore, you shall feel that it is right. But if it be not right you shall have no such feelings, but you shall have a stupor of thought that shall cause you to forget the thing which is wrong; therefore, you cannot write that which is sacred save it be given you from me."

D&C 42:61. "If thou shalt ask, thou shalt receive revelation upon revelation, knowledge upon knowledge, that thou mayest know the mysteries and peaceable things—that which bringeth joy, that which bringeth life eternal."

D&C 90:10–11. "And then cometh the day when the arm of the Lord shall be revealed in power in convincing the nations, the heathen nations, the house of Joseph, of the gospel of their salvation. For it shall come to pass in that day, that every man shall hear the fulness of the gospel in his own tongue, and in his own language, through those who are ordained unto this power, by the administration of the Comforter, shed forth upon them for the revelation of Jesus Christ."

Seventh Article of Faith. "We believe in the gift of tongues, prophecy, revelation, visions, healing, interpretation of tongues, and so forth."

Ninth Article of Faith. "We believe all that God has revealed, all that He does now reveal, and we believe that He will yet reveal many great and important things pertaining to the Kingdom of God."

Words of the Prophets | George Albert Smith on revelation being a great distinction for the Church. "The distinction between this great Church and that of all other churches from the beginning has been that we believe in divine revelation; we believe that our Father speaks to man today as he has done from the time of Adam. We believe and we know—which is more than mere belief—that our Father has set his hand in this world for the salvation of the children of men." —George Albert Smith, *CR*, April, 1917, 37.

RIGHTEOUSNESS [856]. The Father and the Son are perfectly righteous in all dimensions of Their being, Their work, and Their glory. Thus we, as their children, are to be righteous unto perfection by following Their example in all that we think, feel, hope, and do. Righteousness is the enduring pattern of living that will enable us to return one day in valor and obedience to the hallways of the eternal world. Righteousness is the context of our faith, the framework of our view of eternity, the fuel of our lamp of illumination on the pathway of life, the energy of our charitable deeds, and the measure and harmony of all our lasting relationships in mortality. The scriptures are replete with references to the principle of righteousness.

Psalm 15:1–2. "Lord, who shall abide in thy tabernacle? who shall dwell in thy holy hill? He that walketh uprightly, and worketh righteousness, and speaketh the truth in his heart."

Isaiah 41:10. "Fear thou not; for I am with thee: be not dismayed; for I am thy God: I will strengthen thee; yea, I will help thee; yea, I will uphold thee with the right hand of my righteousness." (See also verse 3 of "How Firm a Foundation," Hymns no. 85.)

Isaiah 53:10–11. "Yet it pleased the Lord to bruise him; he hath put him to grief: when thou shalt make his soul an offering for sin, he shall see his seed, he shall prolong his days, and the pleasure of the Lord shall prosper in his hand. He shall see of the travail of his soul, and shall be satisfied: by his knowledge shall my righteous servant justify many; for he shall bear their iniquities." (See also Mosiah 14:10–11.)

Malachi 3:1–3. "Behold, I will send my messenger, and he shall prepare the way before me: and the Lord, whom ye seek, shall suddenly come to his temple, even the messenger of the covenant, whom ye delight in: behold, he shall come, saith the Lord of hosts. But who may abide the day of his coming? and who shall stand when he appeareth? for he is like a refiner's fire, and like fullers' soap: And he shall sit as a refiner and purifier of silver: and he shall purify the sons of Levi, and purge them as gold and silver, that they may offer unto the Lord an offering in righteousness." (See also 3 Nephi 24:1–3.)

2 Timothy 4:7–8. "I have fought a good fight, I have finished my course, I have kept the faith: Henceforth there is laid up for me a crown of righteousness, which the Lord, the righteous judge, shall give me at that day: and not to me only, but unto all them also that love his appearing."

James 5:16. "The effectual fervent prayer of a righteous man availeth much."

1 John 3:7. "Little children, let no man deceive you: he that doeth righteousness is righteous, even as he [the Lord] is righteous."

2 Nephi 1:23. "Awake, my sons; put on the armor of righteousness. Shake off the chains with which ye are bound, and come forth out of obscurity, and arise from the dust."

3 Nephi 25:2. "But unto you that fear my name, shall the Son of Righteousness arise with healing in his wings; and ye shall go forth and grow up as calves in the stall." (See also Malachi 4:2.)

D&C 11:12. "And now, verily, verily, I say unto thee, put your trust in that Spirit which leadeth to do good—yea, to do justly, to walk humbly, to judge righteously; and this is my Spirit."

D&C 25:12. "For my soul delighteth in the song of the heart; yea, the song of the righteous is a prayer unto me, and it shall be answered with a blessing upon their heads."

D&C 58:27–28. "Verily I say, men should be anxiously engaged in a good cause, and do many things of their own free will, and bring to pass much righteousness; For the power is in them, wherein they are agents unto themselves. And inasmuch as men do good they shall in nowise lose their reward."

D&C 59:8–11. "Thou shalt offer a sacrifice unto the Lord thy God in righteousness, even that of a broken heart and a contrite spirit. And that thou mayest more fully keep thyself unspotted from the world, thou shalt go to the house of prayer and offer up thy sacraments upon my holy day; For verily this is a day appointed unto you to rest from your labors, and to pay thy devotions unto the Most High; Nevertheless thy vows shall be offered up in righteousness on all days and at all times."

D&C 59:23–24. "But learn that he who doeth the works of righteousness shall receive his reward, even peace in this world, and eternal life in the world to come. I, the Lord, have spoken it, and the Spirit beareth record."

Words of the Prophets | Spencer W. Kimball on actively being righteous. "People tend often to measure their righteousness by the absence of wrong acts in their lives, as if passivity were the end of being. But God has created 'things to act and things to be acted upon' (2 Nephi 2:14), and man is in the former category. He does not fill the measure of his creation unless he acts, and that in righteousness. 'Therefore to him that knoweth to do good, and doeth it not,' warns James, 'to him it is sin' (James 4:17)." —Spencer W. Kimball, *The Miracle of Forgiveness*, (Salt Lake City: Bookcraft, 1969), 91–92.

SABBATH [180]. The word *sabbath* derives from Hebrew, Greek, and Latin source words meaning "to rest." Just as the Lord created (organized) the world and generated the gospel plan before resting from His labors on the seventh day, similarly, we, as His sons and daughters, work each week to create (organize) our family heritage and generate our offerings toward the building up of the Lord's kingdom on earth—and then, by divine command, we pause for a day to rejoice and rest in renewing our covenants with the Lord and presenting our oblations to the glory and honor of His name. With the mortal mission of the Savior bringing about the Atonement and the Resurrection, the Sabbath shifted from the last day of the week to the first—and Sunday and Sabbath became synonymous. Thus the Sabbath is the Lord's day. He made it for us, commanding: "Remember the sabbath day, to keep it holy" (Exodus 20:8).

The purpose of the Sabbath day is to worship God, rest from our daily labors, renew our covenants, pray together, receive instruction in the ways of the Lord through the word of God, and receive edification to our spirits—all this in order to become more pure and grateful before the Lord. Honoring the Sabbath is not only one of the Ten Commandments but signifies our enduring covenant with God and our willing dependence upon Him.

Exodus 20:8–11. "Remember the sabbath day, to keep it holy. Six days shalt thou labour, and do all thy work: But the seventh day is the sabbath of the Lord thy God: in it thou shalt not do any work, thou, nor thy son, nor thy daughter, thy manservant, nor thy maidservant, nor thy cattle, nor thy stranger that is within thy gates: For in six days the Lord made heaven and earth, the sea, and all that in them is, and rested the seventh day: wherefore the Lord blessed the sabbath day, and hallowed it."

Matthew 12:8. "For the Son of man is Lord even of the sabbath day." (See also Luke 6:5.)

Mark 2:27–28. "And he said unto them, The sabbath was made for man, and not man for the sabbath: Therefore the Son of man is Lord also of the sabbath."

Luke 14:5–6. "And answered them, saying, Which of you shall have an ass or an ox fallen into a pit, and will not straightway pull him out on the sabbath day? And they could not answer him again to these things."

D&C 59:9–17. "And that thou mayest more fully keep thyself unspotted from the world, thou shalt go to the house of prayer and offer up thy sacraments upon my holy day; For verily this is a day appointed unto you to rest from your labors, and to pay thy devotions unto the Most High; Nevertheless thy vows shall be offered up in righteousness on all days and at all times; But remember that on this, the Lord's day, thou shalt offer thine oblations and thy sacraments unto the Most High, confessing thy sins unto thy brethren, and before the Lord. And on this day thou shalt do none other thing, only let thy food be prepared with singleness of heart that thy fasting may be perfect, or, in other words, that thy joy may be full. Verily, this is fasting and prayer, or in other words, rejoicing and prayer. And inasmuch as ye do these things with thanksgiving, with cheerful hearts and countenances, not with much laughter, for this is sin, but with a glad heart and a cheerful countenance—Verily I say, that inasmuch as ye do this, the fulness of the earth is yours, the beasts of the field and the fowls of the air, and that which climbeth upon the trees and walketh upon the earth; Yea, and the herb, and the good things which come of the earth, whether for food or for raiment, or for houses, or for barns, or for orchards, or for gardens, or for vineyards."

What counsel do the scriptures give concerning how to observe the Sabbath?

Avoid commercial activities on the Sabbath (under the law of Moses). Nehemiah 10:31. "And if the people of the land bring ware or any victuals on the sabbath day to sell, that we would not buy it of them on the sabbath, or on the holy day: and that we would leave the seventh year, and the exaction of every debt." (See also Nehemiah 13:15–22.)

Be charitable to the needy; turn away from personal pleasure; honor the Lord. Isaiah 58:6–7, 10, 13–14. "Is not this the fast that I have chosen? to loose the bands of wickedness, to undo the heavy burdens, and to let the oppressed go free, and that ye break every yoke? Is it not to deal thy bread to the hungry, and that thou bring the poor that are cast out to thy house? when thou seest the naked, that thou cover him; and that thou hide not thyself from thine own flesh?. . . And if thou draw out thy soul to the hungry, and satisfy the afflicted soul; then shall thy light rise in obscurity, and thy darkness be as the noonday. . . . If thou turn away thy foot from the sabbath, from doing thy pleasure on my holy day; and call the sabbath a delight, the holy of the Lord, honourable; and shalt honour him, not doing thine own ways, nor finding thine own pleasure, nor speaking thine own words: Then shalt thou delight thyself in the Lord; and I will cause thee to ride upon the high places of the earth, and feed thee with the heritage of Jacob thy father: for the mouth of the Lord hath spoken it."

Choose that which pleases the Lord; take hold of His covenant; love the Lord and be His servant; come to His holy mountain. Isaiah 56:1–8. "Thus saith the Lord, Keep ye judgment, and do justice: for my salvation is near to come, and my righteousness to be revealed. Blessed is the man that doeth this, and the son of man that layeth hold on it; that keepeth the sabbath from polluting it, and keepeth his hand from doing any evil. Neither let the son of the stranger, that hath joined himself to the Lord, speak, saying, The Lord hath utterly separated me from his people: neither let the eunuch say, Behold, I am a dry tree. For thus saith the Lord unto the eunuchs that keep my sabbaths, and choose the things that please me, and take hold of my covenant; Even unto them will I give in mine house and within my walls a place and a name better than of sons and of daughters: I will give them an everlasting name, that shall not be cut off. Also the sons of the stranger, that join themselves to the Lord, to serve him, and to love the name of the Lord, to be his servants, every one that keepeth the sabbath from polluting it, and taketh hold of my covenant; Even them will I bring to my holy mountain, and make them joyful in my house of prayer: their burnt offerings and their sacrifices shall be accepted upon mine altar; for mine house shall be called an house of prayer for all people. The Lord God which gathereth the outcasts of Israel saith, Yet will I gather others to him, beside those that are gathered unto him."

Give thanks. Mosiah 18:23. "And he [Alma the Elder] commanded them that they should observe the sabbath day, and keep it holy, and also every day they should give thanks to the Lord their God."

Heal the afflicted, and "do well" on the Sabbath. Matthew 12:10–13. "And, behold, there was a man which had his hand withered. And they asked him, saying, Is it lawful to heal on the sabbath days? that they might accuse him. And he said unto them, What man shall there be among you, that shall have one sheep, and if it fall into a pit on the sabbath day, will he not lay hold on it, and lift it out? How much then is a man better than a sheep?

Wherefore it is lawful to do well on the sabbath days. Then saith he to the man, Stretch forth thine hand. And he stretched it forth; and it was restored whole, like as the other." (See also Mark 3:1–6; Luke 6:6–11; 13:11–17; 14:1–6.)

Do the works of the Father. John 5:14–18. "Afterward Jesus findeth him in the temple, and said unto him, Behold, thou art made whole: sin no more, lest a worse thing come unto thee. The man departed, and told the Jews that it was Jesus, which had made him whole. And therefore did the Jews persecute Jesus, and sought to slay him, because he had done these things on the sabbath day. But Jesus answered them, My Father worketh hitherto, and I work. Therefore the Jews sought the more to kill him, because he not only had broken the sabbath, but said also that God was his Father, making himself equal with God."

Observe the spirit of the law rather than the letter of the law—according to the example of the Lord in defending His disciples for gathering some grain on the Sabbath. Matthew 12:1–8. "At that time Jesus went on the sabbath day through the corn; and his disciples were an hungred, and began to pluck the ears of corn, and to eat. But when the Pharisees saw it, they said unto him, Behold, thy disciples do that which is not lawful to do upon the sabbath day. But he said unto them, Have ye not read what David did, when he was an hungred, and they that were with him; How he entered into the house of God, and did eat the shewbread, which was not lawful for him to eat, neither for them which were with him, but only for the priests? Or have ye not read in the law, how that on the sabbath days the priests in the temple profane the sabbath, and are blameless? But I say unto you, That in this place is one greater than the temple. But if ye had known what this meaneth, I will have mercy, and not sacrifice, ye would not have condemned the guiltless. For the Son of man is Lord even of the sabbath day." (See also Mark 2:23–28; Luke 6:1–5.)

Partake of the sacrament. 3 Nephi 18:6–7. "And this shall ye always observe to do, even as I have done, even as I have broken bread and blessed it and given it unto you. And this shall ye do in remembrance of my body, which I have shown unto you. And it shall be a testimony unto the Father that ye do always remember me. And if ye do always remember me ye shall have my Spirit to be with you."

Perform no work on the Sabbath, even in harvest time (under the law of Moses). Exodus 34:21. "Six days thou shalt work, but on the seventh day thou shalt rest: in earing time and in harvest thou shalt rest."

Teach the gospel. Mark 1:21-22. "And they went into Capernaum; and straightway on the sabbath day he entered into the synagogue, and taught. And they were astonished at his doctrine: for he taught them as one that had authority, and not as the scribes." (See also Mark 6:1–4; Luke 4:16–19, 31–32; 13:10; Acts 13:14–16, 26–27, 42–45; 15:21; 16:13; 17:1–2; 18:4.)

Words of the Prophets | Spencer W. Kimball on being constructive on the Sabbath. "The Sabbath is a holy day in which to do worthy and holy things. Abstinence from work and recreation is important but insufficient. The Sabbath calls for constructive thoughts and acts, and if one merely lounges about doing nothing on the Sabbath, he is breaking it. To observe it, one will be on his knees in prayer, preparing lessons, studying the gospel, meditating, visiting the ill and distressed, sleeping, reading wholesome material, and attending all the meetings of that day to which he is expected. To fail to do these proper things is a transgression on the omission side." —Spencer W. Kimball, *The Miracle of Forgiveness* (Salt Lake City: Bookcraft, 1969), 96–97.

SACRAMENT [12]. The sacrament of the Lord's supper is a beautiful and hallowed ordinance in which the Atonement and our obedient acceptance of the Lord's sacrifice on our behalf are made a central part of our worship. The sacrament is an extension of our covenant promises to our Father in Heaven and His Only Begotten Son. The blessings we receive on this earth come from God our Father through, and because of, Jesus Christ. By partaking of the sacrament, we symbolically partake of His atoning sacrifice, with all of its accompanying blessings. We take His name upon us in worthiness and covenant to remember Him always and keep His commandments, thus qualifying to have His Spirit with us continually.

We partake of the sacrament not in private but in the congregations of the Saints, emphasizing unity and fellowship in honoring our mutual covenants. The sacramental prayers use the plural form: "*we* ask thee," "that *they* may eat," "that *they* are willing," "that *they* may always have his Spirit" (emphasis added; Moroni 4:3; see also Moroni 5:2; D&C 20:77, 79). It is a weekly reminder that we are truly part of the family of God.

Matthew 26:26–30. "And as they were eating, Jesus took bread, and blessed it, and brake it, and gave it to the disciples, and said, Take, eat; this is my body. And he took the cup, and gave thanks, and gave it to them, saying, Drink ye all of it; For this is my blood of the new testament, which is shed for many for the remission of sins. But I say unto you, I will not drink henceforth of this fruit of the vine, until that day when I drink it new with you in my Father's kingdom. And when they had sung an hymn, they went out into the mount of Olives."

3 Nephi 18:3–12. "And when the disciples had come with bread and wine, he took of the bread and brake and blessed it; and he gave unto the disciples and commanded that they should eat. And when they had eaten and were filled, he commanded that they should give unto the multitude. And when the multitude had eaten and were filled, he said unto the disciples: Behold there shall one be ordained among you, and to him will I give power that he shall break bread and bless it and give it unto the people of my church, unto all those who shall believe and be baptized in my name. And this shall ye always observe to do, even as I have done, even as I have broken bread and blessed it and given it unto you. And this shall ye do in remembrance of my body, which I have shown unto you. And it shall be a testimony unto the Father that ye do always remember me. And if ye do always remember me ye shall have my Spirit to be with you. And it came to pass that when he said these words, he commanded his disciples that they should take of the wine of the cup and drink of it, and that they should also give unto the multitude that they might drink of it. And it came to pass that they did so, and did drink of it and were filled; and they gave unto the multitude, and they did drink, and they were filled. And when the disciples had done this, Jesus said unto them: Blessed are ye for this thing which ye have done, for this is fulfilling my commandments, and this doth witness unto the Father that ye are willing to do that which I have commanded you. And this shall ye always do to those who repent and are baptized in my name; and ye shall do it in remembrance of my blood, which I have shed for you, that ye may witness unto the Father that ye do always remember me. And if ye do always remember me ye shall have my Spirit to be with you. And I give unto you a commandment that ye shall do these things."

Moroni 6:5–6. "And the church did meet together oft, to fast and to pray, and to speak one with another concerning the welfare of their souls. And they did meet together oft to partake of bread and wine, in remembrance of the Lord Jesus."

D&C 20:68–69. "The duty of the members after they are received by baptism.—The elders or priests are to have a sufficient time to expound all things concerning the church of Christ to their understanding, previous to their partaking of the sacrament and being confirmed by the laying on of the hands of the elders, so that all things may be done in order. And the members shall manifest before the church, and also before the elders, by a godly walk and conversation, that they are worthy of it, that there may be works and faith agreeable to the holy scriptures—walking in holiness before the Lord."

D&C 20:75–79. "It is expedient that the church meet together often to partake of bread and wine in the remembrance of the Lord Jesus; And the elder or priest shall administer it; and after this manner shall he administer it—he shall kneel with the church and call upon the Father in solemn prayer, saying: O God, the Eternal Father, we ask thee in the name of thy Son, Jesus Christ, to bless and sanctify this bread to the souls of all those who partake of it, that they may eat in remembrance of the body of thy Son, and witness unto thee, O God, the Eternal Father, that they are willing to take upon them the name of thy Son, and always remember him and keep his commandments which he has given them; that they may always have his Spirit to be with them. Amen. The manner of administering the wine—he shall take the cup also, and say: O God, the Eternal Father, we ask thee in the name of thy Son, Jesus Christ, to bless and sanctify this wine to the souls of all those who drink of it, that they may do it in remembrance of the blood of thy Son, which was shed for them; that they may witness unto thee, O God, the Eternal Father, that they do always remember him, that they may have his Spirit to be with them. Amen." (See also Moroni 4–5.)

D&C 59:9–12. "And that thou mayest more fully keep thyself unspotted from the world, thou shalt go to the house of prayer and offer up thy sacraments upon my holy day; For verily this is a day appointed unto you to rest from your labors, and to pay thy devotions unto the Most High; Nevertheless thy vows shall be offered up in righteousness on all days and at all times; But remember that on this, the Lord's day, thou shalt offer thine oblations and thy sacraments unto the Most High, confessing thy sins unto thy brethren, and before the Lord."

What is the symbolism of the sacrament?

Emblems of new life deriving from the Atonement—living bread and living water.
John 6:50–58. "This is the bread which cometh down from heaven, that a man may eat thereof, and not die. I am the living bread which came down from heaven: if any man eat of this bread, he shall live for ever: and the bread that I will give is my flesh, which I will give for the life of the world. The Jews therefore strove among themselves, saying, How can this man give us his flesh to eat? Then Jesus said unto them, Verily, verily, I say

unto you, Except ye eat the flesh of the Son of man, and drink his blood, ye have no life in you. Whoso eateth my flesh, and drinketh my blood, hath eternal life; and I will raise him up at the last day. For my flesh is meat indeed, and my blood is drink indeed. He that eateth my flesh, and drinketh my blood, dwelleth in me, and I in him. As the living Father hath sent me, and I live by the Father: so he that eateth me, even he shall live by me. This is that bread which came down from heaven: not as your fathers did eat manna, and are dead: he that eateth of this bread shall live for ever." (See also John 4:9–14; 1 Corinthians 10:16–17; 11:23–29.)

Emblems of sacrifice and suffering leading to peace and vitality. Matthew 26:36–39. "Then cometh Jesus with them unto a place called Gethsemane, and saith unto the disciples, Sit ye here, while I go and pray yonder. And he took with him Peter and the two sons of Zebedee, and began to be sorrowful and very heavy. Then saith he unto them, My soul is exceeding sorrowful, even unto death: tarry ye here, and watch with me. And he went a little further, and fell on his face, and prayed, saying, O my Father, if it be possible, let this cup pass from me: nevertheless not as I will, but as thou wilt." (See also Mosiah 3:7; D&C 19:15–20, 23–24.)

Like the Old Testament passover ordinance, the New Testament sacrament was in similitude of Lord's atoning sacrifice. Exodus 12:11–14. "And thus shall ye eat it; with your loins girded, your shoes on your feet, and your staff in your hand; and ye shall eat it in haste: it is the Lord's passover. For I will pass through the land of Egypt this night, and will smite all the firstborn in the land of Egypt, both man and beast; and against all the gods of Egypt I will execute judgment: I am the Lord. And the blood shall be to you for a token upon the houses where ye are: and when I see the blood, I will pass over you, and the plague shall not be upon you to destroy you, when I smite the land of Egypt. And this day shall be unto you for a memorial; and ye shall keep it a feast to the Lord throughout your generations; ye shall keep it a feast by an ordinance for ever."

Partaking of the sacrament (bread and wine or bread and water) with a broken heart and contrite spirit (our sacrifice) is in similitude of the Atonement. 3 Nephi 9:19–20. "And ye shall offer up unto me no more the shedding of blood; yea, your sacrifices and your burnt offerings shall be done away, for I will accept none of your sacrifices and your burnt offerings. And ye shall offer for a sacrifice unto me a broken heart and a contrite spirit. And whoso cometh unto me with a broken heart and a contrite spirit, him will I baptize with fire and with the Holy Ghost, even as the Lamanites, because of their faith in me at the time of their conversion, were baptized with fire and with the Holy Ghost, and they knew it not." (See also Matthew 26:26–30; Mark 14:22–25; Luke 22:19–20; John 6:50–51, 53-58; 1 Corinthians 10:16–17; 11:23–25; 2 Nephi 2:7; 3 Nephi 12:19–20; 18:3–14; 20:1–9; Ether 4:15; Moroni 4–5; 6:1–2, 5–6; D&C 20:37, 75–79.)

Words of the Prophets | Joseph Fielding Smith on remembering why we have the sacrament. "To 'always remember him,' does not mean simply to remember that he was crucified; but to keep in mind constantly the reasons why, and what blessings have come to each of us through his death and resurrection. We are to remember the great suffering and what it cost him to make the great atonement. We are to remember that he did it because of his love, not only for those who believe on him, but also for the whole world." —Joseph Fielding Smith, *Answers to Gospel Questions*, 5 vols. (Salt Lake City: Deseret Book, 1957–1966), 3:4.

SACRIFICE [384]. The eternal Exemplar of sacrifice is Jesus Christ, who gave His life for the "immortality and eternal life of man" (see Moses 1:39). In turn, we are asked to observe our covenants by sacrifice—anything the Lord may command (see D&C 97:8–9). Sacrifice has always been a key element of the plan of salvation. Throughout all dispensations of time, the Lord has required His children to make sacrifice an indispensable dimension of daily living as a constant reminder of the mercy and grace embodied in His own atoning sacrifice on their behalf. With the accomplishment of the infinite and eternal Atonement of the Savior in the meridian of time, blood sacrifice was sublimated into sacrifice of a different nature for the children of God, including the covenant offering of a broken heart and a contrite spirit. Such a sacrificial offering reflects the spirit of true repentance, even "godly sorrow" (2 Corinthians 7:10), leading to the lifting up of a new person and a rebirth spiritually unto the heritage of eternal life. Such a son or daughter of God is imbued with the spirit of charity toward all and the faithful commitment to sacrifice all that is required for the building up of the kingdom of God. In this sense, sacrifice becomes an exalting principle as it flows outwardly from an inner reservoir of love and obedience.

1 Samuel 15:22. "And Samuel said, Hath the Lord as great delight in burnt offerings and sacrifices, as in obeying the voice of the Lord? Behold, to obey is better than sacrifice, and to hearken than the fat of rams."

Psalm 51:17. "The sacrifices of God are a broken spirit: a broken and a contrite heart, O God, thou wilt not despise."

Hosea 6:6. "For I desired mercy, and not sacrifice; and the knowledge of God more than burnt offerings."

2 Nephi 2:7. "Behold, he offereth himself a sacrifice for sin, to answer the ends of the law, unto all those who have a broken heart and a contrite spirit; and unto none else can the ends of the law be answered."

Alma 34:13–16. "Therefore, it is expedient that there should be a great and last sacrifice, and then shall there be, or it is expedient there should be, a stop to the shedding of blood; then shall the law of Moses be fulfilled; yea, it shall be all fulfilled, every jot and tittle, and none shall have passed away. And behold, this is the whole meaning of the law, every whit pointing to that great and last sacrifice; and that great and last sacrifice will be the Son of God, yea, infinite and eternal. And thus he shall bring salvation to all those who shall believe on his name; this being the intent of this last sacrifice, to bring about the bowels of mercy, which overpowereth justice, and bringeth about means unto men that they may have faith unto repentance. And thus mercy can satisfy the demands of justice, and encircles them in the arms of safety, while he that exercises no faith unto repentance is exposed to the whole law of the demands of justice; therefore only unto him that has faith unto repentance is brought about the great and eternal plan of redemption."

D&C 59:8. "Thou shalt offer a sacrifice unto the Lord thy God in righteousness, even that of a broken heart and a contrite spirit."

Moses 5:6–9. "And after many days an angel of the Lord appeared unto Adam, saying: Why dost thou offer sacrifices unto the Lord? And Adam said unto him: I know not, save the Lord commanded me. And then the angel spake, saying: This thing is a similitude of the sacrifice of the Only Begotten of the Father, which is full of grace and truth. Wherefore, thou shalt do all that thou doest in the name of the Son, and thou shalt repent and call upon God in the name of the Son forevermore. And in that day the Holy Ghost fell upon Adam, which beareth record of the Father and the Son, saying: I am the Only Begotten of the Father from the beginning, henceforth and forever, that as thou hast fallen thou mayest be redeemed, and all mankind, even as many as will."

What do the scriptures counsel us to offer as our sacrifice?

A broken heart and a contrite spirit. Psalm 51:16–19. "For thou desirest not sacrifice; else would I give it: thou delightest not in burnt offering. The sacrifices of God are a broken spirit: a broken and a contrite heart, O God, thou wilt not despise. Do good in thy good pleasure unto Zion: build thou the walls of Jerusalem. Then shalt thou be pleased with the sacrifices of righteousness, with burnt offering and whole burnt offering: then shall they offer bullocks upon thine altar." (See also 3 Nephi 9:17–20; D&C 59:8.)

Doing the will of the Lord; preaching righteousness; declaring the lovingkindness of the Lord. Psalm 40:5–10. "Many, O Lord my God, are thy wonderful works which thou hast done, and thy thoughts which are to us-ward: they cannot be reckoned up in order unto thee: if I would declare and speak of them, they are more than can be numbered. Sacrifice and offering thou didst not desire; mine ears hast thou opened: burnt offering and sin offering hast thou not required. Then said I, Lo, I come: in the volume of the book it is written of me, I delight to do thy will, O my God: yea, thy law is within my heart. I have preached righteousness in the great congregation: lo, I have not refrained my lips, O Lord, thou knowest. I have not hid thy righteousness within my heart; I have declared thy faithfulness and thy salvation: I have not concealed thy lovingkindness and thy truth from the great congregation."

Doing well and acting with charity—rather than offering vain oblations. Isaiah 1:13, 16–18. "Bring no more vain oblations. . . . Wash you, make you clean; put away the evil of your doings from before mine eyes; cease to do evil; Learn to do well; seek judgment, relieve the oppressed, judge the fatherless, plead for the widow. Come now, and let us reason together, saith the Lord: though your sins be as scarlet, they shall be as white as snow; though they be red like crimson, they shall be as wool."

Joy and singing. Psalm 27:6. "And now shall mine head be lifted up above mine enemies round about me: therefore will I offer in his tabernacle sacrifices of joy; I will sing, yea, I will sing praises unto the Lord."

Observing the covenants in obedience. D&C 97:8-9. "Verily I say unto you, all among them who know their hearts are honest, and are broken, and their spirits contrite, and are willing to observe their covenants by sacrifice—yea, every sacrifice which I, the Lord, shall command—they are accepted of me. For I, the Lord, will cause them to bring forth as a very fruitful tree which is planted in a goodly land, by a pure stream, that yieldeth much precious fruit." (See also D&C 132:49-51; 132:60.)

Offering your body as a living sacrifice. Romans 12:1–3. "I beseech you therefore, brethren, by the mercies of God, that ye present your bodies a living sacrifice, holy, acceptable unto God, which is your reasonable service. And be not conformed to this world: but be ye transformed by the renewing of your mind, that ye may prove what is that good, and acceptable, and perfect, will of God. For I say, through the grace given unto me, to every man that is among you, not to think of himself more highly than he ought to think; but to think soberly, according as God hath dealt to every man the measure of faith."

Praying unto the Lord. Psalm 141:1–2. "Lord, I cry unto thee: make haste unto me; give ear unto my voice, when I cry unto thee. Let my prayer be set forth before thee as incense; and the lifting up of my hands as the evening sacrifice." (See also Proverbs 15:8; Jeremiah 33:11; Jonah 2:9; Hebrews 13:15–16.)

Repentance. 3 Nephi 12:19. "And behold, I have given you the law and the commandments of my Father, that ye shall believe in me, and that ye shall repent of your sins, and come unto me with a broken heart and a contrite spirit. Behold, ye have the commandments before you, and the law is fulfilled."

Service. Hebrews 5:1–4. "For every high priest taken from among men is ordained for men in things pertaining to God, that he may offer both gifts and sacrifices for sins: Who can have compassion on the ignorant, and on them that are out of the way; for that he himself also is compassed with infirmity. And by reason hereof he ought, as for the people, so also for himself, to offer for sins. And no man taketh this honour unto himself, but he that is called of God, as was Aaron."

Supporting the leaders of the Church. D&C 117:12–13. "And again, I say unto you, I remember my servant Oliver Granger; behold, verily I say unto him that his name shall be had in sacred remembrance from generation to generation, forever and ever, saith the Lord. Therefore, let him contend earnestly for the redemption of the First Presidency of my Church, saith the Lord; and when he falls he shall rise again, for his sacrifice shall be more sacred unto me than his increase, saith the Lord."

Tithing and temple work. D&C 97:10–13. "Verily I say unto you, that it is my will that a house should be built unto me in the land of Zion, like unto the pattern which I have given you. Yea, let it be built speedily, by the tithing of my people. Behold, this is the tithing and the sacrifice which I, the Lord, require at their hands, that there may be a house built unto me for the salvation of Zion— For a place of thanksgiving for all saints, and for a place of instruction for all those who are called to the work of the ministry in all their several callings and offices."

Words of the Prophets | Gordon B. Hinckley on the importance of sacrifice. "Sacrifice is the very essence of religion; it is the keystone of happy home life, the basis of true friendship, the foundation of peaceful community living, of sound relations among people and nations. . . . Without sacrifice there is no true worship of God. I become increasingly convinced of that every day. 'The Father gave his Son, and the Son gave his life,' and we do not worship unless we give—give of our substance, give of our time, give of our strength, give of our talent, give of our faith, give of our testimonies." —Gordon B. Hinckley, "Without Sacrifice There Is No True Worship," *BYU Speeches of the Year*, October 1962, 4.

SAINTS [223]. The word *saint* derives from the Latin word *sanctus*, meaning "holy" or "consecrated." In the gospel context, *Saint* refers to one who has come into the fold of Christ through obedience to the prescribed principles and ordinances of the gospel and is enduring to the end in righteousness. In our day, a Saint is a member of The Church of Jesus Christ of Latter-day Saints. The qualities of a Saint are many: faith, obedience, prayerfulness, and meekness, among others. The blessings accorded the Saints by the Lord—both now and in the future—are abundant and glorious, as the scriptures confirm.

Psalm 50:5. "Gather my saints together unto me; those that have made a covenant with me by sacrifice."

Psalm 89:7. "God is greatly to be feared in the assembly of the saints, and to be had in reverence of all them that are about him."

1 Corinthians 1:2–3. "Unto the church of God which is at Corinth, to them that are sanctified in Christ Jesus, called to be saints, with all that in every place call upon the name of Jesus Christ our Lord, both theirs and ours: Grace be unto you, and peace, from God our Father, and from the Lord Jesus Christ."

1 Corinthians 14:33. "For God is not the author of confusion, but of peace, as in all churches of the saints."

Ephesians 2:19–22. "Now therefore ye are no more strangers and foreigners, but fellowcitizens with the saints, and of the household of God; And are built upon the foundation of the apostles and prophets, Jesus Christ himself being the chief corner stone; In whom all the building fitly framed together groweth unto an holy temple in the Lord: In whom ye also are builded together for an habitation of God through the Spirit."

Ephesians 4:11–15. "And he gave some, apostles; and some, prophets; and some, evangelists; and some, pastors and teachers; For the perfecting of the saints, for the work of the ministry, for the edifying of the body of Christ: Till we all come in the unity of the faith, and of the knowledge of the Son of God, unto a perfect man, unto the measure of the stature of the fulness of Christ: That we henceforth be no more children, tossed to and fro, and carried about with every wind of doctrine, by the sleight of men, and cunning craftiness, whereby they lie in wait to deceive; But speaking the truth in love, may grow up into him in all things, which is the head, even Christ."

2 Nephi 9:18–19. "But, behold, the righteous, the saints of the Holy One of Israel, they who have believed in the Holy One of Israel, they who have endured the crosses of the world, and despised the shame of it, they shall inherit the kingdom of God, which was prepared for them from the foundation of the world, and their joy shall be full forever. O the greatness of the mercy of our God, the Holy One of Israel! For he delivereth his saints from that awful monster the devil, and death, and hell, and that lake of fire and brimstone, which is endless torment."

Mosiah 3:19. "For the natural man is an enemy to God, and has been from the fall of Adam, and will be, forever and ever, unless he yields to the enticings of the Holy Spirit, and putteth off the natural man and becometh a saint through the atonement of Christ the Lord, and becometh as a child, submissive, meek, humble, patient, full of love, willing to submit to all things which the Lord seeth fit to inflict upon him, even as a child doth submit to his father."

D&C 88:106–107. "And again, another angel shall sound his trump, which is the seventh angel, saying: It is finished; it is finished! The Lamb of God hath overcome and trodden the wine-press alone, even the wine-press of the fierceness of the wrath of Almighty God. And then shall the angels be crowned with the glory of his might, and the saints shall be filled with his glory, and receive their inheritance and be made equal with him."

D&C 104:15–17. "And it is my purpose to provide for my saints, for all things are mine. But it must needs be done in mine own way; and behold this is the way that I, the Lord, have decreed to provide for my saints, that the poor shall be exalted, in that the rich are made low. For the earth is full, and there is enough and to spare; yea, I prepared all things, and have given unto the children of men to be agents unto themselves."

D&C 115:3–4. "And also unto my faithful servants who are of the high council of my church in Zion, for thus it shall be called, and unto all the elders and people of my Church of Jesus Christ of Latter-day Saints, scattered abroad in all the world. For thus shall my church be called in the last days, even The Church of Jesus Christ of Latter-day Saints."

SALVATION [315]. Salvation is the state of being saved in the kingdom of God. By the solemn assurance of the Lord Himself, salvation "is the greatest of all the gifts of God; for there is no gift greater than the gift of salvation" (D&C 6:13). Jesus Christ—"even the messenger of salvation" (D&C 93:8)—continues to declare by multiple means the true principles of salvation to all mankind, according to their willingness to hear and respond (see D&C 43:25). Salvation, in its various nuances of meaning, applies to a sequence of interrelated states of being: the predicates of redemption laid down in the premortal realm, the various episodes throughout time where the Lord intervened to liberate His people from their enemies (as in the exodus from Egypt), the everyday lives of all who live by faith and obedience and thus immediately experience the joy and blessings of redemption, and the ultimate state of glory and eternal life reserved for the heirs of salvation in the coming world.

Isaiah 12:2–3. "Behold, God is my salvation; I will trust, and not be afraid: for the Lord Jehovah is my strength and my song; he also is become my salvation. Therefore with joy shall ye draw water out of the wells of salvation." (See also 2 Nephi 22:2–3.)

Romans 1:16. "For I am not ashamed of the gospel of Christ: for it is the power of God unto salvation to every one that believeth; to the Jew first, and also to the Greek."

Hebrews 5:8–9. "Though he were a Son, yet learned he obedience by the things which he suffered; And being made perfect, he became the author of eternal salvation unto all them that obey him."

Omni 1:26. "And now, my beloved brethren, I would that ye should come unto Christ, who is the Holy One of Israel, and partake of his salvation, and the power of his redemption. Yea, come unto him, and offer your whole souls as an offering unto him, and continue in fasting and praying, and endure to the end; and as the Lord liveth ye will be saved."

Mosiah 3:17–18. "And moreover, I say unto you, that there shall be no other name given nor any other way nor means whereby salvation can come unto the children of men, only in and through the name of Christ, the Lord Omnipotent. For behold he judgeth, and his judgment is just; and the infant perisheth not that dieth in his infancy; but men drink damnation to their own souls except they humble themselves and become as little children, and believe that salvation was, and is, and is to come, in and through the atoning blood of Christ, the Lord Omnipotent."

Mosiah 28:3–4. "Now they were desirous that salvation should be declared to every creature, for they could not bear that any human soul should perish; yea, even the very thoughts that any soul should endure endless torment did cause them to quake and tremble. And thus did the Spirit of the Lord work upon them, for they were the very vilest of sinners. And the Lord saw fit in his infinite mercy to spare them; nevertheless they suffered much anguish of soul because of their iniquities, suffering much and fearing that they should be cast off forever."

Alma 26:14–15. "Yea, we have reason to praise him forever, for he is the Most High God, and has loosed our brethren from the chains of hell. Yea, they were encircled about with everlasting darkness and destruction; but behold, he has brought them into his everlasting light, yea, into everlasting salvation; and they are encircled about with the matchless bounty of his love; yea, and we have been instruments in his hands of doing this great and marvelous work."

D&C 4:4. "For behold the field is white already to harvest; and lo, he that thrusteth in his sickle with his might, the same layeth up in store that he perisheth not, but bringeth salvation to his soul."

D&C 6:13. "If thou wilt do good, yea, and hold out faithful to the end, thou shalt be saved in the kingdom of God, which is the greatest of all the gifts of God; for there is no gift greater than the gift of salvation."

D&C 128:15. "And now, my dearly beloved brethren and sisters, let me assure you that these are principles in relation to the dead and the living that cannot be lightly passed over, as pertaining to our salvation. For their salvation is necessary and essential to our salvation, as Paul says concerning the fathers—that they without us cannot be made perfect—neither can we without our dead be made perfect."

Moses 6:59–62. "That by reason of transgression cometh the fall, which fall bringeth death, and inasmuch as ye were born into the world by water, and blood, and the spirit, which I have made, and so became of dust a living soul, even so ye must be born again into the kingdom of heaven, of water, and of the Spirit, and be cleansed by blood, even the blood of mine Only Begotten; that ye might be sanctified from all sin, and enjoy the words of eternal life in this world, and eternal life in the world to come, even immortal glory; For by the water ye keep the commandment; by the Spirit ye are justified, and by the blood ye are sanctified; Therefore it is given to abide in you; the record of heaven; the Comforter; the peaceable things of immortal glory; the truth of all things; that which quickeneth all things, which maketh alive all things; that which knoweth all things, and hath all power according to wisdom, mercy, truth, justice, and judgment. And now, behold, I say unto you: This is the plan of salvation unto all men, through the blood of mine Only Begotten, who shall come in the meridian of time."

How are we to obtain salvation?

Being as little children—who are saved in innocence. Moroni 8:17. "And I am filled with charity, which is everlasting love; wherefore, all children are alike unto me; wherefore, I love little children with a perfect love; and they are all alike and partakers of salvation." (See also Mosiah 3:19.)

Being meek. Psalm 149:4. "For the Lord taketh pleasure in his people: he will beautify the meek with salvation."

Being sealed by the Holy Spirit of promise. Ephesians 1:12–13. "That we should be to the praise of his glory, who first trusted in Christ. In whom ye also trusted, after that ye heard the word of truth, the gospel of your salvation: in whom also after that ye believed, ye were sealed with that holy Spirit of promise."

Being wise, receptive of the truth, and heeding the Spirit. D&C 45:57–59. "For they that are wise and have received the truth, and have taken the Holy Spirit for their guide, and have not been deceived—verily I say unto you, they shall not be hewn down and cast into the fire, but shall abide the day. And the earth shall be given unto them for an inheritance; and they shall multiply and wax strong, and their children shall grow up without sin unto salvation. For the Lord shall be in their midst, and his glory shall be upon them, and he will be their king and their lawgiver."

Coming unto Christ and enduring to the end. Omni 1:26. "And now, my beloved brethren, I would that ye should come unto Christ, who is the Holy One of Israel, and partake of his salvation, and the power of his redemption. Yea, come unto him, and offer your whole souls as an offering unto him, and continue in fasting and praying, and endure to the end; and as the Lord liveth ye will be saved."

Doing missionary work. D&C 4:4. "For behold the field is white already to harvest; and lo, he that thrusteth in his sickle with his might, the same layeth up in store that he perisheth not, but bringeth salvation to his soul." (See also D&C 6:3; 11:3; 12:3; 14:3.)

Following the scriptures. 2 Timothy 3:15–17. "And that from a child thou hast known the holy scriptures, which are able to make thee wise unto salvation through faith which is in Christ Jesus. All scripture is given by inspiration of God, and is profitable for doctrine, for reproof, for correction, for instruction in righteousness: That the man of God may be perfect, throughly furnished unto all good works."

Following the witness of the prophets. Jacob 4:12–13. "And now, beloved, marvel not that I tell you these things; for why not speak of the atonement of Christ, and attain to a perfect knowledge of him, as to attain to the knowledge of a resurrection and the world to come? Behold, my brethren, he that prophesieth, let him prophesy to the understanding of men; for the Spirit speaketh the truth and lieth not. Wherefore, it speaketh of things as they really are, and of things as they really will be; wherefore, these things are manifested unto us plainly, for the salvation of our souls. But behold, we are not witnesses alone in these things; for God also spake them unto prophets of old."

Obeying the commandments, preaching, and being clean. D&C 38:40–42. "And again, I say unto you, I give unto you a commandment, that every man, both elder, priest, teacher, and also member, go to with his might, with the labor of his hands, to prepare and accomplish the things which I have commanded. And let your preaching be the warning voice, every man to his neighbor, in mildness and in meekness. And go ye out from among the wicked. Save yourselves. Be ye clean that bear the vessels of the Lord." (See also D&C 46:7.)

Receiving the words of the Lord. 3 Nephi 28:34–35. "And wo be unto him that will not hearken unto the words of Jesus, and also to them whom he hath chosen and sent among them; for whoso receiveth not the words of Jesus and the words of those whom he hath sent receiveth not him; and therefore he will not receive them at the last day; And it would be better for them if they had not been born. For do ye suppose that ye can get rid of the justice of an offended God, who hath been trampled under feet of men, that thereby salvation might come?"

Repenting. 2 Corinthians 7:10. "For godly sorrow worketh repentance to salvation not to be repented of: but the sorrow of the world worketh death." (See also Helaman 5:11; 3 Nephi 18:31–32.)

Supporting the work of the temple. D&C 42:35–36. "And for the purpose of purchasing lands for the public benefit of the church, and building houses of worship, and building up of the New Jerusalem which is hereafter to be revealed— That my covenant people may be gathered in one in that day when I shall come to my temple. And this I do for the salvation of my people." (See also D&C 97:10–12; 128:5, 8, 11–15, 23; Official Declaration—1.)

SATAN [150]. Satan is the devil, the arch-enemy of all righteousness, the primary opponent against Heavenly Father's divine plan of salvation and exaltation, the principal adversary of the Son of God, the fallen angel who misled a third part of the hosts of heaven in the premortal existence, the tempter and deceiver of those born into mortality, and the ultimate leader of the dominion of eternal darkness destined to house those children of God who refuse all truth, deny all light, defy all saving principles, and earn no glory.

Genesis 3:14–15. "And the Lord God said unto the serpent, Because thou hast done this, thou art cursed above all cattle, and above every beast of the field; upon thy belly shalt thou go, and dust shalt thou eat all the days of thy life: And I will put enmity between thee and the woman, and between thy seed and her seed [i.e., Jesus Christ]; it shall bruise thy head, and thou shalt bruise his heel." (See also Moses 4:20–21.)

Isaiah 14:12–15. "How art thou fallen from heaven, O Lucifer, son of the morning! how art thou cut down to the ground, which didst weaken the nations! For thou hast said in thine heart, I will ascend into heaven, I will exalt my throne above the stars of God: I will sit also upon the mount of the congregation, in the sides of the north: I will ascend above the heights of the clouds; I will be like the most High. Yet thou shalt be brought down to hell, to the sides of the pit." (See also 2 Peter 2:4; Jude 1:6; Revelation 12:3–4; 2 Nephi 24:12–15.)

Luke 10:17–19. "And the seventy returned again with joy, saying, Lord, even the devils are subject unto us through thy name. And he said unto them, I beheld Satan as lightning fall from heaven. Behold, I give unto you power to tread on serpents and scorpions, and over all the power of the enemy: and nothing shall by any means hurt you."

2 Nephi 2:27. "Wherefore, men are free according to the flesh; and all things are given them which are expedient unto man. And they are free to choose liberty and eternal life, through the great Mediator of all men, or to choose captivity and death, according to the captivity and power of the devil; for he seeketh that all men might be miserable like unto himself."

2 Nephi 9:7–10. "Wherefore, it must needs be an infinite atonement—save it should be an infinite atonement this corruption could not put on incorruption . . . For behold, if the flesh should rise no more our spirits must become subject to that angel who fell from before the presence of the Eternal God, and became the devil, to rise no more. And our spirits must have become like unto him, and we become devils, angels to a devil, to be shut out from the presence of our God, and to remain with the father of lies, in misery, like unto himself; yea, to that being who beguiled our first parents, who transformeth himself nigh unto an angel of light, and stirreth up the children of men unto secret combinations of murder and all manner of secret works of darkness."

Helaman 6:30. "And behold, it is he who is the author of all sin. And behold, he doth carry on his works of darkness and secret murder, and doth hand down their plots, and their oaths, and their covenants, and their plans of awful wickedness, from generation to generation according as he can get hold upon the hearts of the children of men."

D&C 29:36–39. "And it came to pass that Adam, being tempted of the devil—for, behold, the devil was before Adam, for he rebelled against me, saying, Give me thine honor, which is my power; and also a third part of the hosts of heaven turned he away from me because of their agency; And they were thrust down, and thus came the devil and his angels; And, behold, there is a place prepared for them from the beginning, which place is hell. And it must needs be that the devil should tempt the children of men, or they could not be agents unto themselves; for if they never should have bitter they could not know the sweet."

D&C 88:110–116. "And so on, until the seventh angel shall sound his trump; and he shall stand forth upon the land and upon the sea, and swear in the name of him who sitteth upon the throne, that there shall be time no longer; and Satan shall be bound, that old serpent, who is called the devil, and shall not be loosed for the space of a thousand years. And then he shall be loosed for a little season, that he may gather together his armies. And Michael, the seventh angel, even the archangel, shall gather together his armies, even the hosts of heaven. And the devil shall gather together his armies; even the hosts of hell, and shall come up to battle against Michael and his armies. And then cometh the battle of the great God; and the devil and his armies shall be cast away into their own place, that they shall not have power over the saints any more at all. For Michael shall fight their battles, and shall overcome him who seeketh the throne of him who sitteth upon the throne, even the Lamb. This is the glory of God, and the sanctified; and they shall not any more see death." (See also Revelation 12:7–10.)

Moses 4:1–4. "And I, the Lord God, spake unto Moses, saying: That Satan, whom thou hast commanded in the name of mine Only Begotten, is the same which was from the beginning, and he came before me, saying—Behold, here am I, send me, I will be thy son, and I will redeem all mankind, that one soul shall not be lost, and surely I will do it;

wherefore give me thine honor. But, behold, my Beloved Son, which was my Beloved and Chosen from the beginning, said unto me—Father, thy will be done, and the glory be thine forever. Wherefore, because that Satan rebelled against me, and sought to destroy the agency of man, which I, the Lord God, had given him, and also, that I should give unto him mine own power; by the power of mine Only Begotten, I caused that he should be cast down; And he became Satan, yea, even the devil, the father of all lies, to deceive and to blind men, and to lead them captive at his will, even as many as would not hearken unto my voice."

ADDITIONAL INFORMATION—**The names of Satan.** The word *Satan,* in its Greek, Latin, and Hebrew sources, means "adversary"—the perfect characterization of the fallen angel's defining role in opposing the Father's plan of redemption and rejecting the choice of Jehovah as Redeemer from the foundations of the world. The word *devil,* in its Latin and Greek etymological derivation, means, in general, "slanderer"—an accurate characterization of the fallen angel's strategy in opposing the eternal source of truth. The word *perdition* in English usage comes from the Latin verb *perdere,* meaning "to lose." Assuredly, Satan is the archetype of the loser, for as an angel in authority in the premortal existence who rebelled against the Almighty God, he lost forever the divinely appointed opportunity to receive an inheritance of glory. The word *Lucifer* literally means "the shining one" or "the lightbringer" (see Bible Dictionary, 726). *Lucifer* is the Latin word for "light" (see also the related word *lucid*) and is the equivalent of the appellation "son of the morning." The case of Lucifer (Perdition, Satan, devil, etc.) is the most fundamental example of irony in the scriptures, for how could a being of light (son of the morning) transform himself into the archetypal representative of darkness? The benighted personality of Satan, the old serpent, stands in infinite contrast to the grandeur of the eternal source of light and truth, even the Father and the Son.

SCRIPTURES [134]. The word of God—given unto His children by His own voice, or by the voice of holy angels and chosen prophets—is compelling evidence of His boundless love. The central objective of the scriptures is to provide a continuous flow of light to illuminate the pathway leading to Christ. By following the word of God, we can come unto Christ and partake of the blessings of the gospel and eternal life (see 2 Nephi 32:3, 5).

In its broadest sense, the word of God constitutes the divine directive to bring about "the immortality and eternal life of man" (see Moses 1:39). It caused the Creation to unfold (see Hebrews 11:3; Psalm 33:6; Moses 3:7). The word of God was and is the guiding force that sustains the forward progress of God's Church and kingdom upon the earth (see Mosiah 26:38). And the Word of God is the Son of God—Jesus Christ, Himself, the Author of eternal salvation through the power of the Atonement (see Revelation 19:11–13).

The Restoration in the latter days has enriched our treasure of scriptural truth concerning the eternal covenant between God and His children. The Book of Mormon has brought back the "the fulness of the gospel of Jesus Christ" (D&C 20:9); the Doctrine and Covenants has restored the foundation of priesthood precepts and principles for unfolding the kingdom of God on the earth; the Pearl of Great Price has confirmed the eternal pattern of how God relates to mankind—past, present, and future. This restored word of

God, when written in the hearts of the Saints and infused in their thoughts, actions, and patterns of living, becomes the testament of salvation and the constitution of exaltation unto all who will yield to the will of the Father and the Son. The scriptures testify and witness that Jesus Christ is indeed the promised Messiah—the Savior and Redeemer of the world—and that through Him and through obedience to His word, we can gain eternal life (see 2 Nephi 31:20).

Luke 4:4. "It is written, That man shall not live by bread alone, but by every word of God."

2 Timothy 3:14–17. "But continue thou in the things which thou hast learned and hast been assured of, knowing of whom thou hast learned them; And that from a child thou hast known the holy scriptures, which are able to make thee wise unto salvation through faith which is in Christ Jesus. All scripture is given by inspiration of God, and is profitable for doctrine, for reproof, for correction, for instruction in righteousness: That the man of God may be perfect, throughly [i.e., thoroughly] furnished unto all good works."

1 Peter 1: 24–25. "For all flesh is as grass, and all the glory of man as the flower of grass. The grass withereth, and the flower thereof falleth away: But the word of the Lord endureth for ever. And this is the word which by the gospel is preached unto you."

2 Peter 1:19–21. "We have also a more sure word of prophecy; whereunto ye do well that ye take heed, as unto a light that shineth in a dark place, until the day dawn, and the day star arise in your hearts: Knowing this first, that no prophecy of the scripture is of any private interpretation. For the prophecy came not in old time by the will of man: but holy men of God spake as they were moved by the Holy Ghost."

2 Nephi 29:10–14. "Wherefore, because that ye have a Bible ye need not suppose that it contains all my words; neither need ye suppose that I have not caused more to be written. For I command all men, both in the east and in the west, and in the north, and in the south, and in the islands of the sea, that they shall write the words which I speak unto them; for out of the books which shall be written I will judge the world, every man according to their works, according to that which is written. For behold, I shall speak unto the Jews and they shall write it; and I shall also speak unto the Nephites and they shall write it; and I shall also speak unto the other tribes of the house of Israel, which I have led away, and they shall write it; and I shall also speak unto all nations of the earth and they shall write it. And it shall come to pass that the Jews shall have the words of the Nephites, and the Nephites shall have the words of the Jews; and the Nephites and the Jews shall have the words of the lost tribes of Israel; and the lost tribes of Israel shall have the words of the Nephites and the Jews. And it shall come to pass that my people, which are of the house of Israel, shall be gathered home unto the lands of their possessions; and my word also shall be gathered in one. And I will show unto them that fight against my word and against my people, who are of the house of Israel, that I am God, and that I covenanted with Abraham that I would remember his seed forever."

2 Nephi 32:3. "Angels speak by the power of the Holy Ghost; wherefore, they speak the words of Christ. Wherefore, I said unto you, feast upon the words of Christ; for behold, the words of Christ will tell you all things what ye should do." (See also 2 Nephi 31:20).

Alma 37:8. "And now, it has hitherto been wisdom in God that these things should be preserved; for behold, they have enlarged the memory of this people, yea, and convinced many of the error of their ways, and brought them to the knowledge of their God unto the salvation of their souls."

3 Nephi 28:33. "And if ye had all the scriptures which give an account of all the marvelous works of Christ, ye would, according to the words of Christ, know that these things must surely come. And wo be unto him that will not hearken unto the words of Jesus, and also to them whom he hath chosen and sent among them; for whoso receiveth not the words of Jesus and the words of those whom he hath sent receiveth not him; and therefore he will not receive them at the last day."

Moroni 10:3–5. "Behold, I would exhort you that when ye shall read these things, if it be wisdom in God that ye should read them, that ye would remember how merciful the Lord hath been unto the children of men, from the creation of Adam even down until the time that ye shall receive these things, and ponder it in your hearts. And when ye shall receive these things, I would exhort you that ye would ask God, the Eternal Father, in the name of Christ, if these things are not true; and if ye shall ask with a sincere heart, with real intent, having faith in Christ, he will manifest the truth of it unto you, by the power of the Holy Ghost. And by the power of the Holy Ghost ye may know the truth of all things."

D&C 20:69. "And the members shall manifest before the church, and also before the elders, by a godly walk and conversation, that they are worthy of it, that there may be works and faith agreeable to the holy scriptures—walking in holiness before the Lord."

D&C 35:20. "And a commandment I give unto thee—that thou [Sydney Rigdon] shalt write for him; and the scriptures shall be given, even as they are in mine own bosom, to the salvation of mine own elect."

D&C 84:45. "For the word of the Lord is truth, and whatsoever is truth is light, and whatsoever is light is Spirit, even the Spirit of Jesus Christ."

Eighth Article of Faith. "We believe the Bible to be the word of God as far as it is translated correctly; we also believe the Book of Mormon to be the word of God."

How does one obtain a testimony of the truth of the scriptures?

By honoring God and accepting His word. D&C 20:35–36. "And we know that these things are true and according to the revelations of John, neither adding to, nor diminishing from the prophecy of his book, the holy scriptures, or the revelations of God which shall come hereafter by the gift and power of the Holy Ghost, the voice of God, or the ministering of angels. And the Lord God has spoken it; and honor, power and glory be rendered to his holy name, both now and ever."

By searching daily. Acts 17:1–2, 11–12. "Now when they had passed through Amphipolis and Apollonia, they came to Thessalonica, where was a synagogue of the Jews: And Paul, as his manner was, went in unto them, and three sabbath days reasoned with them out of the scriptures. . . . These were more noble than those in Thessalonica, in that they received the word with all readiness of mind, and searched the scriptures daily, whether those things were so. Therefore many of them believed; also of honourable women which were Greeks, and of men, not a few."

Through continual heed and diligence. Alma 12:9–11. "It is given unto many to know the mysteries of God; nevertheless they are laid under a strict command that they shall not impart only according to the portion of his word which he doth grant unto the children of men, according to the heed and diligence which they give unto him. And therefore, he that will harden his heart, the same receiveth the lesser portion of the word; and he that will not harden his heart, to him is given the greater portion of the word, until it is given unto him to know the mysteries of God until he know them in full. And they that will harden their hearts, to them is given the lesser portion of the word until they know nothing concerning his mysteries." (See also Alma 17:2–3.)

Through the sincere prayer of faith. Moroni 10:3–5. "Behold, I would exhort you that when ye shall read these things, if it be wisdom in God that ye should read them, that ye would remember how merciful the Lord hath been unto the children of men, from the creation of Adam even down until the time that ye shall receive these things, and ponder it in your hearts. And when ye shall receive these things, I would exhort you that ye would ask God, the Eternal Father, in the name of Christ, if these things are not true; and if ye shall ask with a sincere heart, with real intent, having faith in Christ, he will manifest the truth of it unto you, by the power of the Holy Ghost. And by the power of the Holy Ghost ye may know the truth of all things."

Through gradual enlightenment. D&C 98:12. "For he will give unto the faithful line upon line, precept upon precept; and I will try you and prove you herewith." (See also Isaiah 28:9–10; 2 Nephi 28:30; D&C 50:24.)

What scriptures will yet come forth?

Book of remembrance during the days of Adam. Moses 6:5. "And a book of remembrance was kept, in the which was recorded, in the language of Adam, for it was given unto as many as called upon God to write by the spirit of inspiration."

Book of Enoch. D&C 107:56–57. "And Adam stood up in the midst of the congregation; and, notwithstanding he was bowed down with age, being full of the Holy Ghost, predicted whatsoever should befall his posterity unto the latest generation. These things were all written in the book of Enoch, and are to be testified of in due time." (See also Jude 1:14.)

Records from other prophets who have been shown all things. 1 Nephi 14:25–26. "But the things which thou [Nephi] shalt see hereafter thou shalt not write; for the Lord God hath ordained the apostle of the Lamb of God that he should write them. And also others who have been, to them hath he shown all things, and they have written them; and they are sealed up to come forth in their purity, according to the truth which is in the Lamb, in the own due time of the Lord, unto the house of Israel."

Records of the lost tribes and other nations. 2 Nephi 29:11–14. "For I command all men, both in the east and in the west, and in the north, and in the south, and in the islands of the sea, that they shall write the words which I speak unto them; for out of the books which shall be written I will judge the world, every man according to their works, according to that which is written. For behold, I shall speak unto the Jews and they shall write it; and I shall also speak unto the Nephites and they shall write it; and I shall also speak unto the other tribes of the house of Israel, which I have led away, and they shall write it; and I shall also speak unto all nations of the earth and they shall write it. And it shall come to pass that the Jews shall have the words of the Nephites, and the Nephites shall have the words of the Jews; and the Nephites and the Jews shall have the words of the lost tribes of Israel; and the lost tribes of Israel shall have the words of the Nephites and the Jews. And it shall come to pass that my people, which are of the house of Israel, shall be gathered home unto the lands of their possessions; and my word also shall be gathered in one."

Many great and important things yet to be revealed. Ninth Article of Faith. "We believe all that God has revealed, all that He does now reveal, and we believe that He will yet reveal many great and important things pertaining to the Kingdom of God."

Missing scriptures that may one day be revealed. Exodus 24:7 ("book of the covenant"); Numbers 21:14 ("book of the wars of the Lord"); Joshua 10:13 ("book of Jasher"); 1 Kings 11:41 ("book of the acts of Solomon"); 1 Chronicles 29:29 ("the book of Samuel the seer," "the book of Nathan the prophet," "the book of Gad the seer"); 2 Chronicles 9:29 ("the book of Nathan the prophet," "the prophecy of Ahijah the Shilonite," "the visions of Iddo the seer"); 2 Chronicles 12:15 ("the book of Shemaiah the prophet, and of Iddo the seer"); 2 Chronicles 20:34 ("the book of Jehu the son of Hanani"); 2 Chronicles 26:22 ("the acts of Uzziah"); 2 Chronicles 33:19 ("the sayings of the seers"); 1 Corinthians 5:9 ("I wrote unto you in an epistle not to company with fornicators"); Ephesians 3:3–4 (Epistle testifying of Christ); Colossians 4:16 (Epistle to "the church in Laodiceans . . . the epistle from Laodicea"); Jude 1:3 (Epistle on salvation and faith); 1 Nephi 19:10 (the book of Neum); Helaman 8:19 (the book of Zenos); 8:20 (the book of Zenock, the book of Ezias).

WORDS OF THE PROPHETS | **Joseph Smith on the Book of Mormon.** "Take away the Book of Mormon and the revelations, and where is our religion? We have none." —Joseph Smith, *HC* 2:52.

Gordon B. Hinckley on the joy of the scriptures. "I am grateful for emphasis on reading the scriptures. I hope that for you this will become something far more enjoyable than a duty; that, rather, it will become a love affair with the word of God. I promise you that as you read, your minds will be enlightened and your spirits will be lifted. At first it may seem tedious, but that will change into a wondrous experience with thoughts and words of things divine." —Gordon B. Hinckley, "The Light within You," *Ensign*, May 1995, 99.

Cross reference to "Scriptures": see Preach My Gospel, *180–182.*

SECOND COMING [1]. The Second Coming of our Lord is a reality soon to occur. The tenth Article of Faith confirms that "Christ will reign personally upon the earth; and, that the earth will be renewed and receive its paradisiacal glory." His return will take place amidst overwhelming power and all-encompassing glory, cloaked as He will be in the brilliance of His red robes of judgment (see D&C 133:48; Isaiah 63:2) and surrounded by the consuming radiance of His presence. He will instill in all the inhabitants of the world, at an instant, the awe of His majesty; all will proclaim His Saviorhood—the wicked will be constrained to testify, and the Saints will joyfully testify (see D&C 88:104). At the time of the Second Coming, the Millennium will be ushered in, accompanied by enormous upheaval and cataclysmic change—a nightmare for the wayward and a long-awaited blessing for the faithful. The Son of Man will fulfill His commission to judge the inhabitants of the earth and receive the faithful in a cloud of angelic choirs. We can prepare ourselves to participate in this supernal event by following the admonition of the Lord to prepare ourselves spiritually and temporally.

Malachi 4:5–6. "Behold, I will send you Elijah the prophet before the coming of the great and dreadful day of the Lord: And he shall turn the heart of the fathers to the children, and the heart of the children to their fathers, lest I come and smite the earth with a curse." (See also 3 Nephi 25:5–6; D&C 2; 110:13–16; 128:17; JS—H 1:38–39.)

Matthew 24:35–36. "Heaven and earth shall pass away, but my words shall not pass away. But of that day and hour knoweth no man, no, not the angels of heaven, but my Father only."

Mark 13:31–32. "Heaven and earth shall pass away: but my words shall not pass away. But of that day and that hour knoweth no man, no, not the angels which are in heaven, neither the Son, but the Father." (See also Matthew 24:36.)

D&C 38:30. "But if ye are prepared ye shall not fear."

D&C 45:32. "But my disciples shall stand in holy places, and shall not be moved; but among the wicked, men shall lift up their voices and curse God and die."

D&C 45:44. "And then they shall look for me, and, behold, I will come; and they shall see me in the clouds of heaven, clothed with power and great glory; with all the holy angels; and he that watches not for me shall be cut off."

D&C 76:61–63. "Wherefore, let no man glory in man, but rather let him glory in God, who shall subdue all enemies under his feet. These shall dwell in the presence of God and his Christ forever and ever. These are they whom he shall bring with him, when he shall come in the clouds of heaven to reign on the earth over his people."

D&C 87:8. "Wherefore, stand ye in holy places, and be not moved, until the day of the Lord come; for behold, it cometh quickly, saith the Lord."

D&C 101:22–23. "Behold, it is my will, that all they who call on my name, and worship me according to mine everlasting gospel, should gather together, and stand in holy places; And prepare for the revelation which is to come, when the veil of the covering of my temple, in my tabernacle, which hideth the earth, shall be taken off, and all flesh shall see me together."

D&C 101:36–38. "Wherefore, fear not even unto death; for in this world your joy is not full, but in me your joy is full. Therefore, care not for the body, neither the life of the body; but care for the soul, and for the life of the soul. And seek the face of the Lord always, that in patience ye may possess your souls, and ye shall have eternal life."

How are we to prepare for the Second Coming?

Abound in love toward all. 1 Thessalonians 3:12–13. "And the Lord make you to increase and abound in love one toward another, and toward all men, even as we do toward you: To the end he may stablish your hearts unblameable in holiness before God, even our Father, at the coming of our Lord Jesus Christ with all his saints."

Be cheerful and fear not, for the Lord is with you. D&C 68:6. "Wherefore, be of good cheer, and do not fear, for I the Lord am with you, and will stand by you; and ye shall bear record of me, even Jesus Christ, that I am the Son of the living God, that I was, that I am, and that I am to come."

Be pure and free of sin. D&C 88:86. "Abide ye in the liberty wherewith ye are made free; entangle not yourselves in sin, but let your hands be clean, until the Lord comes."

Believe and cry repentance to the world through the power of the Holy Ghost. D&C 34:5–6, 10. "And more blessed are you because you are called of me to preach my gospel—To lift up your voice as with the sound of a trump, both long and loud, and cry repentance unto a crooked and perverse generation, preparing the way of the Lord for his second coming. Wherefore, lift up your voice and spare not, for the Lord God hath spoken; therefore prophesy, and it shall be given by the power of the Holy Ghost."

Know Christ now. John 4:25–26. "The woman saith unto him, I know that Messias cometh, which is called Christ: when he is come, he will tell us all things. Jesus saith unto her, I that speak unto thee am he."

Prove all things and hold fast to the good. 1 Thessalonians 5:21–23. "Prove all things; hold fast that which is good. Abstain from all appearance of evil. And the very God of peace sanctify you wholly; and I pray God your whole spirit and soul and body be preserved blameless unto the coming of our Lord Jesus Christ."

Receive the truth and take the Holy Spirit as guide. D&C 45:56–57. "And at that day, when I shall come in my glory, shall the parable be fulfilled which I spake concerning the ten virgins. For they that are wise and have received the truth, and have taken the Holy Spirit for their guide, and have not been deceived—verily I say unto you, they shall not be hewn down and cast into the fire, but shall abide the day."

Rejoice, be pure, and do temple work. D&C 128:24. "Behold, the great day of the Lord is at hand; and who can abide the day of his coming, and who can stand when he appeareth? For he is like a refiner's fire, and like fuller's soap; and he shall sit as a refiner and purifier of silver, and he shall purify the sons of Levi, and purge them as gold and silver, that they may offer unto the Lord an offering in righteousness. Let us, therefore, as a church and a people, and as Latter-day Saints, offer unto the Lord an offering in righteousness; and let us present in his holy temple, when it is finished, a book containing the records of our dead, which shall be worthy of all acceptation."

Stand in holy places and be not moved. D&C 87:8. "Wherefore, stand ye in holy places, and be not moved, until the day of the Lord come; for behold, it cometh quickly, saith the Lord." (See also D&C 45:32.)

Use the scriptures as your guide. D&C 33:16–18. "And the Book of Mormon and the holy scriptures are given of me for your instruction; and the power of my Spirit quickeneth all things. Wherefore, be faithful, praying always, having your lamps trimmed and burning, and oil with you, that you may be ready at the coming of the Bridegroom—For behold, verily, verily, I say unto you, that I come quickly."

WORDS OF THE PROPHETS | **Heber J. Grant on the Church's mission to prepare the world for the coming of Christ.** "The mission of the Church of Jesus Christ of Latter-day

Saints is one of peace. It aims to prepare the people of the world for the second coming of Christ, and for the inauguration of that blessed day when the Millennium shall come and Christ shall reign as King of kings, standing at the head of the universal brotherhood of man. —Heber J. Grant, "A Marvelous Work and a Wonder," *Improvement Era*, 1920, 23:473

ADDITIONAL INFORMATION—**The clouds of heaven.** Could it be that the "clouds" spoken of in association with the Second Coming are not merely natural phenomena but the numberless concourses of the righteous Saints caught up to meet the Redeemer at His advent, along with the returning city of Enoch (see Moses 7:63)? Joseph Smith rendered the opening part of the book of Revelation this way: "For behold, he cometh in the clouds with ten thousands of his saints in the kingdom, clothed with the glory of his Father" (JST Revelation 1:7). It is our lot to remain on the pathway of righteousness, and to prepare ourselves for this final coming, that we might be caught up in the "clouds of heaven" (D&C 45:16) on that grand day.

SELF-CONTROL/TEMPERANCE [0, 18]. The Savior provided the consummate example of self-control and temperance by accomplishing the infinite Atonement (see 3 Nephi 11:11). We are to follow His example through self-discipline and mastery of our God-given talents, moderating our devotion to worldly cares in order to fully serve the Lord with all of our "heart, might, mind and strength" (D&C 4:2). The qualities of self-control and temperance are manifested in various ways in the lives of the Lord's sons and daughters: setting aside self-interest and pride in favor of devoting one's life to building up the kingdom of heaven on earth; consecrating one's talents and resources for the good of family, community, and Church; bridling passions, appetites, and excessive joviality in order to harvest the blessings of love and spirituality; cultivating patience in acquiring more fully the divine qualities exemplified by the Savior; learning and fulfilling one's duty in faith and valor, including stepping forward and opening one's mouth boldly to declare the gospel message to others through the strength of the Lord and the power of His Spirit; even applying the discipline of authentic "boasting"—not in one's own accomplishments but rather in rejoicing over how the Lord unfolds His work. That kind of self-control and temperance—fueled by humility, meekness, and love unfeigned—reaps marvelous blessings for self and others and leads to miracles of service along the pathway to eternal life.

Matthew 25:19–21. "After a long time the lord of those servants cometh, and reckoneth with them. And so he that had received five talents came and brought other five talents, saying, Lord, thou deliveredst unto me five talents: behold, I have gained beside them five talents more. His lord said unto him, Well done, thou good and faithful servant: thou hast been faithful over a few things, I will make thee ruler over many things: enter thou into the joy of thy lord." (See also Matthew 25:14–29; Luke 19:11–27.)

Mark 8:34. "And when he had called the people unto him with his disciples also, he said unto them, Whosoever will come after me, let him deny himself, and take up his cross, and follow me." (See also Mark 8:34; Luke 9:23; 3 Nephi 12:30.)

Luke 21:19. "In your patience possess ye your souls."

Luke 21:34–36. "And take heed to yourselves, lest at any time your hearts be overcharged with surfeiting, and drunkenness, and cares of this life, and so that day come upon you unawares. For as a snare shall it come on all them that dwell on the face of the whole earth. Watch ye therefore, and pray always, that ye may be accounted worthy to escape all these things that shall come to pass, and to stand before the Son of man."

Hebrews 13:5–6. "Let your conversation [manner of life] be without covetousness; and be content with such things as ye have: for he hath said, I will never leave thee, nor forsake thee. So that we may boldly say, The Lord is my helper, and I will not fear what man shall do unto me."

2 Peter 1:4–8. "Whereby are given unto us exceeding great and precious promises: that by these ye might be partakers of the divine nature, having escaped the corruption that is in the world through lust. And beside this, giving all diligence, add to your faith virtue; and to virtue knowledge; And to knowledge temperance; and to temperance patience; and to patience godliness; And to godliness brotherly kindness; and to brotherly kindness charity. For if these things be in you, and abound, they make you that ye shall neither be barren nor unfruitful in the knowledge of our Lord Jesus Christ."

Alma 7:22–24. "And now my beloved brethren, I have said these things unto you that I might awaken you to a sense of your duty to God, that ye may walk blameless before him, that ye may walk after the holy order of God, after which ye have been received. And now I would that ye should be humble, and be submissive and gentle; easy to be entreated; full of patience and long-suffering; being temperate in all things; being diligent in keeping the commandments of God at all times; asking for whatsoever things ye stand in need, both spiritual and temporal; always returning thanks unto God for whatsoever things ye do receive. And see that ye have faith, hope, and charity, and then ye will always abound in good works."

Alma 26:35–36. "Now have we not reason to rejoice? Yea, I say unto you, there never were men that had so great reason to rejoice as we, since the world began; yea, and my joy is carried away, even unto boasting in my God; for he has all power, all wisdom, and all understanding; he comprehendeth all things, and he is a merciful Being, even unto salvation, to those who will repent and believe on his name. Now if this is boasting, even so will I boast; for this is my life and my light, my joy and my salvation, and my redemption from everlasting wo. Yea, blessed is the name of my God, who has been mindful of this people, who are a branch of the tree of Israel, and has been lost from its body in a strange land; yea, I say, blessed be the name of my God, who has been mindful of us, wanderers in a strange land."

Alma 38:11–12. "See that ye are not lifted up unto pride; yea, see that ye do not boast in your own wisdom, nor of your much strength. Use boldness, but not overbearance; and also see that ye bridle all your passions, that ye may be filled with love; see that ye refrain from idleness."

Moroni 10:32. "Yea, come unto Christ, and be perfected in him, and deny yourselves of all ungodliness; and if ye shall deny yourselves of all ungodliness, and love God with all your might, mind and strength, then is his grace sufficient for you, that by his grace ye may be perfect in Christ; and if by the grace of God ye are perfect in Christ, ye can in nowise deny the power of God."

D&C 3:3–4. "Remember, remember that it is not the work of God that is frustrated, but the work of men; For although a man may have many revelations, and have power to do many mighty works, yet if he boasts in his own strength, and sets at naught the counsels of God, and follows after the dictates of his own will and carnal desires, he must fall and incur the vengeance of a just God upon him."

D&C 4:5–7. "And faith, hope, charity and love, with an eye single to the glory of God, qualify him for the work. Remember faith, virtue, knowledge, temperance, patience, brotherly kindness, godliness, charity, humility, diligence. Ask, and ye shall receive; knock, and it shall be opened unto you."

D&C 33:8–11. "Open your mouths and they shall be filled, and you shall become even as Nephi of old, who journeyed from Jerusalem in the wilderness. Yea, open your mouths and spare not, and you shall be laden with sheaves upon your backs, for lo, I am with you. Yea, open your mouths and they shall be filled, saying: Repent, repent, and prepare ye the way of the Lord, and make his paths straight; for the kingdom of heaven is at hand; Yea, repent and be baptized, every one of you, for a remission of your sins; yea, be baptized even by water, and then cometh the baptism of fire and of the Holy Ghost."

WORDS OF THE PROPHETS | **James E. Faust concerning self-control.** "Self-discipline and self-control are consistent and permanent characteristics of the followers of Jesus." —James E. Faust, *To Reach Even unto You* (Salt Lake City: Deseret Book, 1990), 114.

TALENTS, DEVELOPING OUR [70]. Our word *talent* comes from the Greek word *talanton*, meaning balance or weight, and refers to any of a variety of weights of gold or silver and the value of such in terms of currency in ancient cultures. Most of the seventy occurrences of the word *talent* (or *talents*) in the scriptures refer to money in this sense, including the parable of Jesus concerning the king who became the model of compassion by forgiving one of his servants a debt of "ten thousand talents" (Matthew 18:24). However, in His other well-known "parable of the talents" (see Matthew 25:14–30), the Lord uses the metaphorical transition of the meaning of the word from currency to our modern sense: the ability to use one's gifts and capabilities in the achievement of worthwhile goals and objectives. In this same sense, the gifts and talents the Lord grants unto us for the purpose of building the kingdom of heaven on earth come with a covenant responsibility: when we serve the Lord with all of our "heart, might, mind and strength" (D&C 4:2), we can "stand blameless before God at the last day" and bring "salvation to [our] soul" (D&C 4:4). Gifts and abilities—our talents—come to us through the blessings of the Spirit. Developing them with a commitment to service and using them wisely for the cause of Zion—"that all may be profited thereby" (D&C 46:12)—brings joy, comfort, and enduring blessings.

1 Peter 4:11. "If any man speak, let him speak as the oracles of God; if any man minister, let him do it as of the ability which God giveth: that God in all things may be glorified through Jesus Christ, to whom be praise and dominion for ever and ever."

Ether 12:35–36. "Wherefore, I [Moroni] know by this thing which thou hast said, that if the Gentiles have not charity [by accepting the record contained in the Book of Mormon], because of our weakness [in writing the record], that thou wilt prove them, and take away their talent, yea, even that which they have received, and give unto them who shall have more abundantly. And it came to pass that I prayed unto the Lord that he would give unto the Gentiles grace, that they might have charity."

Moroni 10:8. "And again, I exhort you, my brethren, that ye deny not the gifts of God, for they are many; and they come from the same God. And there are different ways that these gifts are administered; but it is the same God who worketh all in all; and they are given by the manifestations of the Spirit of God unto men, to profit them."

D&C 46:8–12. "Wherefore, beware lest ye are deceived; and that ye may not be deceived seek ye earnestly the best gifts, always remembering for what they are given; For verily I say unto you, they are given for the benefit of those who love me and keep all my commandments, and him that seeketh so to do; that all may be benefited that seek or that ask of me, that ask and not for a sign that they may consume it upon their lusts. And again, verily I say unto you, I would that ye should always remember, and always retain in your minds what those gifts are, that are given unto the church. For all have not every gift given unto them; for there are many gifts, and to every man is given a gift by the Spirit of God. To some is given one, and to some is given another, that all may be profited thereby."

D&C 60:2–3. "But with some I am not well pleased, for they will not open their mouths, but they hide the talent which I have given unto them, because of the fear of man. Wo unto such, for mine anger is kindled against them. And it shall come to pass, if they are not more faithful unto me, it shall be taken away, even that which they have."

D&C 60:12–13. "And now I speak of the residue who are to come unto this land. Behold, they have been sent to preach my gospel among the congregations of the wicked; wherefore, I give unto them a commandment, thus: Thou shalt not idle away thy time, neither shalt thou bury thy talent that it may not be known."

D&C 82:18. "And all this [United Order in those days] for the benefit of the church of the living God, that every man may improve upon his talent, that every man may gain other talents, yea, even an hundred fold, to be cast into the Lord's storehouse, to become the common property of the whole church."

D&C 88:33–34. "For what doth it profit a man if a gift is bestowed upon him, and he receive not the gift? Behold, he rejoices not in that which is given unto him, neither rejoices in him who is the giver of the gift. And again, verily I say unto you, that which is governed by law is also preserved by law and perfected and sanctified by the same."

TEACHING [568]. Teaching the gospel is a service of inestimable worth to the children of God. It is not a supplementary service, nor a secondary duty or ancillary addition to the cause of Zion. It is central, pivotal, indispensable, vital, and essential to the operation of the plan of salvation. And those who are God's faithful and devoted teachers carry on a work on which all salvation depends. Without the divine mandate and system to teach the gospel to all the world, there would be no gospel in operation, no enlightenment leading to the pathway of celestial glory, no chance to act upon our God-given agency in choosing to follow the Lord's way to eternal life and exaltation. God the Father is the supreme Exemplar of divine teaching; His Only Begotten Son, the Redeemer, is the anointed Regent for dispensing all truth under the direction of the Father; the Holy Ghost is the agent of light and comfort that empowers all teaching and learning through the process of revelation. The army of teachers throughout the dispensations of time—chosen and commissioned to act under the aegis of the Godhead for the salvation of mankind—include the angel ministrants of the Lord, who act as founts of wisdom and authority; the prophets, seers, and revelators who hold the keys and convey the will of God; the priesthood servants and messengers of truth who spread the good news of salvation at every turn; the parents who exercise their covenant blessing to teach their children gospel values; and all the Saints of God who act with valor and courage to share the gospel message with the world. These are they who ascend the mountain of the Lord to raise with courage the ensign of truth. Teaching is dynamic. It is love in action. It is the banner of charity unfurled.

Isaiah 2:2–3. "And it shall come to pass in the last days, that the mountain of the Lord's house shall be established in the top of the mountains, and shall be exalted above the hills; and all nations shall flow unto it. And many people shall go and say, Come ye, and let us go up to the mountain of the Lord, to the house of the God of Jacob; and he will teach us of his ways, and we will walk in his paths: for out of Zion shall go forth the law, and the word of the Lord from Jerusalem." (See also Micah 4:1–2; 2 Nephi 12:2–3.)

Isaiah 28:9–10, 26. "Whom shall he teach knowledge? and whom shall he make to understand doctrine? them that are weaned from the milk, and drawn from the breasts. For precept must be upon precept, precept upon precept; line upon line, line upon line; here a little, and there a little. . . . For his God doth instruct him to discretion, and doth teach him." (See also 2 Nephi 28:30; D&C 98:12; 128:21.)

Matthew 28:19–20. "Go ye therefore, and teach all nations, baptizing them in the name of the Father, and of the Son, and of the Holy Ghost: Teaching them to observe all things whatsoever I have commanded you: and, lo, I am with you alway, even unto the end of the world."

John 14:26–27. "But the Comforter, which is the Holy Ghost, whom the Father will send in my name, he shall teach you all things, and bring all things to your remembrance, whatsoever I have said unto you. Peace I leave with you, my peace I give unto you: not as the world giveth, give I unto you. Let not your heart be troubled, neither let it be afraid."

2 Nephi 33:6, 10. "I glory in plainness; I glory in truth; I glory in my Jesus, for he hath redeemed my soul from hell. . . . And now, my beloved brethren, and also Jew, and all ye ends of the earth, hearken unto these words and believe in Christ; and if ye believe not in these words believe in Christ. And if ye shall believe in Christ ye will believe in these words, for they are the words of Christ, and he hath given them unto me; and they teach all men that they should do good."

Alma 17:2–4. "Now these sons of Mosiah . . . had waxed strong in the knowledge of the truth; for they were men of a sound understanding and they had searched the scriptures diligently, that they might know the word of God. But this is not all; they had given themselves to much prayer, and fasting; therefore they had the spirit of prophecy, and the spirit of revelation, and when they taught, they taught with power and authority of God. And they had been teaching the word of God for the space of fourteen years among the Lamanites, having had much success in bringing many to the knowledge of the truth;

yea, by the power of their words many were brought before the altar of God, to call on his name and confess their sins before him."

D&C 38:23–25. "But, verily I say unto you, teach one another according to the office wherewith I have appointed you; And let every man esteem his brother as himself, and practise virtue and holiness before me. And again I say unto you, let every man esteem his brother as himself."

D&C 42:12–14. "And again, the elders, priests and teachers of this church shall teach the principles of my gospel, which are in the Bible and the Book of Mormon, in the which is the fulness of the gospel. And they shall observe the covenants and church articles to do them, and these shall be their teachings, as they shall be directed by the Spirit. And the Spirit shall be given unto you by the prayer of faith; and if ye receive not the Spirit ye shall not teach."

D&C 68:25–28. "And again, inasmuch as parents have children in Zion, or in any of her stakes which are organized, that teach them not to understand the doctrine of repentance, faith in Christ the Son of the living God, and of baptism and the gift of the Holy Ghost by the laying on of the hands, when eight years old, the sin be upon the heads of the parents. For this shall be a law unto the inhabitants of Zion, or in any of her stakes which are organized. And their children shall be baptized for the remission of their sins when eight years old, and receive the laying on of the hands. And they shall also teach their children to pray, and to walk uprightly before the Lord."

D&C 88:76–78, 81. "Also, I give unto you a commandment that ye shall continue in prayer and fasting from this time forth. And I give unto you a commandment that you shall teach one another the doctrine of the kingdom. Teach ye diligently and my grace shall attend you, that you may be instructed more perfectly in theory, in principle, in doctrine, in the law of the gospel, in all things that pertain unto the kingdom of God, that are expedient for you to understand. . . . Behold, I sent you out to testify and warn the people, and it becometh every man who hath been warned to warn his neighbor."

According to the scriptures, what are the qualities of a good and devoted teacher?

Don't reason according to the philosophy of the audience but reason according to the truth of the gospel as it is. D&C 49:3–4. "Wherefore, I send you, my servants Sidney and Parley, to preach the gospel unto them. And my servant Leman shall be ordained unto this work, that he may reason with them, not according to that which he has received of them, but according to that which shall be taught him by you my servants; and by so doing I will bless him, otherwise he shall not prosper."

Live what you teach. Romans 2:21. "Thou therefore which teachest another, teachest thou not thyself? thou that preachest a man should not steal, dost thou steal?"

Look upon teaching as a special gift, and cultivate it for the good of others. Romans 12:4–8. "For as we have many members in one body, and all members have not the same office: So we, being many, are one body in Christ, and every one members one of another. Having then gifts differing according to the grace that is given to us, whether prophecy, let us prophesy according to the proportion of faith; Or ministry, let us wait on our ministering: or he that teacheth, on teaching; Or he that exhorteth, on exhortation: he that giveth, let him do it with simplicity; he that ruleth, with diligence; he that sheweth mercy, with cheerfulness." (See also 1 Corinthians 12:28-31; Moroni 10:9-10; D&C 46:17.)

Magnify your office with all diligence by teaching the word of God. Jacob 1:17–19. "Wherefore I, Jacob, gave unto them these words as I taught them in the temple, having first obtained mine errand from the Lord. For I, Jacob, and my brother Joseph had been consecrated priests and teachers of this people, by the hand of Nephi. And we did magnify our office unto the Lord, taking upon us the responsibility, answering the sins of the people upon our own heads if we did not teach them the word of God with all diligence; wherefore, by laboring with our might their blood might not come upon our garments; otherwise their blood would come upon our garments, and we would not be found spotless at the last day."

Never be ashamed of the cause of the gospel of Jesus Christ. 2 Timothy 1:8–11. "Be not thou therefore ashamed of the testimony of our Lord, nor of me his prisoner: but be thou partaker of the afflictions of the gospel according to the power of God; Who hath saved us, and called us with an holy calling, not according to our works, but according to his own purpose and grace, which was given us in Christ Jesus before the world began, But is now made manifest by the appearing of our Saviour Jesus Christ, who hath abolished death, and hath brought life and immortality to light through the gospel: Whereunto I am appointed a preacher, and an apostle, and a teacher of the Gentiles." (See also Romans 1:16.)

Obey the commandments of the Lord. 1 Nephi 2:22. "And inasmuch as thou shalt keep my commandments, thou [Nephi] shalt be made a ruler and a teacher over thy brethren." (See also 2 Nephi 5:18-19.)

Preach the gospel by the Spirit. D&C 50:13–14. "Wherefore, I the Lord ask you this question—unto what were ye ordained? To preach my gospel by the Spirit, even the Comforter which was sent forth to teach the truth." (See also D&C 42:12–17.)

Receive all the scriptures, then teach them to all people. D&C 42:56–58. "Thou shalt ask, and my scriptures shall be given as I have appointed, and they shall be preserved in safety; And it is expedient that thou shouldst hold thy peace concerning them, and not teach them until ye have received them in full. And I give unto you a commandment that then ye shall teach them unto all men; for they shall be taught unto all nations, kindreds, tongues and people."

Study the scriptures prayerfully. Alma 17:2–4. "Now these sons of Mosiah were with Alma at the time the angel first appeared unto him; therefore Alma did rejoice exceedingly to see his brethren; and what added more to his joy, they were still his brethren in the Lord; yea, and they had waxed strong in the knowledge of the truth; for they were men of a sound understanding and they had searched the scriptures diligently, that they might know the word of God. But this is not all; they had given themselves to much prayer, and fasting; therefore they had the spirit of prophecy, and the spirit of revelation, and when they taught, they taught with power and authority of God. And they had been teaching the word of God for the space of fourteen years among the Lamanites, having had much success in bringing many to the knowledge of the truth; yea, by the power of their words many were brought before the altar of God, to call on his name and confess their sins before him." (See also 3 Nephi 26:6–14.)

Teach with patience. 2 Timothy 2:23–26. "But foolish and unlearned questions avoid, knowing that they do gender strifes. And the servant of the Lord must not strive; but be gentle unto all men, apt to teach, patient, In meekness instructing those that oppose themselves; if God peradventure will give them repentance to the acknowledging of the truth; And that they may recover themselves out of the snare of the devil, who are taken captive by him at his will."

Teach with plainness. 2 Nephi 25:4, 7–8, 28. "Wherefore I shall prophesy according to the plainness which hath been with me from the time that I came out from Jerusalem with my father; for behold, my soul delighteth in plainness unto my people, that they may learn. . . . But behold, I proceed with mine own prophecy, according to my plainness; in the which I know that no man can err; nevertheless, in the days that the prophecies of Isaiah shall be fulfilled men shall know of a surety, at the times when they shall come to pass. Wherefore, they are of worth unto the children of men, and he that supposeth that they are not, unto them will I speak particularly, and confine the words unto mine own people; for I know that they shall be of great worth unto them in the last days; for in that day shall they understand them; wherefore, for their good have I written them . . . And now behold, my people, ye are a stiffnecked people; wherefore, I have spoken plainly unto you, that ye cannot misunderstand." (See also 2 Nephi 33:1–6, 10.)

Use boldness but with temperance and love, not overbearance. Alma 38:10–15. "And now, as ye have begun to teach the word even so I would that ye should continue to teach; and I would that ye would be diligent and temperate in all things. See that ye are not lifted up unto pride; yea, see that ye do not boast in your own wisdom, nor of your much strength. Use boldness, but not overbearance; and also see that ye bridle all your passions, that ye may be filled with love; see that ye refrain from idleness. Do not pray as the Zoramites do, for ye have seen that they pray to be heard of men, and to be praised for their wisdom. Do not say: O God, I thank thee that we are better than our brethren; but rather say: O Lord, forgive my unworthiness, and remember my brethren in mercy—yea, acknowledge your unworthiness before God at all times. And may the Lord bless your soul, and receive you at the last day into his kingdom, to sit down in peace. Now go, my son, and teach the word unto this people. Be sober. My son, farewell."

Words of the Prophets | Gordon B. Hinckley on adding to the good. "Bring all the good that you have and let us see if we can add to it." —Gordon B. Hinckley, "The BYU Experience," BYU devotional address, Nov. 4, 1997, 4.

Cross-reference to "Teaching": see Preach My Gospel, *175–194.*

TEMPLES AND FAMILY HISTORY [254]. Among all the doctrines and practices that distinguish The Church of Jesus Christ of Latter-day Saints and set it apart from all other churches of the world, perhaps the most unique and compelling is the vast, encompassing work of the temples of God. Temple work is the evidence that God has extended to every individual who has ever lived upon the earth and who will ever be born into this mortal experience the blessings and opportunities of salvation, immortality, and eternal life. The Lord's holy house is an ensign of God's love for His children, the venue of sacred truths and holy covenants that open the gateway to the presence of the Father and the Son. The temple is the Missionary Training Center of the eternities. It is the ultimate venue for gathering in the dispersed of Israel. It is the place where eternal families are sealed together forever. Through temple work, the sanctioning hand of grace and mercy is extended to the vast hosts of the Almighty's spirit children, who languish in the spirit realm, awaiting their turn to receive the truths of the gospel (see D&C 138). The armies of workers in the temples of God are missionaries on the Lord's errand, opening the floodgates of salvation through vicarious service administered by the priesthood of God! These are the "saviours [who] shall come up on mount Zion" (Obadiah 1:21), bringing the records of their forebears to "offer unto the Lord an offering in righteousness" (D&C 128:24) and ensure, through the sealing power of the priesthood, an inheritance of "crowns of eternal lives in the eternal worlds" (D&C 132:55).

From the beginning of time, there have always been places provided for the ordinances of exaltation. The Garden of Eden itself was a holy place in which celestial marriage could be performed (see Moses 2:28; 3:23–25; 4:26–29). Mountaintops served as a site for the endowment of truth when so ordained of the Lord (see Exodus 19:3; Matthew 17:1; Moses 1:1). Following the Exodus, the Tabernacle served as a portable temple for sacred priesthood rites in ancient Israel (see Exodus 25:8; D&C 124:38). The Lord promised David that his son would build a temple (1 Kings 5:5), and Solomon followed through with this destined project by erecting a magnificent temple complex for sacred worship about a millennium before the birth of Christ (see 1 Kings 8). Temple services were restored in the days of Hezekiah and Isaiah (eighth century BC), but the original temple edifice was destroyed in the Babylonian conquest around 587 BC (see Jeremiah 44:30; 52:12–13; 2 Kings 25:8–10). It was later rebuilt by Zerubbabel, appointed by the Persians as governor over the Holy Land, and dedicated in 516 BC (see Ezra 6:15–16). Herod reconstructed this temple during the days of Jesus, but it was completely destroyed by the Romans in AD 70, thus interrupting the tradition of temple service in that part of the world until the days of the Restoration. Meanwhile, the people of Nephi, in the New World, constructed temples for sacred rites and gatherings (see 2 Nephi 5:16; Jacob 1:17; Mosiah 2:5–7; 3 Nephi 11:1).

In our day, the Restoration of the gospel has brought about the building of temples throughout the world. Joseph Smith stated: "The Church is not fully organized, in its proper order, and cannot be, until the Temple is completed, where places will be provided for the administration of the ordinances of the Priesthood" (*HC* 4:603). The first of the modern temples was dedicated in Kirtland, Ohio, on March 27, 1836—thus launching the groundswell of temple work as the fulfillment of Isaiah's vision: "And it shall come to pass in the last days, that the mountain of the Lord's house shall be established in the top of the mountains, and shall be exalted above the hills; and all nations shall flow unto it. And many people shall go and say, Come ye, and let us go up to the mountain of the Lord, to the house of the God of Jacob; and he will teach us of his ways, and we will walk in his paths: for out of Zion shall go forth the law, and the word of the Lord from Jerusalem" (Isaiah 2:2–3). It was in the Kirtland Temple that Jesus Christ Himself appeared to Joseph Smith and Oliver Cowdery to accept the sacrifice and offering of the Saints (D&C 110:7), followed by the ministration of Moses, Elias, and Elijah, who restored essential keys for the work of the kingdom. In current times, the living prophets have escalated the effort to make temples more readily accessible to members of the Church throughout the world. Family history and temple work is the culmination of the Lord's plan to perfect and preserve the family and prepares us for our future roles in the worlds to come.

1 Kings 7:23, 25. "And he [Solomon] made a molten sea [i.e., baptismal font of the temple]. . . . It stood upon twelve oxen . . . and the sea was set above upon them." (See also Jeremiah 52:20.)

1 Kings 9:3. "I have hallowed this house, which thou hast built, to put my name there for ever; and mine eyes and mine heart shall be there perpetually."

Isaiah 2:2–3. "And it shall come to pass in the last days, that the mountain of the Lord's house shall be established in the top of the mountains, and shall be exalted above the hills; and all nations shall flow unto it. And many people shall go and say, Come ye, and let us go up to the mountain of the Lord, to the house of the God of Jacob; and he will teach us of his ways, and we will walk in his paths: for out of Zion shall go forth the law, and the word of the Lord from Jerusalem." (See also Micah 4:1–2 and 2 Nephi 12:2–3.)

Malachi 4:5–6. "Behold, I will send you Elijah the prophet before the coming of the great and dreadful day of the Lord: And he shall turn the heart of the fathers to the children, and the heart of the children to their fathers, lest I come and smite the earth with a curse." (See also 3 Nephi 25:5–6; D&C 2; D&C 110:13–16; JS—H 1:38–39.)

Matthew 16:19. "And I will give unto thee [Peter] the keys of the kingdom of heaven: and whatsoever thou shalt bind on earth shall be bound in heaven: and whatsoever thou shalt loose on earth shall be loosed in heaven."

1 Corinthians 3:16–17. "Know ye not that ye are the temple of God, and that the Spirit of God dwelleth in you? If any man defile the temple of God, him shall God destroy; for the temple of God is holy, which temple are ye."

1 Corinthians 15:29. "Else what shall they do which are baptized for the dead, if the dead rise not at all? why are they then baptized for the dead?"

Revelation 20:12. "And I saw the dead, small and great, stand before God; and the books were opened: and another book was opened, which is the book of life: and the dead were judged out of those things which were written in the books, according to their works." (See also D&C 128:7.)

3 Nephi 15:9. "Behold, I am the law, and the light. Look unto me, and endure to the end, and ye shall live; for unto him that endureth to the end will I give eternal life."

D&C 88:119 "Organize yourselves; prepare every needful thing; and establish a house, even a house of prayer, a house of fasting, a house of faith, a house of learning, a house of glory, a house of order, a house of God."

D&C 97:15–17. "And inasmuch as my people build a house unto me in the name of the Lord, and do not suffer any unclean thing to come into it, that it be not defiled, my glory shall rest upon it; Yea, and my presence shall be there, for I will come into it, and all the pure in heart that shall come into it shall see God. But if it be defiled I will not come into it, and my glory shall not be there; for I will not come into unholy temples."

D&C 110:13–16. "After this vision had closed, another great and glorious vision burst upon us; for Elijah the prophet, who was taken to heaven without tasting death, stood before us, and said: Behold, the time has fully come, which was spoken of by the mouth of Malachi—testifying that he [Elijah] should be sent, before the great and dreadful day of the Lord come—To turn the hearts of the fathers to the children, and the children to the fathers, lest the whole earth be smitten with a curse—Therefore, the keys of this dispensation are committed into your hands; and by this ye may know that the great and dreadful day of the Lord is near, even at the doors."

D&C 124:39–41, 55. "Therefore, verily I say unto you, that your anointings, and your washings, and your baptisms for the dead, and your solemn assemblies, and your memorials for your sacrifices by the sons of Levi, and for your oracles in your most holy places wherein you receive conversations, and your statutes and judgments, for the beginning of the revelations and foundation of Zion, and for the glory, honor, and endowment of all her municipals, are ordained by the ordinance of my holy house, which my people are always commanded to build unto my holy name. And verily I say unto you, let this house be built unto my name, that I may reveal mine ordinances therein unto my people; For I deign to reveal unto my church things which have been kept hid from before the foundation of the world, things that pertain to the dispensation of the fulness of times. . . . And again, verily I say unto you, I command you again to build a house to my name, even in this place, that you may prove yourselves unto me that ye are faithful in all things whatsoever I command you, that I may bless you, and crown you with honor, immortality, and eternal life."

Moses 6:5–8. "And a book of remembrance was kept . . . and a genealogy was kept of the children of God. And this was the book of the generations of Adam."

What are the blessings of the temple?

The power of the priesthood. D&C 109:22, 24, 26. "And we ask thee, Holy Father, that thy servants may go forth from this house armed with thy power, and that thy name may be upon them, and thy glory be round about them, and thine angels have charge over them. . . . We ask thee, Holy Father, to establish the people that shall worship, and honorably hold a name and standing in this thy house, to all generations and for eternity. . . . That no combination of wickedness shall have power to rise up and prevail over thy people upon whom thy name shall be put in this house."

Eternal perpetuation of loving relationships. 1 Corinthians 11:11. "Nevertheless neither is the man without the woman, neither the woman without the man, in the Lord."

Peace, comfort, and joy. D&C 59:23. "But learn that he who doeth the works of righteousness shall receive his reward, even peace in this world, and eternal life in the world to come."

Safety and protection. D&C 84:88. "There I will be also, for I will go before your face. I will be on your right hand and on your left, and my Spirit shall be in your hearts, and mine angels round about you, to bear you up."

Instruction and revelation. John 17:3. "And this is life eternal, that they might know thee the only true God, and Jesus Christ, whom thou hast sent."

Opportunities for service. D&C 103:9. "For they were set to be a light unto the world, and to be the saviors of men." (See also Obadiah 1:21.)

Fellowship through temple work. Ephesians 2:19–21. "Now therefore ye are no more strangers and foreigners, but fellowcitizens with the saints, and of the household of God; And are built upon the foundation of the apostles and prophets, Jesus Christ himself being the chief corner stone; In whom all the building fitly framed together groweth unto an holy temple in the Lord."

Spirituality. 2 Nephi 2:8. "Wherefore, how great the importance to make these things known unto the inhabitants of the earth, that they may know that there is no flesh that can dwell in the presence of God, save it be through the merits, and mercy, and grace of the Holy Messiah."

Greater harvest for our lives. John 15:5, 8. "I am the vine, ye are the branches: He that abideth in me, and I in him, the same bringeth forth much fruit: for without me ye can do nothing. . . . Herein is my Father glorified, that ye bear much fruit; so shall ye be my disciples."

Exaltation in the celestial kingdom. Matthew 25:21. "Well done, thou good and faithful servant: thou hast been faithful over a few things, I will make thee ruler over many things: enter thou into the joy of thy lord." (See also D&C 76:69.)

Words of the Prophets | Spencer W. Kimball on the vast work of the temple. "Missionary work is not limited to proclaiming the gospel to every nation, kindred, tongue, and people now living on the earth. Missionary work is also continuing beyond the veil among the millions and even billions of the children of our Heavenly Father who have died either without hearing the gospel or without accepting it while they lived on the earth. Our great part in this aspect of missionary work is to perform on this earth the ordinances required for those who accept the gospel over there. The spirit world is full of spirits who are anxiously awaiting the performance of these earthly ordinances for them. I hope to see us dissolve the artificial boundary line we so often place between missionary work and temple and genealogical work, because it is the same great redemptive work!" —Spencer W. Kimball, "The Things of Eternity—Stand We in Jeapardy?" *Ensign*, January 1977, 3.

Cross reference to "Temples and Family History": see Preach My Gospel, *85–87.*

TEMPTATION [129]. The plan of happiness is anchored in the power and love of God and unfolds as a magnificent blessing for His children who make wise choices along the pathway of life. Temptation is an element encountered along that pathway, "For it must needs be, that there is an opposition in all things" (2 Nephi 2:11)—this opposition contributing to the probationary nature of the mortal experience, according the design of the Almighty (see Abraham 3:25). Through the mercy and guidance of the Lord, the righteous can overcome the insidious "temptations of the devil, which blindeth the eyes, and hardeneth the hearts of the children of men, and leadeth them away into broad roads, that they perish and are lost" (1 Nephi 12:17). Continual watchfulness and prayer will sustain the devoted saints of God and enable them to defeat all temptation as they abide by the sacred and healing counsel to "trust in the Lord with all thine heart; and lean not unto thine own understanding. In all thy ways acknowledge him, and he shall direct thy paths" (Proverbs 3:5–6).

Matthew 6:13. "And lead us not into temptation, but deliver us from evil: For thine is the kingdom, and the power, and the glory, for ever. Amen." (See also Luke 11:4; JST Matthew 6:13; 3 Nephi 13:12.)

Matthew 26:40–41. "And he cometh unto the disciples, and findeth them asleep, and saith unto Peter, What, could ye not watch with me one hour? Watch and pray, that ye enter not into temptation: the spirit indeed is willing, but the flesh is weak." (See also Mark 14:37–38; Luke 22:45–46.)

Luke 8:13. "They on the rock are they, which, when they hear, receive the word with joy; and these have no root, which for a while believe, and in time of temptation fall away."

1 Corinthians 10:13. "There hath no temptation taken you but such as is common to man: but God is faithful, who will not suffer you to be tempted above that ye are able; but will with the temptation also make a way to escape, that ye may be able to bear it."

Alma 13:27–30. "And now, my brethren, I wish from the inmost part of my heart, yea, with great anxiety even unto pain, that ye would hearken unto my words, and cast off your sins, and not procrastinate the day of your repentance; But that ye would humble yourselves before the Lord, and call on his holy name, and watch and pray continually, that ye may not be tempted above that which ye can bear, and thus be led by the Holy Spirit, becoming humble, meek, submissive, patient, full of love and all long-suffering; Having faith on the Lord; having a hope that ye shall receive eternal life; having the love of God always in your hearts, that ye may be lifted up at the last day and enter into his rest. And may the Lord grant unto you repentance, that ye may not bring down his wrath upon you, that ye may not be bound down by the chains of hell, that ye may not suffer the second death."

3 Nephi 18:14–15. "Therefore blessed are ye if ye shall keep my commandments, which the Father hath commanded me that I should give unto you. Verily, verily, I say unto you, ye must watch and pray always, lest ye be tempted by the devil, and ye be led away captive by him."

D&C 23:1. "Behold, I speak unto you, Oliver [Cowdery], a few words. Behold, thou art blessed, and art under no condemnation. But beware of pride, lest thou shouldst enter into temptation."

D&C 95:1. "Verily, thus saith the Lord unto you whom I love, and whom I love I also chasten that their sins may be forgiven, for with the chastisement I prepare a way for their deliverance in all things out of temptation, and I have loved you."

How can we overcome temptation?

Avoid pride. D&C 23:1. "Behold, I speak unto you, Oliver [Cowdery], a few words. Behold, thou art blessed, and art under no condemnation. But beware of pride, lest thou shouldst enter into temptation."

Be accepting of others and bear their burdens. Galatians 6:1–2. "Brethren, if a man be overtaken in a fault, ye which are spiritual, restore such an one in the spirit of meekness; considering thyself, lest thou also be tempted. Bear ye one another's burdens, and so fulfil the law of Christ."

Follow the word of God by holding to the iron rod. 1 Nephi 15:23–25. "And they said unto me: What meaneth the rod of iron which our father saw, that led to the tree? And I said unto them that it was the word of God; and whoso would hearken unto the word of

God, and would hold fast unto it, they would never perish; neither could the temptations and the fiery darts of the adversary overpower them unto blindness, to lead them away to destruction."

Have faith and do good works. 1 Thessalonians 3:5–7. "For this cause, when I could no longer forbear, I sent to know your faith, lest by some means the tempter have tempted you, and our labour be in vain. But now when Timotheus came from you unto us, and brought us good tidings of your faith and charity, and that ye have good remembrance of us always, desiring greatly to see us, as we also to see you: Therefore, brethren, we were comforted over you in all our affliction and distress by your faith." (See also 1 Timothy 6:7–12; Alma 37:32–35.)

Lean on the strength of the Lord. Alma 26:12. "Yea, I know that I [Ammon] am nothing; as to my strength I am weak; therefore I will not boast of myself, but I will boast of my God, for in his strength I can do all things."

Pray continually in faith; be watchful: Matthew 6:13. "And lead us not into temptation, but deliver us from evil: For thine is the kingdom, and the power, and the glory, for ever. Amen." (See also Luke 11:2–4; Alma 13:27–30; 31:8–11; 34:37–41; 3 Nephi 13:9–13;18:14–21, 25; D&C 31:11–13; 61:36–39.)

Realize that because of the blessing of the Lord, you cannot be tempted above that which you can bear. 1 Corinthians 10:13. "There hath no temptation taken you but such as is common to man: but God is faithful, who will not suffer you to be tempted above that ye are able; but will with the temptation also make a way to escape, that ye may be able to bear it." (See also Alma 13:28; D&C 64:20.)

Stand fast in the work you are called to do, for that will protect you from temptation. D&C 9:11–14. "Behold, it was expedient when you commenced; but you feared, and the time is past, and it is not expedient now; For, do you not behold that I have given unto my servant Joseph sufficient strength, whereby it is made up? And neither of you have I condemned. Do this thing which I have commanded you, and you shall prosper. Be faithful, and yield to no temptation. Stand fast in the work wherewith I have called you, and a hair of your head shall not be lost, and you shall be lifted up at the last day."

Take heed, for even the sanctified who love and serve God completely might slip and fall from grace. D&C 20:29–34. "And we know that all men must repent and believe on the name of Jesus Christ, and worship the Father in his name, and endure in faith on his name to the end, or they cannot be saved in the kingdom of God. And we know that justification through the grace of our Lord and Savior Jesus Christ is just and true; And we know also, that sanctification through the grace of our Lord and Savior Jesus Christ is just and true, to all those who love and serve God with all their mights, minds, and strength. But there is a possibility that man may fall from grace and depart from the living God; Therefore let the church take heed and pray always, lest they fall into temptation; Yea, and even let those who are sanctified take heed also."

View temptation as an opportunity to prove your faith through the love of Christ. 1 Peter 1:6–9. "Wherein ye greatly rejoice, though now for a season, if need be, ye are in heaviness through manifold temptations: That the trial of your faith, being much more precious than of gold that perisheth, though it be tried with fire, might be found unto praise and honour and glory at the appearing of Jesus Christ: Whom having not seen, ye love; in whom, though now ye see him not, yet believing, ye rejoice with joy unspeakable and full of glory: Receiving the end of your faith, even the salvation of your souls."

Words of the Prophets | Howard W. Hunter on avoiding temptation. "Strive to build a personal testimony of Jesus Christ and the atonement. A study of the life of Christ and a testimony of his reality is something each of us should seek. As we come to understand his mission, and the atonement which he wrought, we will desire to live more like him. We especially encourage the young men and young women to come to know the reason for the atoning sacrifice of our Lord. When temptations come, as they surely will, an understanding of the Savior's agony in Gethsemane and his eventual death on the cross will be a reminder to you to avoid any activity that would cause the Savior more pain. Listen to his words, 'For behold, I, God, have suffered these things for all, that they might not suffer if they would repent; But if they would not repent, they must suffer even as I' (D&C 19:16–17)." —Howard W. Hunter, *The Teachings of Howard W. Hunter*, edited by Clyde J. Williams (Salt Lake City: Bookcraft, 1997), 30–31.

TESTIMONY [220]. A personal testimony is a divine endowment of truth and light and is essential for our salvation and exaltation. It is a revealed conviction—given unto the faithful and prayerful by the Holy Ghost—that Jesus is the Christ and that His living Church—The Church of Jesus Christ of Latter-day Saints—has been restored in our day for the blessing of all mankind through the power and authority of His holy priesthood. A testimony is a gift from heaven, as the Apostle Paul confirmed: "Wherefore I give you to understand, that no man . . . can say that Jesus is the Lord, but by the Holy Ghost" (1 Corinthians 12:3). When we bear our testimony to others with full purpose of heart, we bless their lives in our role as emissaries of the Lord (see D&C 100:8). A testimony serves as the anchor of faith, the armor of gospel strength, the peaceful assurance that we are doing the will of God, and the inner flame of certainty that our vision of future blessings of glory and everlasting life is true and inexorable. The seed of testimony, when cultivated with desire and courage, unfolds as a "tree springing up unto everlasting life" (Alma 32:41). This miracle happens when we "feast upon the words of Christ" (2 Nephi 32:3), pray for divine confirmation through the Spirit (see Moroni 10:4–5), and work ceaselessly in doing the will of God (see John 7:17).

Psalm 19:7. "The law of the Lord is perfect, converting the soul: the testimony of the Lord is sure, making wise the simple."

Psalm 132:12. "If thy children will keep my covenant and my testimony that I shall teach them, their children shall also sit upon thy throne for evermore."

Isaiah 8:16. "Bind up the testimony, seal the law among my disciples." (See also D&C 88:84; 109:46; 133:72.)

Matthew 18:16. "In the mouth of two or three witnesses every word may be established."

Romans 1:16. "For I am not ashamed of the gospel of Christ: for it is the power of God unto salvation to every one that believeth."

Revelation 19:10. "And I [John] fell at his feet to worship him. And he said unto me, See thou do it not: I am thy fellowservant, and of thy brethren that have the testimony of Jesus: worship God: for the testimony of Jesus is the spirit of prophecy."
2 Nephi 11:2–3, 6. "And now I, Nephi, write more of the words of Isaiah, for my soul delighteth in his words. For I will liken his words unto my people, and I will send them forth unto all my children, for he verily saw my Redeemer, even as I have seen him. And my brother, Jacob, also has seen him as I have seen him; wherefore, I will send their words forth unto my children to prove unto them that my words are true. Wherefore, by the words of three, God hath said, I will establish my word. Nevertheless, God sendeth more witnesses, and he proveth all his words. . . . And my soul delighteth in proving unto my people that save Christ should come all men must perish."
2 Nephi 29:8. "Wherefore murmur ye, because that ye shall receive more of my word? Know ye not that the testimony of two nations is a witness unto you that I am God, that I remember one nation like unto another? Wherefore, I speak the same words unto one nation like unto another. And when the two nations shall run together the testimony of the two nations [Bible and Book of Mormon] shall run together also."
Alma 4:19. "And this he did [appoint another as chief judge] that he himself might go forth among his people, or among the people of Nephi, that he might preach the word of God unto them, to stir them up in remembrance of their duty, and that he might pull down, by the word of God, all the pride and craftiness and all the contentions which were among his people, seeing no way that he might reclaim them save it were in bearing down in pure testimony against them."
Alma 7:13. "Now the Spirit knoweth all things; nevertheless the Son of God suffereth according to the flesh that he might take upon him the sins of his people, that he might blot out their transgressions according to the power of his deliverance; and now behold, this is the testimony which is in me [Alma]."
Alma 30:41. "But, behold, I have all things as a testimony that these things are true; and ye also have all things as a testimony unto you that they are true; and will ye deny them? Believest thou that these things are true?"
D&C 6:31. "But if they reject not my words, which shall be established by the testimony which shall be given, blessed are they, and then shall ye have joy in the fruit of your labors."
D&C 58:47. "Let them preach by the way, and bear testimony of the truth in all places, and call upon the rich, the high and the low, and the poor to repent."
D&C 62:3. "Nevertheless, ye are blessed, for the testimony which ye have borne is recorded in heaven for the angels to look upon; and they rejoice over you, and your sins are forgiven you."
D&C 76:22–24. "And now, after the many testimonies which have been given of him, this is the testimony, last of all, which we give of him: That he lives! For we saw him, even on the right hand of God; and we heard the voice bearing record that he is the Only Begotten of the Father— That by him, and through him, and of him, the worlds are and were created, and the inhabitants thereof are begotten sons and daughters unto God."
D&C 109:38–39. "Put upon thy servants the testimony of the covenant, that when they go out and proclaim thy word they may seal up the law, and prepare the hearts of thy

saints for all those judgments thou art about to send, in thy wrath, upon the inhabitants of the earth, because of their transgressions, that thy people may not faint in the day of trouble. And whatsoever city thy servants shall enter, and the people of that city receive their testimony, let thy peace and thy salvation be upon that city; that they may gather out of that city the righteous, that they may come forth to Zion, or to her stakes, the places of thine appointment, with songs of everlasting joy."

Moses 7:62. "And righteousness will I send down out of heaven; and truth will I send forth out of the earth, to bear testimony of mine Only Begotten; his resurrection from the dead; yea, and also the resurrection of all men; and righteousness and truth will I cause to sweep the earth as with a flood, to gather out mine elect from the four quarters of the earth, unto a place which I shall prepare, an Holy City, that my people may gird up their loins, and be looking forth for the time of my coming; for there shall be my tabernacle, and it shall be called Zion, a New Jerusalem."

How do we strengthen our testimony of Jesus Christ?

Covenant to serve the Lord and bless the lives of His children. Mosiah 18:9, 13. "Yea, and are willing to mourn with those that mourn; yea, and comfort those that stand in need of comfort, and to stand as witnesses of God at all times and in all things, and in all places that ye may be in, even until death, that ye may be redeemed of God, and be numbered with those of the first resurrection, that ye may have eternal life. . . . And when he [Alma the Elder] had said these words, the Spirit of the Lord was upon him, and he said: Helam, I baptize thee, having authority from the Almighty God, as a testimony that ye have entered into a covenant to serve him until you are dead as to the mortal body; and may the Spirit of the Lord be poured out upon you; and may he grant unto you eternal life, through the redemption of Christ, whom he has prepared from the foundation of the world." (See also Mosiah 21:35.)

Cultivate a sincere desire to strengthen our faith and learn more about the gospel. Alma 32:26–27. "Now, as I said concerning faith—that it was not a perfect knowledge—even so it is with my words. Ye cannot know of their surety at first, unto perfection, any more than faith is a perfect knowledge. But behold, if ye will awake and arouse your faculties, even to an experiment upon my words, and exercise a particle of faith, yea, even if ye can no more than desire to believe, let this desire work in you, even until ye believe in a manner that ye can give place for a portion of my words."

Do the will of the Lord. John 7:17. "If any man will do his will, he shall know of the doctrine, whether it be of God, or whether I speak of myself."

Fast and pray. Alma 5:45–47. "And this is not all. Do ye not suppose that I know of these things myself? Behold, I testify unto you that I do know that these things whereof I have spoken are true. And how do ye suppose that I know of their surety? Behold, I say unto you they are made known unto me by the Holy Spirit of God. Behold, I have fasted and prayed many days that I might know these things of myself. And now I do know of myself that they are true; for the Lord God hath made them manifest unto me by his Holy Spirit; and this is the spirit of revelation which is in me. And moreover, I say unto you that it has thus been revealed unto me, that the words which have been spoken by our fathers are true, even so according to the spirit of prophecy which is in me, which is also by the manifestation of the Spirit of God." (See also Moroni 10:4–5; JS—H 1:26; James 1:5.)

Listen receptively. D&C 8:2–3. "Yea, behold, I will tell you in your mind and in your heart, by the Holy Ghost, which shall come upon you and which shall dwell in your heart. Now, behold, this is the spirit of revelation."

Partake frequently of the sacrament as a witness that you will always remember the Lord and keep His commandments. 3 Nephi 18:7. "And this shall ye do in remembrance of my body, which I have shown unto you. And it shall be a testimony unto the Father that ye do always remember me. And if ye do always remember me ye shall have my Spirit to be with you." (See also Moroni 4:3; 5:2; D&C 20:77, 79.)

Prepare our hearts to bear testimony to others in the spirit of obedience. D&C 58:6. "Behold, verily I say unto you, for this cause I have sent you—that you might be obedient, and that your hearts might be prepared to bear testimony of the things which are to come."

Sacrifice willingly for the gospel cause. 2 Timothy 1:8. "Be not thou therefore ashamed of the testimony of our Lord, nor of me his prisoner: but be thou partaker of the afflictions of the gospel according to the power of God."

Search the scriptures diligently. John 5:39. "Search the scriptures; for in them ye think ye have eternal life: and they are they which testify of me."

Cross-reference to "Testimony": see Preach My Gospel, *198–200.*

TITHES AND OFFERINGS [52; 1,480]. The Lord, who has given His all for the blessing of God's children, extends to them, in turn, the sacred opportunity to serve Him (see D&C 4:2). This consecrated service involves the willing offering of one's time, talents, and resources for the building up of the kingdom of God on the earth, including the contribution of an honest tithe amounting to "one-tenth of all their interest annually" (D&C 119:4)—plus a generous fast offering for the blessing of the needy. Such a spiritual investment unto the Lord is a covenant act that results in an outpouring of heavenly blessings upon the donor in such abundance "that there shall not be room enough to receive it" (Malachi 3:10). The ongoing payment of tithes and offerings constitutes an opportunity for all those with a broken heart and a contrite spirit to manifest their love for the Lord and confirm their valiant commitment to support the cause of Zion with enduring faith and unabated loyalty.

Proverbs 3:9–10. "Honour the Lord with thy substance, and with the firstfruits of all thine increase: So shall thy barns be filled with plenty, and thy presses shall burst out with new wine."

Malachi 3:8–10. "Will a man rob God? Yet ye have robbed me. But ye say, Wherein have we robbed thee? In tithes and offerings. Ye are cursed with a curse: for ye have robbed me, even this whole nation. Bring ye all the tithes into the storehouse, that there may be meat in mine house, and prove me now herewith, saith the Lord of hosts, if I will not open you the windows of heaven, and pour you out a blessing, that there shall not be room enough to receive it." (See also 3 Nephi 24:8–10.)

D&C 64:23. "Behold, now it is called today until the coming of the Son of Man, and verily it is a day of sacrifice, and a day for the tithing of my people; for he that is tithed shall not be burned at his coming." (See also D&C 85:3.)

D&C 97:10–15. "Verily I say unto you, that it is my will that a house should be built unto me in the land of Zion, like unto the pattern which I have given you. Yea, let it be built speedily, by the tithing of my people. Behold, this is the tithing and the sacrifice which I, the Lord, require at their hands, that there may be a house built unto me for the salvation of Zion— For a place of thanksgiving for all saints, and for a place of instruction for all those who are called to the work of the ministry in all their several callings and offices; That they may be perfected in the understanding of their ministry, in theory, in principle, and in doctrine, in all things pertaining to the kingdom of God on the earth, the keys of which kingdom have been conferred upon you. And inasmuch as my people build a house unto me in the name of the Lord, and do not suffer any unclean thing to come into it, that it be not defiled, my glory shall rest upon it."

D&C 119:3–4. "And this shall be the beginning of the tithing of my people. And after that, those who have thus been tithed shall pay one-tenth of all their interest annually; and this shall be a standing law unto them forever, for my holy priesthood, saith the Lord."

How do the scriptures confirm that tithing has been a principle of the gospel from the beginning?

Abel. Genesis 4:4. "And Abel, he also brought of the firstlings of his flock and of the fat thereof. And the Lord had respect unto Abel and to his offering."

Melchizedek and Abraham. Genesis 14:18–20. "And Melchizedek king of Salem brought forth bread and wine: and he was the priest of the most high God. And he blessed him, and said, Blessed be Abram of the most high God, possessor of heaven and earth: And blessed be the most high God, which hath delivered thine enemies into thy hand. And he gave him tithes of all." (See also JST Genesis 14:36–40; Hebrews 7:4–10; Alma 13:14–15.)

Jacob. Genesis 28:20–22. "And Jacob vowed a vow, saying, If God will be with me, and will keep me in this way that I go, and will give me bread to eat, and raiment to put on, So that I come again to my father's house in peace; then shall the Lord be my God: And this stone, which I have set for a pillar, shall be God's house: and of all that thou shalt give me I will surely give the tenth unto thee."

Moses and the ensuing generations. Leviticus 27:30. "And all the tithe of the land, whether of the seed of the land, or of the fruit of the tree, is the Lord's: it is holy unto the Lord." (See also Deuteronomy 14:22.)

WORDS OF THE PROPHETS | **Gordon B. Hinckley on the blessing of tithing.** "The law of tithing is a law designed to bless us. It does not take from us, it adds to us. It is not so much a matter of money as it is a matter of faith, and great are the promises of the Lord to those who live honestly with Him in the payment of their tithes and their offerings."
—Gordon B. Hinckley, *Teachings of Gordon B. Hinckley* (Salt Lake City: Deseret Book, 1997), 405.

Cross-reference to "Tithes and Offerings": see Preach My Gospel, *78–80.*

TRUTH (408) God is the supreme manifestation and source of truth. His plan of happiness is anchored in the verity and truth of the Atonement brought about through divine mercy, love, and grace. The message of the missionaries of the Lord is centered in truth—truth concerning the restored fulness of the gospel leading to salvation and exaltation. Truth is radiated through the light of Christ, "Which light proceedeth forth from the presence of God to fill the immensity of space" (D&C 88:12), sustaining all creation, giving light to all things, quickening our understanding, prompting us to choose the right, and—through the power of the Holy Ghost—confirming that we are sons and daughters of God. Truth encompasses the very essence of being (see D&C 93:24). Truth is the governing principle of our God-given moral agency (see D&C 93:30). Truth is the radiating dimension of divine glory (see D&C 93:36). Faithful obedience to the truth is the only gateway to liberation and redemption, the only pathway leading us back once again to the celestial home of the Father and the Son (see D&C 75:5).

Joshua 24:14–15. "Now therefore fear the Lord, and serve him in sincerity and in truth; . . . [C]hoose you this day whom ye will serve; . . . but as for me and my house, we will serve the Lord."

John 8:31–32. "Then said Jesus to those Jews which believed on him, If ye continue in my word, then are ye my disciples indeed; And ye shall know the truth, and the truth shall make you free."

John 16:13–14. "Howbeit when he, the Spirit of truth, is come, he will guide you into all truth: for he shall not speak of himself; but whatsoever he shall hear, that shall he speak: and he will shew you things to come. He shall glorify me: for he shall receive of mine, and shall shew it unto you."

1 John 5:5–7. "Who is he that overcometh the world, but he that believeth that Jesus is the Son of God? This is he that came by water and blood, even Jesus Christ; not by water only, but by water and blood. And it is the Spirit that beareth witness, because the Spirit is truth. For there are three that bear record in heaven, the Father, the Word, and the Holy Ghost: and these three are one."

2 Nephi 33:6. "I glory in plainness; I glory in truth; I glory in my Jesus, for he hath redeemed my soul from hell."

Mosiah 4:14–15. "And ye will not suffer your children that they go hungry, or naked; neither will ye suffer that they transgress the laws of God, and fight and quarrel one with another, and serve the devil, who is the master of sin, or who is the evil spirit which hath been spoken of by our fathers, he being an enemy to all righteousness. But ye will teach them to walk in the ways of truth and soberness; ye will teach them to love one another, and to serve one another."

Alma 17: 2–3. "They [sons of Mosiah] had waxed strong in the knowledge of the truth; for they were men of a sound understanding and they had searched the scriptures diligently, that they might know the word of God. But this is not all; they had given themselves to much prayer, and fasting; therefore they had the spirit of prophecy, and the spirit of revelation, and when they taught, they taught with power and authority of God."

Moroni 10:4–5. "And when ye shall receive these things, I would exhort you that ye would ask God, the Eternal Father, in the name of Christ, if these things are not true; and if ye shall ask with a sincere heart, with real intent, having faith in Christ, he will manifest the truth of it unto you, by the power of the Holy Ghost. And by the power of the Holy Ghost ye may know the truth of all things."

D&C 45:56–57. "And at that day, when I shall come in my glory, shall the parable be fulfilled which I spake concerning the ten virgins. For they that are wise and have received the truth, and have taken the Holy Spirit for their guide, and have not been deceived—verily I say unto you, they shall not be hewn down and cast into the fire, but shall abide the day."

D&C 50:9, 24–25, 40. "Wherefore, let every man beware lest he do that which is not in truth and righteousness before me. . . . That which is of God is light; and he that receiveth light, and continueth in God, receiveth more light; and that light groweth brighter and brighter until the perfect day. And again, verily I say unto you, and I say it that you may know the truth, that you may chase darkness from among you; . . . Behold, ye are little children and ye cannot bear all things now; ye must grow in grace and in the knowledge of the truth."

D&C 84:43–47. "And I now give unto you a commandment to beware concerning yourselves, to give diligent heed to the words of eternal life. For you shall live by every word that proceedeth forth from the mouth of God. For the word of the Lord is truth, and whatsoever is truth is light, and whatsoever is light is Spirit, even the Spirit of Jesus Christ. And the Spirit giveth light to every man that cometh into the world; and the Spirit enlighteneth every man through the world, that hearkeneth to the voice of the Spirit. And every one that hearkeneth to the voice of the Spirit cometh unto God, even the Father."

D&C 93:24. "And truth is knowledge of things as they are, and as they were, and as they are to come."

D&C 123:12. "For there are many yet on the earth among all sects, parties, and zenominations, who are blinded by the subtle craftiness of men, whereby they lie in wait to deceive, and who are only kept from the truth because they know not where to find it."

WORKS, GOOD [107]. When we think of the term "good works," we are reminded of the opportunity and covenant responsibility we have to serve others faithfully and contribute to their enduring happiness. Heavenly Father and Jesus Christ present to us the supreme model of good works as manifested in the Creation, the plan of salvation, the Atonement, the delegation of the power and authority of the holy priesthood unto the righteous, the unfolding of the kingdom of God upon the earth, and the continual flow of revelation through the Holy Spirit—all of this constituting the good works of mercy, love, and glory that we are to emulate. Our good works constitute the eternal book of remembrance from which we will ultimately be judged as candidates for celestial glory and eternal life. As the scriptures confirm, good works are defined by, and are reflected in daily life through the application of, divine qualities, such as faith, hope, charity, humility, patience, obedience, prayerfulness, gratitude, peacefulness, purity, joy, love of God, and faithfully following the Spirit. From good works flow magnificent blessings: spiritual awakening, peace and rest, comfort and honor, happiness and joy, opening the windows of opportunity for leadership and service, and the endowment of divine grace leading to a crown of exaltation and eternal life.

Matthew 5:16. "Let your light so shine before men, that they may see your good works, and glorify your Father which is in heaven." (See also 3 Nephi 12:16.)
Matthew 25:40. "And the King shall answer and say unto them, Verily I say unto you, Inasmuch as ye have done it unto one of the least of these my brethren, ye have done it unto me."
John 7:17. "If any man will do his will, he shall know of the doctrine, whether it be of God, or whether I speak of myself."
John 13:15–17. "For I have given you an example, that ye should do as I have done to you. Verily, verily, I say unto you, The servant is not greater than his lord; neither he that is sent greater than he that sent him. If ye know these things, happy are ye if ye do them."
2 Timothy 3:16–17. "All scripture is given by inspiration of God, and is profitable for doctrine, for reproof, for correction, for instruction in righteousness: That the man of God may be perfect, throughly furnished unto all good works."
Hebrews 13:20–21. "Now the God of peace, that brought again from the dead our Lord Jesus, that great shepherd of the sheep, through the blood of the everlasting covenant, Make you perfect in every good work to do his will, working in you that which is wellpleasing in his sight, through Jesus Christ; to whom be glory for ever and ever."
James 1:27. "Pure religion and undefiled before God and the Father is this, To visit the fatherless and widows in their affliction, and to keep himself unspotted from the world."
James 2:18, 24, 26. "Yea, a man may say, Thou hast faith, and I have works: shew me thy faith without thy works, and I will shew thee my faith by my works. . . . Ye see then how that by works a man is justified, and not by faith only. . . . For as the body without the spirit is dead, so faith without works is dead also."
2 Nephi 25:23. "For we labor diligently to write, to persuade our children, and also our brethren, to believe in Christ, and to be reconciled to God; for we know that it is by grace that we are saved, after all we can do."
Mosiah 2:17. "And behold, I tell you these things that ye may learn wisdom; that ye may learn that when ye are in the service of your fellow beings ye are only in the service of your God."
Mosiah 4:9–10. "Believe in God; believe that he is, and that he created all things, both in heaven and in earth; believe that he has all wisdom, and all power, both in heaven and in earth; believe that man doth not comprehend all the things which the Lord can comprehend. And again, believe that ye must repent of your sins and forsake them, and humble yourselves before God; and ask in sincerity of heart that he would forgive you; and now, if you believe all these things see that ye do them."
Mosiah 5:15. "Therefore, I would that ye should be steadfast and immovable, always abounding in good works, that Christ, the Lord God Omnipotent, may seal you his, that you may be brought to heaven, that ye may have everlasting salvation and eternal life, through the wisdom, and power, and justice, and mercy of him who created all things, in heaven and in earth, who is God above all."
Alma 7:23–24. "And now I would that ye should be humble, and be submissive and gentle; easy to be entreated; full of patience and long-suffering; being temperate in all things; being diligent in keeping the commandments of God at all times; asking for whatsoever things ye stand in need, both spiritual and temporal; always returning thanks

unto God for whatsoever things ye do receive. And see that ye have faith, hope, and charity, and then ye will always abound in good works."

Ether 12:4. "Wherefore, whoso believeth in God might with surety hope for a better world, yea, even a place at the right hand of God, which hope cometh of faith, maketh an anchor to the souls of men, which would make them sure and steadfast, always abounding in good works, being led to glorify God."

D&C 4:5. "And faith, hope, charity and love, with an eye single to the glory of God, qualify him for the work."

D&C 20:69. "And the members shall manifest before the church, and also before the elders, by a godly walk and conversation, that they are worthy of it, that there may be works and faith agreeable to the holy scriptures—walking in holiness before the Lord."

D&C 90:24. "Search diligently, pray always, and be believing, and all things shall work together for your good, if ye walk uprightly and remember the covenant wherewith ye have covenanted one with another."

Words of the Prophets | Gordon B. Hinckley on serving others. "Those who are engaged in this service [temple work and other good works] know that out of it all comes a sweet and satisfying feeling. This sweet blessing of the Spirit becomes literally a medicine to cure many of the ailments of our lives. From such experiences we come to realize that only when we serve others do we truly serve the Lord." —Gordon B. Hinckley, *Faith: The Essence of True Religion* (Salt Lake City: Deseret Book, 1989), 40.

WORSHIP [276]. We are to worship "the true and the living God" (Alma 7:6)—and Him alone. In doing so, we witness unto Him that we honor and remember Him in the spirit of enduring love, humility, gratitude, devotion, and sacrifice—always in recognition of His eternal glory, majesty, and perfection, and always in the name of the Son. Though we are to gather together regularly and worship in holy places—homes, congregations, and temples of God—we are nevertheless committed to worship at all times and in all places, that our hearts will continually be filled with songs of praise and prayers of faith and testimony.

Exodus 34:14. "For thou shalt worship no other god: for the Lord, whose name is Jealous, is a jealous God."

John 4:23. "But the hour cometh, and now is, when the true worshippers shall worship the Father in spirit and in truth: for the Father seeketh such to worship him."

Alma 34:37–38. "And now, my beloved brethren, I desire that ye should remember these things, and that ye should work out your salvation with fear before God, and that ye should no more deny the coming of Christ; That ye contend no more against the Holy Ghost, but that ye receive it, and take upon you the name of Christ; that ye humble yourselves even to the dust, and worship God, in whatsoever place ye may be in, in spirit and in truth; and that ye live in thanksgiving daily, for the many mercies and blessings which he doth bestow upon you."

D&C 20:29. "And we know that all men must repent and believe on the name of Jesus Christ, and worship the Father in his name, and endure in faith on his name to the end, or they cannot be saved in the kingdom of God."

D&C 59:9–14. "And that thou mayest more fully keep thyself unspotted from the world, thou shalt go to the house of prayer and offer up thy sacraments upon my holy day; For verily this is a day appointed unto you to rest from your labors, and to pay thy devotions unto the Most High; Nevertheless thy vows shall be offered up in righteousness on all days and at all times; But remember that on this, the Lord's day, thou shalt offer thine oblations and thy sacraments unto the Most High, confessing thy sins unto thy brethren, and before the Lord. And on this day thou shalt do none other thing, only let thy food be prepared with singleness of heart that thy fasting may be perfect, or, in other words, that thy joy may be full. Verily, this is fasting and prayer, or in other words, rejoicing and prayer."

D&C 93:19–20. "I give unto you these sayings that you may understand and know how to worship, and know what you worship, that you may come unto the Father in my name, and in due time receive of his fulness. For if you keep my commandments you shall receive of his fulness, and be glorified in me as I am in the Father; therefore, I say unto you, you shall receive grace for grace."

D&C 101:22. "Behold, it is my will, that all they who call on my name, and worship me according to mine everlasting gospel, should gather together, and stand in holy places."

Moses 1:15, 17, 20. "Blessed be the name of my God . . . for God said unto me: Worship God, for him only shalt thou serve. . . . Call upon God in the name of mine Only Begotten, and worship me. . . . for this one God only will I worship, which is the God of glory."

Eleventh Article of Faith. "We claim the privilege of worshiping Almighty God according to the dictates of our own conscience, and allow all men the same privilege, let them worship how, where, or what they may."

What qualities should characterize the nature of our worship?

Authenticity, by expunging any semblance of doubt. Matthew 28:16–17. "Then the eleven disciples went away into Galilee, into a mountain where Jesus had appointed them. And when they saw him, they worshipped him: but some doubted."

Doing it in the spirit of belonging to the Lord. Psalm 95:6–7. "O come, let us worship and bow down: let us kneel before the Lord our maker. For he is our God; and we are the people of his pasture, and the sheep of his hand."

Fearing the Lord (having awe and reverence for Him). Psalm 5:7. "But as for me, I will come into thy house in the multitude of thy mercy: and in thy fear will I worship toward thy holy temple."

Full compliance with the will of God. John 9:31. "Now we know that God heareth not sinners: but if any man be a worshipper of God, and doeth his will, him he heareth."

Having faith in the remission of sins. Alma 7:6. "But behold, I trust that ye are not in a state of so much unbelief as were your brethren; I trust that ye are not lifted up in the pride of your hearts; yea, I trust that ye have not set your hearts upon riches and the vain things of the world; yea, I trust that you do not worship idols, but that ye do worship the true and the living God, and that ye look forward for the remission of your sins, with an everlasting faith, which is to come."

Humble devotion. Matthew 28:9–10. "And as they went to tell his disciples, behold, Jesus met them, saying, All hail. And they came and held him by the feet, and worshipped him. Then said Jesus unto them, Be not afraid: go tell my brethren that they go into Galilee, and there shall they see me."

Spirit of giving. 1 Chronicles 16:28–29. "Give unto the Lord, ye kindreds of the people, give unto the Lord glory and strength. Give unto the Lord the glory due unto his name: bring an offering, and come before him: worship the Lord in the beauty of holiness." (See also Psalm 29:1–2; 96:8–9; Matthew 2:1–2, 11; Moses 5:4–8.)

Spirit of gratitude. John 9:35–38. "Jesus heard that they had cast him out [after he had been healed of his blindness]; and when he had found him, he said unto him, Dost thou believe on the Son of God? He answered and said, Who is he, Lord, that I might believe on him? And Jesus said unto him, Thou hast both seen him, and it is he that talketh with thee. And he said, Lord, I believe. And he worshipped him."

Spirit of learning. D&C 19: 23. "Learn of me, and listen to my words; walk in the meekness of my Spirit, and you shall have peace in me."

Investing all our might, mind, strength, and soul. 2 Nephi 25:29. "And now behold, I say unto you that the right way is to believe in Christ, and deny him not; and Christ is the Holy One of Israel; wherefore ye must bow down before him, and worship him with all your might, mind, and strength, and your whole soul; and if ye do this ye shall in nowise be cast out."

Praising the Lord for His love and truth. Psalm 138:2. "I will worship toward thy holy temple, and praise thy name for thy lovingkindness and for thy truth: for thou hast magnified thy word above all thy name."

Watching and praying continually. Alma 15:17. "Therefore, after Alma having established the church at Sidom, seeing a great check, yea, seeing that the people were checked as to the pride of their hearts, and began to humble themselves before God, and began to assemble themselves together at their sanctuaries to worship God before the altar, watching and praying continually, that they might be delivered from Satan, and from death, and from destruction."

With acute awareness and remembrance of the atoning sacrifice of the Lord: 3 Nephi 11:15–17. "And it came to pass that the multitude went forth, and thrust their hands into his side, and did feel the prints of the nails in his hands and in his feet; and this they did do, going forth one by one until they had all gone forth, and did see with their eyes and did feel with their hands, and did know of a surety and did bear record, that it was he, of whom it was written by the prophets, that should come. And when they had all gone forth and had witnessed for themselves, they did cry out with one accord, saying: Hosanna! Blessed be the name of the Most High God! And they did fall down at the feet of Jesus, and did worship him." (See also 3 Nephi 17:10; Moroni 4:3; 5:2; D&C 20:77, 79.)

With songs of devotion and joy. 2 Chronicles 29:28–30. "And all the congregation worshipped, and the singers sang, and the trumpeters sounded: and all this continued until the burnt offering was finished. And when they had made an end of offering, the king and all that were present with him bowed themselves, and worshipped. Moreover Hezekiah the king and the princes commanded the Levites to sing praise unto the Lord with the words of David, and of Asaph the seer. And they sang praises with gladness, and they bowed their heads and worshipped." (See also Psalm 66:4.)

WORTH OF SOULS [1]. We are told by the Lord: "Remember the worth of souls is great in the sight of God" (D&C 18:10). Even though this is the only place in the scriptures where the phrase "the worth of souls" is used, the word of God throughout the sacred canon makes abundantly clear that mortals have a divine and glorious heritage as the supreme creation of the Almighty—and a majestic and everlasting destiny to return again to their celestial home though obedience to gospel principles that are empowered and enabled by the "merits, and mercy, and grace of the Holy Messiah" (2 Nephi 2:8). Thus mortals can learn that they are the sons and daughters of God, created in His own image to be the beneficiaries of His work and glory (see Moses 1:39). They are the children of God, the children of the prophets, the children of the covenant, and joint-heirs with Christ of the treasures of eternal life. They become, through the process of divine adoption, the generation of Christ—His seed given Him of the Father to be equal with their Redeemer throughout the eternities. As they ply the pathway of mortality—this probationary opportunity to manifest their obedience and worthiness by the wise use of their God-given agency—they learn to be the temple of God and serve as the friends of the Lord in helping to build the Church and kingdom of God on earth. In all of this they are supported by the esteem and faith of their fellow Saints and guided by the Holy Spirit, who is granted as a comforting gift to ensure that no matter what happens, God knows them and they are His beloved children. If they follow the Spirit, their actions will enable them to become perfect, even as Christ and His Father are perfect.

John 15:14–15. "Ye are my friends, if ye do whatsoever I command you. Henceforth I call you not servants; for the servant knoweth not what his lord doeth: but I have called you friends; for all things that I have heard of my Father I have made known unto you."

Romans 8:16–17. "The Spirit itself beareth witness with our spirit, that we are the children of God: And if children, then heirs; heirs of God, and joint-heirs with Christ; if so be that we suffer with him, that we may be also glorified together."

1 Peter 2:9–10. "But ye are a chosen generation, a royal priesthood, an holy nation, a peculiar people [i.e., belonging to God]; that ye should shew forth the praises of him who hath called you out of darkness into his marvellous light: Which in time past were not a people, but are now the people of God: which had not obtained mercy, but now have obtained mercy."

1 Nephi 17:35. "Behold, the Lord esteemeth all flesh in one; he that is righteous is favored of God."

Mosiah 15:10–11. "And now I say unto you, who shall declare his generation? Behold, I say unto you, that when his soul has been made an offering for sin he shall see his seed. And now what say ye? And who shall be his seed? Behold I say unto you, that whosoever has heard the words of the prophets, yea, all the holy prophets who have prophesied concerning the coming of the Lord—I say unto you, that all those who have hearkened unto their words, and believed that the Lord would redeem his people, and have looked forward to that day for a remission of their sins, I say unto you, that these are his seed, or they are the heirs of the kingdom of God."

3 Nephi 12:48. "Therefore I would that ye should be perfect even as I, or your Father who is in heaven is perfect." (See also Matthew 5:48.)
3 Nephi 20:25–26. "And behold, ye are the children of the prophets; and ye are of the house of Israel; and ye are of the covenant which the Father made with your fathers, saying unto Abraham: And in thy seed shall all the kindreds of the earth be blessed. The Father having raised me up unto you first, and sent me to bless you in turning away every one of you from his iniquities; and this because ye are the children of the covenant."
D&C 18:10. "Remember the worth of souls is great in the sight of God."
D&C 25:1. "For verily I say unto you, all those who receive my gospel are sons and daughters in my kingdom."
D&C 38:24–25. "And let every man esteem his brother as himself, and practise virtue and holiness before me. And again I say unto you, let every man esteem his brother as himself."
D&C 76:22–24. "And now, after the many testimonies which have been given of him, this is the testimony, last of all, which we give of him: That he lives! For we saw him, even on the right hand of God; and we heard the voice bearing record that he is the Only Begotten of the Father— That by him, and through him, and of him, the worlds are and were created, and the inhabitants thereof are begotten sons and daughters unto God."
D&C 76:68–70. "These are they whose names are written in heaven, where God and Christ are the judge of all. These are they who are just men made perfect through Jesus the mediator of the new covenant, who wrought out this perfect atonement through the shedding of his own blood. These are they whose bodies are celestial, whose glory is that of the sun, even the glory of God, the highest of all, whose glory the sun of the firmament is written of as being typical."
D&C 84:36–39. "For he that receiveth my servants receiveth me; And he that receiveth me receiveth my Father; And he that receiveth my Father receiveth my Father's kingdom; therefore all that my Father hath shall be given unto him. And this is according to the oath and covenant which belongeth to the priesthood."
D&C 88:106–107. "And again, another angel shall sound his trump, which is the seventh angel, saying: It is finished; it is finished! The Lamb of God hath overcome and trodden the wine-press alone, even the wine-press of the fierceness of the wrath of Almighty God. And then shall the angels be crowned with the glory of his might, and the saints shall be filled with his glory, and receive their inheritance and be made equal with him."
D&C 98:1–2. "Verily I say unto you my friends, fear not, let your hearts be comforted; yea, rejoice evermore, and in everything give thanks; Waiting patiently on the Lord, for your prayers have entered into the ears of the Lord of Sabaoth, and are recorded with this seal and testament—the Lord hath sworn and decreed that they shall be granted."
Moses 1:39. "For behold, this is my work and my glory—to bring to pass the immortality and eternal life of man."
Moses 2:26–28. "And I, God, said unto mine Only Begotten, which was with me from the beginning: Let us make man in our image, after our likeness; and it was so. And I, God, said: Let them have dominion over the fishes of the sea, and over the fowl of the air, and over the cattle, and over all the earth, and over every creeping thing that creepeth upon the earth. And I, God, created man in mine own image, in the image of mine Only

Begotten created I him; male and female created I them. And I, God, blessed them, and said unto them: Be fruitful, and multiply, and replenish the earth, and subdue it, and have dominion over the fish of the sea, and over the fowl of the air, and over every living thing that moveth upon the earth." (See also Genesis 1:26–28; Abraham 4:26–28.)

ZION [436]. Originally, the name *Zion* (from a Hebrew source) applied to a hill near Jerusalem used by the Canaanites as a fortress location prior to its capture by David (see 2 Samuel 5:7). Today, the term "Zion" is a place, an institution, a state of mind, a noble destination, a people, a vision of perfection, and an abode of God. Among all the vocabulary words of the gospel, the term "Zion" is perhaps the closest thing to a free-standing linguistic emblem or ensign for the state of being to which the Saints of God aspire.

Zion is not a utopia nestled beyond mortal access; it is a reality that has already been manifested at times upon the earth among mortals (as in the days of Enoch)—mortals who have risen to such a noble level of covenant righteousness that their exemplary level of peace, unity, and spiritual attainment has evoked upon them the highest blessings of our Father in Heaven. The dispensation of the fulness of times provides the unique framework for the unfolding of a Zion people and a Zion city. It is the will of the Lord that such an establishment be forthcoming. It is the responsibility of the Saints of God to be enlisted in such a magnificent work of edification and eternal progression. It is a great responsibility to be engaged in the Lord's errand during the final period of the earth's history, leading up to the inauguration of the millennial reign—the ultimate Zion.

Isaiah 2:2–3. "And it shall come to pass in the last days, that the mountain of the Lord's house shall be established in the top of the mountains, and shall be exalted above the hills; and all nations shall flow unto it. And many people shall go and say, Come ye, and let us go up to the mountain of the Lord, to the house of the God of Jacob; and he will teach us of his ways, and we will walk in his paths: for out of Zion shall go forth the law, and the word of the Lord from Jerusalem." (See also in Micah 4:1–2; 2 Nephi 12:2–3.)

Isaiah 4:5–6. "And the Lord will create upon every dwelling place of mount Zion, and upon her assemblies, a cloud and smoke by day, and the shining of a flaming fire by night: for upon all the glory shall be a defence. And there shall be a tabernacle for a shadow in the daytime from the heat, and for a place of refuge, and for a covert from storm and from rain." (See also 2 Nephi 14:5–6.)

Isaiah 52:7–8. "How beautiful upon the mountains are the feet of him that bringeth good tidings, that publisheth peace; that bringeth good tidings of good, that publisheth salvation; that saith unto Zion, Thy God reigneth! Thy watchmen shall lift up the voice; with the voice together shall they sing: for they shall see eye to eye, when the Lord shall bring again Zion." (See also Mosiah 12:21–22; 15:16–18; 3 Nephi 20:40; D&C 128:19.)

Isaiah 62:1. "For Zion's sake will I not hold my peace, and for Jerusalem's sake I will not rest, until the righteousness thereof go forth as brightness, and the salvation thereof as a lamp that burneth."

D&C 45:66–71. "And it shall be called the New Jerusalem, a land of peace, a city of refuge, a place of safety for the saints of the Most High God; And the glory of the Lord shall be there, and the terror of the Lord also shall be there, insomuch that the wicked will not come unto it, and it shall be called Zion. And it shall come to pass among the wicked, that every man that will not take his sword against his neighbor must needs flee unto Zion for safety. And there shall be gathered unto it out of every nation under heaven; and it shall be the only people that shall not be at war one with another. And it shall be said among the wicked: Let us not go up to battle against Zion, for the inhabitants of Zion are terrible; wherefore we cannot stand. And it shall come to pass that the righteous shall be gathered out from among all nations, and shall come to Zion, singing with songs of everlasting joy."

D&C 64:33–34, 41–43. "Wherefore, be not weary in well-doing, for ye are laying the foundation of a great work. And out of small things proceedeth that which is great. Behold, the Lord requireth the heart and a willing mind; and the willing and obedient shall eat the good of the land of Zion in these last days. . . . For, behold, I say unto you that Zion shall flourish, and the glory of the Lord shall be upon her; And she shall be an ensign unto the people, and there shall come unto her out of every nation under heaven. And the day shall come when the nations of the earth shall tremble because of her, and shall fear because of her terrible ones. The Lord hath spoken it."

D&C 68:25–26. "And again, inasmuch as parents have children in Zion, or in any of her stakes which are organized, that teach them not to understand the doctrine of repentance, faith in Christ the Son of the living God, and of baptism and the gift of the Holy Ghost by the laying on of the hands, when eight years old, the sin be upon the heads of the parents. For this shall be a law unto the inhabitants of Zion, or in any of her stakes which are organized."

D&C 97:21. "Therefore, verily, thus saith the Lord, let Zion rejoice, for this is Zion—THE PURE IN HEART; therefore, let Zion rejoice, while all the wicked shall mourn."

D&C 105:5–6. "And Zion cannot be built up unless it is by the principles of the law of the celestial kingdom; otherwise I cannot receive her unto myself. And my people must needs be chastened until they learn obedience, if it must needs be, by the things which they suffer."

Moses 7:18. "And the Lord called his people ZION, because they were of one heart and one mind, and dwelt in righteousness; and there was no poor among them."

Moses 7:53, 62. "And the Lord said: Blessed is he through whose seed Messiah shall come; for he saith—I am Messiah, the King of Zion, the Rock of Heaven, which is broad as eternity; whoso cometh in at the gate and climbeth up by me shall never fall; wherefore, blessed are they of whom I have spoken, for they shall come forth with songs of everlasting joy. . . . And righteousness will I send down out of heaven; and truth will I send forth out of the earth, to bear testimony of mine Only Begotten; his resurrection from the dead; yea, and also the resurrection of all men; and righteousness and truth will I cause to sweep the earth as with a flood, to gather out mine elect from the four quarters of the earth, unto a place which I shall prepare, an Holy City, that my people may gird up their loins, and be looking forth for the time of my coming; for there shall be my tabernacle, and it shall be called Zion, a New Jerusalem."

Articles of Faith 1:10. "We believe in the literal gathering of Israel and in the restoration of the Ten Tribes; that Zion (the New Jerusalem) will be built upon the American continent;

that Christ will reign personally upon the earth; and, that the earth will be renewed and receive its paradisiacal glory."

Words of the Prophets | Gordon B. Hinckley on how to build Zion. "If we are to build that Zion of which the prophets have spoken and of which the Lord has given mighty promise, we must set aside our consuming selfishness. We must rise above our love for comfort and ease, and in the very process of effort and struggle, even in our extremity, we shall become better acquainted with our God." —Gordon B. Hinckley, "Our Mission of Saving," *Ensign*, November 1991, 59.

ABOUT THE AUTHOR

Richard J. Allen is a husband, father, teacher, and writer. He has served several times as high priests group leader, on several stake high councils, in several stake presidencies, in a branch presidency at the MTC, and as a bishop. Richard's teaching assignments in the Church have included service as a full-time missionary, instructor in various priesthood quorums, and frequently as a Gospel Doctrine teacher. He and his wife, Carol Lynn, have served together as stake institute directors, stake missionary preparation instructors, and stake welfare specialists. Richard has served as a faculty member at Brigham Young University (where he received his B.A. and M.A.) and at The Johns Hopkins University (where he received his Ph.D. and also served in the senior administration of the university). Richard has authored or coauthored many articles, manuals, and books and has served on a number of national educational boards. Richard and Carol Lynn have four children and five grandchildren.